Constantin-Francois V⌐

Travels Through Egypt and Syria, in tⁱ   ⌐/85

Containing the present natural and political sta   es; their

productions, arts, manufactures, and commerce; wiⱼ   vations on the

manners, customs, and government. Vol. 2

Constantin-Francois Volney

Travels Through Egypt and Syria, in the Years 1783, 1784, and 1785
Containing the present natural and political state of those countries; their productions, arts, manufactures, and commerce; with observations on the manners, customs, and government. Vol. 2

ISBN/EAN: 9783337245245

Printed in Europe, USA, Canada, Australia, Japan

Cover: Foto ©Andreas Hilbeck / pixelio.de

More available books at **www.hansebooks.com**

TRAVELS

THROUGH

EGYPT AND SYRIA,

IN THE YEARS 1783, 1784 & 1785.

CONTAINING

THE PRESENT NATURAL AND POLITICAL STATE OF
THOSE COUNTRIES ;

THEIR

PRODUCTIONS, ARTS, MANUFACTURES & COMMERCE ;

WITH

OBSERVATIONS ON THE MANNERS, CUS-
TOMS AND GOVERNMENT

OF THE

TURKS & ARABS.

By M. C—F VOLNEY.

Translated from the French,

IN TWO VOLUMES.

VOL. II.

NEW YORK:

PRINTED BY J. TIEBOUT, FOR E. DUYCKINCK & CO. BOOKSELLERS.

1798

TRAVELS

IN

EGYPT AND SYRIA.

STATE of SYRIA.

CHAP V.

Of the Cultivating, or Sedentary Inhabitants of Syria.

S E C T. I.

Of the Anfarians.

THE firſt people who ſhould be diſtinguiſhed from the reſt of the inhabitants of Syria among thoſe who employ themſelves in cultivation, are thoſe, called in that country by the plural name Anſaria, in Deliſle's maps ſtiled Enſyrians, and, in thoſe of Danville, Naſ-ſaris. The territory occupied by theſe Anſaria is that chain of mountains which extends from Antakia to the rivulet called *Nahr-el-Kabir*, or the Great Ri-ver. The hiſtory of their origin, though little known, is yet inſtructive : I ſhall give it in the words of a writer who has drawn his materials from the beſt authorities.*

" In the year of the Greeks 1202, (A. D. 891),
" there lived at the village of *Naſar*, in the environs
" of Koufa, an old man, who from his faſtings, his
" continual prayers and his poverty, paſſed for a

* Aſſemani, *Bibliotheque orientale.*

" faint : feveral of the common people declaring
" themfelves his partizans, he felected from among
" them twelve difciples to propagate his doctrine.
" But the commandant of the place, alarmed at his
" proceedings, feized the old man, and confined him
" in prifon.   In this reverfe of fortune, his fituation
" excited the pity of a girl who was a flave to the
" goaler, and fhe determined to give him his liberty ;
" an opportunity foon offered to effect her defign.
" One day when the goaler was gone to bed intoxi-
" cated, and in a profound fleep, fhe gently took the
" keys from under his pillow, and, after opening
" the door to the old man, returned them to their
" place unperceived by her mafter : the next day,
" when the goaler went to vifit his prifoner, he was
" extremely aftonifhed at finding he had made his
" efcape, and the more fo fince he could perceive no
" marks of violence.   He therefore judicioufly con-
" cluded he had been delivered by an angel, and ea-
" gerly fpread the report, to avoid the reprehenfion
" he merited ; the old man, on the other hand affert-
" ed the fame thing to his difciples, and preached
" his doctrine with more earneftnefs than ever.   He
" even wrote a book, in which, among other things,
" he fays : *I, fuch a one, of the village of Nafar, have*
" *feen Chrift who is the word of God, who is Ahmed,*
" *fon of Mohammad, fon of Hanafa, of the race of Ali ;*
" *who alfo is Gabriel, and he faid to me : Thou art*
" *he who readeth, (with underftanding.) thou art the*
" *man who fpeaketh truth ; thou art the camel which*
" *preferveth the faithful from wrath ; thou art the beaft*
" *which carrieth their burthen : thou art the (Holy)*
" *Spirit, and John, the fon of Zachary, Go, and preach*
" *to men that they make four genuflections in praying ;*
" *two before the rifing of the fun, and two before his*
" *fetting, turning their faces towards Jerufalem : and*
" *let them fay, three times : God Almighty, God moft*
" *high, God moft great : let them obferve only the fecond*

" *and third festival ; let them fast but two days annu-*
" *ally ; let them not wash the prepuce, nor drink beer,*
" *but as much wine as they think proper ; and, lastly,*
" *let them abstain from the flesh of carnivorous animals.*
" This old man, passing into Syria, propagated his
" opinions among the lower orders of the country
" people, numbers of whom believed in him. And,
" after a few years, he went away, and nobody ever
" knew what became of him.",

Such was the origin of these Anfarians, who are,
for the most part, inhabitants of the mountains before mentioned. A little more than a century after
this, the crusaders, carrying the war into these countries, and marching from Marrah, along the Orontes,
towards Lebanon, fell in with some of these *Nafireans,*
a great number of whom they flew. William of
Tyre*, who reports this fact, confounds them with
the *assassins,* and possibly they might have resembled
each other; as to what he adds, that the Franks, as
well as the Arabs, employ the term *assassins,* without
being able to give any account of its origin; it is a
problem easy of solution. Hassassin†, in the vulgar
Arabic, signifies *Robbers of the night ;* persons who
lie in ambush to kill ; and is still understood in this
sense at Cairo, and in Syria; for which reason it was
applied to the Bâtenians, who flew by surprize. The
crusaders, who happened to be in Syria at the time
this practice was most frequent, must have adopted
the use of the term in question. What they have
related of the old man of the mountain, is in confequence of an improper translation of the phrase *Shaik-
el-Djebal,* which signifies *Lord of the mountains,* the
title the Arabs gave to the chief of the Bâtenians,

* Lib. xx. chap. 30.

† The root *hafs,* with an afpirated *h,* fignifies to kill, to affaffinate, to liften, to furprife ; but the compound *haffás* is not
to be found in Golius.

whofe refidence was to the eaft of Kourd-eftan, in the mountains of the ancient Media.

The *Anfaria* are, as I have faid, divided into feveral tribes or fects; among which we diftinguifh the Shamfia, or adorers of the fun; the Kelbia, or worfhippers of the dog, and the Kadmoufia, who, as I am affured, pay a particular homage to that part in women, which correfponds to the Priapus*.

M. Niebuhr, to whom the fame circumftances were related as to me, could not believe them, becaufe, fays he, it is not probable that mankind fhould *fo far* degrade themfelves; but this mode of reafoning is contradicted, both by the hiftory of all nations, which proves how capable the human mind is of the moft extravagant exceffes, and even by the prefent ftate of almoft all countries, efpecially of the eaftern world, where we meet with a degree of ignorance and rediculity fufficient to receive the moft palpable abfurdities. The whimfical fuperftitions I have mentioned, may the rather be believed ftill to exift among the Anfaria, as they feem to have been preferved there by a regular tranfmiffion from thofe ancient times in which they are known to have prevailed. Hiftorians remark that, notwithftanding the vicinity of Antioch, Chriftianity penetrated with the greateft difficulty into thefe countries; very few profelytes were made here, even after the reign of Julian: and from that period to the invafion of the Arabs there was not much time for its eftablifhment: in fact, revolutions in opinion feldom take place fo readily in the provinces as in great cities, where the facility of the communication diffufes new ideas with more rapidity, fo that they are foon either univerfally received or

---

* I am affured, likewife, that they hold nocturnal affemblies, in which, after certain difcourfes, they extinguifh the lights, and indulge promifcuous luft, as has been reported of the ancient Gnoftics.

entirely exploded. The progrefs made by Chriftianity among thefe rude mountaineers, could only ferve to prepare the way for Mahometanifm, more fuitable to their habits and inclinations ; and to this abfurd med-ley of ancient and modern doctrines the old man of Nafar owed his fuccefs. One hundred and fifty years after, *Mohammed-el-Dourzi* having, in his turn, form-ed a fect, the Anfarians did not admire its principal article, the Divinity of the Kalif Hakem,: for this reafon they remain diftinct from the Druzes, though they refemble each other in feveral points. Many of the *Anfaria* believe in the Metempfychofis ; others reject the immortality of the foul ; and, in general, in that civil and religious anarchy, that ignorance and rudenefs which prevail among them, thefe pea-fants adopt what opinions they think proper, follow-ing the fect they like beft, and, frequently, attaching themfelves to none.

Their country is divided into three principal dif-tricts farmed by the chiefs called *Mokaddamim.* Their tribute is paid to the Pacha of Tripoli, from whom they annually receive their title. Their mountains are in general not fo fteep as thofe of Lebanon ; and, confequently, are better adapted to cultivation ; but they are alfo more expofed to the Turks, and hence doubtlefs, it happens, that, with greater plenty of corn, tobacco, wines, and olives, they are more thinly inhabited than thofe of their neighbours the Maronites, and the Druzes, of whom' I fhall next fpeak.

S e c t. II.

Of the Maronites.

Between the Anfarians, to the north, and the Dru-zes to the fouth, we find an inconfiderable people long known under the name of *Macuárna* or *Maro-*

nites. Their origin, and the minute difference between them and the Latins, whose communion they
follow, have been much discussed by ecclesiastical
writers. All that is worth notice, and known with
certainty, concerning them, may be reduced to what
follows :

Towards the end of the sixth age of the church,
while the spirit of retirement from the world was
equally novel and fervid, a hermit, of the name of
Mâroun, lived on the banks of the Orontes, who,
by his fasting, his solitary mode of life, and his auste-
rities, became much respected by the neighbouring
people. It seems that, in the disputes which at that
time arose between Rome and Constantinople, he
employed his credit in favour of the western Christians. His death, far from abating the ardor of his
followers, gave new energy to their zeal : it was reported that miracles had been wrought by his remains, and, in consequence, many persons assembled
from Kinesrin, from Aouasem and other places, who
built at Hama a chapel and a tomb whence soon arose
a convent, very celebrated in that part of Syria. The
quarrels of the two Metropolitan churches encreased,
and the whole empire entered warmly into the dissen-
tions of the priests and princes. Matters were thus
situated, when about the end of the seventh century,
a monk, named John the Maronite, obtained, by his
talents for preaching, the reputation of being one of
the most powerful supporters of the cause of the Latins, or Partisans of the Pope. Their opponents, who
espoused the cause of the Emperor, and were therefore named *Melkites*, or Royalists, made at that time
great progress in Lebanon. To oppose them with
success, the Latins determined to send thither John
the Maronite : they presented him accordingly to the
agent of the Pope, at Antioch, who after consecrating
him bishop of Djebail, sent him to preach in those
countries. John lost no time in rallying his parti-

fans, and in augmenting their number ; but oppofed
by the intrigues, and even by the open attacks, of
the Melkites, thought it neceffary to refift force by
force ; he collected all the Latins, and fettled himfelf
with them in Lebanon, where they formed a fociety
independent both with refpect to its civil and religious government. This is related by an Hiftorian of
the Lower Empire in the following words : " In the
" eighth year of the reign of Conftantine Pogonatus,
" (A. D. 676), the Mardaïtes, collecting themfelves
" together, took poffeffion of Lebanon, which be-
" came the afylum of vagabonds, flaves, and other
" forts of people. They grew fo powerful there, as
" to ftop the progrefs of the Arabs, and to compel
" the Kalif Moâouia to requeft of the Greek a truce
" for thirty years, obliging himfelf to pay a tribute of
" fifty horfes, one hundred flaves, and ten thoufand
" pieces of gold.*"
The name of Mardaïtes, here ufed by this Author,
is derived from a Syriac word fignifying Rebel, and
is oppofed to *Melkites*, or Royalifts, which proves
both that the Syriac was ftill in ufe at that time, and
that the fchifm which rent the empire was as much
civil as religious. Befides, it appears that the origin of thefe two factions, and the exiftence of an
infurrection in thefe countries, were prior to thefe
times, for, from the firft ages of Mahometanifm (A. D.
622), mention is made of petty independent princes,
one of whom, named Youfeph, was fovereign of
Djebail ; and the other, called Kefrou, governed the
interior parts of the country, which, from him, took
the name of *Kefraouan*. We read likewife of another who made an expedition againft Jerufalem, and
died at a very advanced age at Befkonta,† where he
refided. Thus, before Conftantine Pogonatus, thefe
mountains were become the refuge of malecontents,

---

* Cedrenus.   † A village of Kefraouan.

or rebels, who fled from the bigotry of the Emperors
and their governors.   It was doubtlefs for this reafon,
and from a fimilarity in their opinions, that John and
his difciples took refuge there ; and it was from the
afcendency they acquired, or already poffeffed, that
the whole nation took the name of Maronites, which
was lefs difgraceful than that of Mardaïtes.   Be this
as it may, John, having eftablifhed order and military
difcipline among the Mountaineers, having provided
them with arms and leaders, they employed their
liberty in combating the common enemies of the empire and their little ftate, and prefently become mafters
of almoft all the mountains as far as Jerufalem.   The
fchifm which took place at this juncture among the
Mahometans, facilitated their conquefts.   Moaouia
rebelling againft Ali at Damafcus, Kalif a Koufa,
found himfelf obliged, in order to avoid being engaged in two wars at once, to make in 678, a difadvan-
tageous treaty with the Greeks.   Seven years after,
Abd-el-Malek renewed it with Juftinian II. on condition, however that the Emperor fhould free him
from the Maronites.   To this propofal, Juftinian had
the imprudence to confent, and was bafe enough to
get their chief affaffinated by an ambaffador, whom
the too generous man had received into his houfe
without fufpicion of treachery.   After this murder,
the fame agent fucceeded fo well by his intrigues,
that he perfuaded twelve thoufand inhabitants to quit
their country, leaving a free paffage to the Mahometan arms.   Soon after another perfecution menaced
the Maronites with total ruin ; for the fame Juftinian
fent troops againft them under Marcian and Maurice,
who deftroyed the monaftery of Hama, and maffacred
five hundred monks, after which they carried the war
quite into Kefraouan ; but happily at this moment,
Juftinian was depofed, when on the point of caufing
a general maffacre at Conftantinople ; and the Maronites, authorized by his fucceffor, falling upon Mau-

rice, cut his enemy to pieces in an engagement wherein he himfelf perifhed. From this period we lofe
fight of them till the invafion of the Crufaders, with
whom they were fometimes in alliance, and fometimes at variance. In this interval, of more than
three centuries, they loft part of their poffeffions,
and were reduced to their prefent limits, paying tribute no doubt, as often as the Arabian or Turcoman
governors were able to compel them. This was the
cafe with the Kalif of Egypt, Hakem-Bàmr-Ellah,
who about the year 1014, ceded their territory to
a Turcoman, Prince of Aleppo. Two hundred years
after, Selah-el-din having driven out the Europeans
from this country, they were obliged to fubmit to
his power, and purchafe peace by contributions. At
this period, that is, about the year 1215, the Maronites effected a reunion with Rome, from which they
never were widely feparated, and which ftill fubfifts.
William of Tyre, who relates this, obferves, that
they had forty thoufand men able to bear arms. The
peace they enjoyed under the Mamlouks was difturbed by Selim the Second, but this prince, occupied by
more important objects, did not take the trouble to
fubject them. This negligence emboldened them;
and, in concert with the Druzes, and their Emir,
the celebrated *Faker-el-din*, they made daily encroach-
ments on the Ottomans; but thefe commotions had
an unfortunate iffue; for Amurath the Third, fending againft them Ibrahim, Pacha of Cairo, that General reduced them to obedience, in 1588, and fubjected them to the annual tribute they ftill pay.

Since that period, the Pachas, defirous of extending their authority and extortions, have frequently
attempted to introduce their garrifons and Agas into
the mountains of the Maronites; but being conftantly repulfed, they have been compelled to abide
by the treaty. The fubjection of the Maronites
therefore only confifts in the payment of a tribute to

the Pacha of Tripoli, of whom they hold their country, which he annually farms out to one or more
Shaiks,* that is to fay, perfons of eminence and property, who affign their refpective fhares to the diftricts
and villages. The impoft is levied, chiefly, on the
Mulberry-trees and vineyards, which are the principal, and almoft the fole objects of culture. It varies
according to the feafons, and the refiftance they can
make to the Pacha. Cuftom houfes are eftablifhed likewife in the maritime towns, fuch as Djebail, and Bât-
roun ; but the produce of thefe is but inconfiderable.

The form of government is not founded on exprefs conventions, but merely on ufages and cuftoms.
This inconvenience would doubtlefs, long ere this,
have produced difagreeable effects, but for the inter-
vention of many fortunate circumftances. The principal of thefe is religion, which, placing an infur-
mountable barrier between the Maronites and the
Mahometans, has prevented ambitious men from
leaguing themfelves with foreigners to enflave their
country, which, every where affording ftrong defen-
ces, enables every village, and almoft every family,
to oppofe, by its fingle force, all ufurpation of fovereign power. A third reafon may be derived even
from the weaknefs of this fociety, which having always been furrounded by powerful enemies, has only
been able to refift them by maintaining union among
its members. which union can only exift by abftain-
ing from oppreffing each other, and by reciprocally
guarding the fafety of each others perfon and property. Thus the government preferves itfelf in a
natural equilibrium, and cuftoms fupplying the place
of laws, the Maronites are to this day equally ftrangers to the oppreffion of defpotifm, and the diforders
of anarchy.

* In the mountains, the word Shaik fignifies, properly, a
man of property, or country gentleman.

The nation may be confidered as divided into two claffes; the people and the Shaiks, by which muft be underftood the moft eminent of the inhabitants, who, from the antiquity of their families, and the opulence of their fortunes, are fuperior to the common clafs. They all live difperfed in the mountains, in villages, hamlets, and even detached houfes; which is never the cafe in the plains. The whole nation confifts of cultivators. Every man improves the little domain he poffeffes, or farms, with his own hands. Even the Shaiks live in the fame manner, and they are only diftinguifhed from the people by a bad Peliffe, a horfe, and a few flight advantages in food and lodging; they all live frugally, without many enjoyments, but alfo with few wants, as they are little acquainted with the inventions of luxury. In general, the nation is poor, but no man wants neceffaries; and if beggars are fometimes feen, they come rather from the fea-coaft than the country itfelf. Property is as facred among them as in Europe, nor do we fee there thofe robberies and extortions fo frequent with the Turks. Travellers may journey there, either by night or day, with a fecurity unknown in any other part of the empire, and the ftranger meets with hofpitality, as among the Arabs; it muft be owned however, that the Maronites are lefs generous, and rather inclined to the vice of parfimony. Conformably to the doctrines of Chriftianity, they have only one wife, whom they efpoufe, frequently, without having feen, and, always, without having been much in her company. Contrary to the precepts of that fame religion, however, they have admitted, or retained, the Arab cuftom of retaliation, and the neareft relation of a murdered perfon is bound to avenge him. From a habit founded on diftruft, and the political ftate of the country, every one, whether Shaik, or peafant, walks continually armed with a fufil and poniards. This is perhaps an inconvenience; but this advantage re-

fults from it, that they have no novices in the ufe of
arms among them, when it is neceffary to employ
them againft the Turks. As the country maintains
no regular troops, every man is obliged to join the
army in time of war, and if this militia were well
conducted, it would be fuperior to many European
armies. From accounts taken in late years, the number of men, fit to bear arms, amounts to thirty-five
thoufand. According to the ufual mode of computation, this would imply a population of about a hundred and five thoufand fouls; and, if we add the
priefts, monks, and nuns, difperfed in upwards of
two hundred convents, and the inhabitants of the
maritime towns, fuch as Djebail, Bàtroun, &c. we
cannot fuppofe it lefs than a hundred and fifteen
thoufand.

This number, compared with the extent of the
country, which is about a hundred and fifty leagues
fquare, gives feven hundred and fixty inhabitants
for each fquare league; which will not appear a fmall
population, when we confider that great part of Lebanon confifts only of barren rocks, and that the
foil, even where it can be cultivated, produces very
little.

In religious matters, the Maronites are dependent
on Rome. Though they acknowledge the fupremacy
of the Pope, their clergy continue, as heretofore, to
elect a head, with the title of Batrak, or patriarch of
Antioch. Their priefts, marry as in the firft ages
of the church; and their wives muft be maidens,
and not widows, nor can they marry a fecond time.
They celebrate mafs in Syriac, of which the greateft
part of them comprehend not a word. The gofpel,
alone, is read aloud in Arabic, that it may be underftood by the people. The communion is adminiftered
in both kinds. The Hoft is a fmall round loaf, un-
leavened, of the thicknefs of a finger, and fometimes
larger than a crown piece. On it is the impreffion

of a feal, which is eaten by the prieft, who cuts the remainder into fmall pieces, and, putting them into the cup, adminifters to each perfon with a fpoon, which ferves every body. Thefe priefts have not, as among us, benefices or ftated revenues; but they fubfift partly on the produce of their maffes, the bounty of their hearers, and the labour of their hands. Some of them exercife trades, others cultivate a fmall piece of land; and all are induftrioufly employed, for the maintenance of their families and the edification of their flock. Their poverty is recompenfed by the great refpect which is paid them. Their vanity is inceffantly flattered; whoever approaches them, whether rich or poor, great or fmall, is anxious to kifs their hands, which they fail not to prefent; nor are they pleafed that the Europeans withhold this mark of reverence, fo repugnant to our manners, though not thought humiliating by the natives, who are accuftomed to it from their infancy. In other refpects, the ceremonies of the Catholic religion are not performed more publicly, or with lefs reftraint, in Europe than in Kefraouan. Each village has its chapel and its prieft, and each chapel its bell: a thing unheard of in any other part of Turkey. The Maronites are vain of this privilege, and that they may not be deprived of it, will not fuffer a Mahometan to live among them. They affume to themfelves, alfo, the privilege of wearing the Green Turban, which, except in their territories, would coft a Chriftian his life.

Italy itfelf has not more bifhops than this little corner of Syria; they here ftill retain the fimplicity of the primative ages; and may be often met on the roads, mounted on a mule, and followed by a fingle Sacriftan. The greater part of them live in convents, where their food and drefs does not differ from that of the other monks; nor does their ufual revenue exceed fifteen hundred livres, (about fifty-three pounds) which, in this country, where every article of life is cheap, enables them to live comfortably. They, as well as the priests, are chosen from the class of monks; and are generally elected for their pre-eminence in learning, which is not difficult to acquire, since the bulk of the monks and priests know nothing but the catechism and the bible. It is nevertheless remarkable, that these two subordinate classes are more amiable in their manners and live more edifying lives; while the bishop and the patriarch, on the contrary, constantly engaged in cabals, disputes of precedency, and religious distinctions, throw the whole country into commotion. Under pretext of exercising ecclesiastical discipline, according to the ancient rules of the church, they mutually excommunicate each other, and their respective adherents; they suspend priests, interdict the monks, and inflict public penance on the laity; in a word, they have retained the turbulent and intriguing spirit, which was the scourge of the Lower Empire. The court of Rome, frequently embarrassed by their disputes, strives to pacify them, in order to preserve the only asylum in her power, remaining in these countries. It is not long since she was obliged to interpose in a singular affair, an acccount of which may give some idea of the character of the Maronites.

About the year 1755, there was in the neighbourhood of the Jesuit Missionaries, a Maronite girl, named Hendia, whose extraordinary mode of life began to attract the attention of the people. She fasted, wore the hair-cloth, possessed the gift of tears; and, in a word, had all the exterior of the ancient hermits, and soon acquired a similar reputation. Every body considered her as a model of piety, and many esteemed her a saint; from such a reputation to miracles the transition is very easy, and in fact, it was soon reported that she worked miracles. To have a proper conception of the effects of this report, we must not forget that the state of mens minds, in Lebanon, is nearly the same as in the earliest ages. There were

neither infidels therefore, nor wits, nor even doubt-
ers. Hendia availed herself of this enthusiasm for
the completion of her designs; and, imitating the
conduct of her predecessors in the same career, she
wished to become the foundress of a new order. In
vain does the human heart endeavour to conceal its
passions, they are invariably the same; nor does the
conqueror differ from the monk; both are alike actuated by ambition and the lust of power; and the
pride of pre-eminence displays itself even in the excess
of humility. To build the convent, money was necessary; the foundress solicited the pious charity of
her followers, whose contributions were so abundant
as to enable her, in a few years, to erect two vast
stone houses, which could not have cost less than one
hundred and twenty thousand livres (five thousand
pounds). They are called the Kourket, and are situated on the ridge of a hill, to the north-west of Antoura, having to the west a view of the sea, which is
very near, and an extensive prospect, to the south as far
as the road of Bairout, which is four leagues distant.
The Kourket soon filled with monks and nuns. The
Patriarch for the time being was director-general,
and other employments, of various kinds were con-
ferred on the different priests and candidates, to whom
one of these houses was allotted. Every thing succeeded as well as could have been wished; it is true
that many of the nuns died, but this was imputed to the
air, and the real cause was not easy to be discovered.
Hendia had reigned over her little kingdom near
twenty years, when an unforeseen accident threw
every thing into confusion. A factor travelling from
Damascus to Bairout, in the summer, was overtaken
by night near this convent: the gates were shut, the
hour unseasonable; and, as he did not wish to give
any trouble, he contented himself with a bed of
straw, and laid himself down in the outer court,
waiting the return of day. He had only slept a few

hours, when a sudden noise of doors and bolts awakened him. From one of the doors came out three
women, with spades and shovels in their hands; who
were followed by two men, bearing a long white
bundle, which appeared very heavy. They proceeded towards an adjoining piece of ground, full of
stones and rubbish, where the men deposited their
load, dug a hole into which they put it, and covering it with earth, trod it down with their feet, after
which they all returned to the house. The fight of men
with nuns, and this bundle thus mysteriously buried
by night, could not but furnish matter of reflection
to the traveller. Astonishment at first kept him silent,
but, to this, anxiety and fear soon succeeded; he,
therefore, hastily set out for Bairout at break of day.
In this town he was acquainted with a merchant, who,
some months before, had placed two of his daughters
in the *Kourket*, with a portion of about four hundred
pounds. He went in search of him, still hesitating,
yet burning with impatience to relate his adventure.
They seated themselves crofs-legged, the long pipe
was lighted, and the coffee brought. The merchant
then proceeded to enquire of his visitor concerning
his journey, who answered, he had paffed the night
near the Kourket. This produced fresh questions, to
which he replied by further particulars, and, at length,
no longer able to contain himself, whispered to his
host what he had seen. The merchant was greatly
surprised, the circumstance of burying the bundle
alarmed him: and the more he considered it, the
more his uneasiness increased. He knew that one of
his daughters was ill, and could not but remark that
a great many nuns died. Tormented with these
thoughts, he knows not how either to admit or reject
the dismal suspicions they occasion; he mounts his
horse, and, accompanied by a friend, they repair
together to the convent, where he asks to fee his
daughters;—He is told they are fick; he insists they

fhall be brought to him; this is angrily refufed: and the more he perfifts, the more peremptory is the refufal, till, his fufpicions are converted into certainty. Leaving the convent, in an agony of defpair, he went to Dair-el-Kamar; and laid all the circumftances before Saad, Kiaya* of prince *Youfef*, chief of the mountain. The Kiaya was greatly aftonifhed, and ordered a body of horfe to accompany him, and, if refufed admiffion, to force the convent; the Kadi took part with the merchant, and the affair was referred to the law; the ground where the bundle had been buried was opened, and a dead body found, which the unhappy father difcovered to be that of his youngeft daughter; the other was found confined in the convent, and almoft dead: fhe revealed a fcene of fuch abominable wickednefs, as makes human nature fhudder, and to which, fhe, like her fifter, was about to fall a victim. The pretended faint being feized, acted her part with firmnefs; and a profecution was commenced againft the priefts and the patriarch. The enemies of the latter united to effect his ruin, in order to fhare his fpoils, and he was fufpended and depofed. The affair was removed to Rome in 1776, and the fociety *de Propaganda*, on examination, difcovered the moft infamous fcenes of debauchery, and the moft horrible cruelties. It was proved that Hendia procured the death of the nuns, fometimes to get poffeffion of their property, at others, becaufe they would not comply with her defires: that this infamous woman not only communicated, but even confecrated the hoft, and faid mafs: that fhe had holes under her bed, by which perfumes were introduced at the moment fhe pretended to be in extacy, and under the influence of the Holy Ghoft; that fhe had a faction who cried her up, and publifhed that fhe was the mother of God, returned upon earth, and a

* The title of the minifter of thefe petty princes.

thoufand other extravagancies. Notwithftanding this, fhe ·retained·a party powerful enough to prevent the fevere punifhment fhe merited : fhe has been fhut up in different convents, from whence fhe has frequently efcaped. In 1783, fhe was prefent at the vifitation of Antoura, and the brother of the Emir of the Druzes was defirous to give her her liberty. Numbers ftill believe in her fanctity ; and, but for the accident of the traveller, her prefent enemies would not have doubted it. What muft we think of reputations for piety, when they may depend on fuch trifling circumftances!

In the fmall country of the Maronites, there are reckoned upwards of two hundred convents for men and women. Thefe religious are of the order of St. Anthony, whofe rules they obferve with an exactnefs which reminds us of earlier times. The drefs of the monks is of brown clumfy woollen, much like that of our capuchin friars. Their food is the fame as that of the peafants, with this exception, that they never eat flefh. They have frequently fafts, and make long prayers, day and night ; the remainder of their time is imployed in cultivating the earth, or breaking the rocks to form the walls of the terraces which fupport their vineyards and mulberry plantations. Each convent has a brother fhoemaker, a brother taylor, a brother weaver, a brother baker ; in a word, an artift of every neceffary trade. We almoft always find a convent of women clofe to one of men ; yet it is rare to hear of any fcandalous report. Thefe women themfelves lead a very laborious life, and it is this activity, doubtlefs, which fecures them againft all mifchiefs attendant on idlenefs. So far, therefore, from being injurious to population, we may affirm that thefe convents have contributed to promote it, by increafing by culture every article in a proportion greater than its confumption. The moft remarkable of the houfes of the Maronite Monks is Kozhaia,

fix hours journey to the eaft of Tripoli. There they
exorcife, as in the firft ages of the church, thofe who
are poffeffed with devils; for fuch perfons are ftill to
be found in thefe countries. A very few years ago,
our merchants at Tripoli faw one of them who put
the patience and learning of the monks to the proof:
This man, to outward appearance healthy, was fubject to fudden convulfions, which threw him into a
kind of madnefs, fometimes fullen, at others violent. He tore, he bit, he foamed at the mouth;
his ufual expreffion was,—*The fun is my mother, let
me adore her.* The priefts almoft drowned him with
ablutions, tormented him with fafting and prayer,
and, at length, as they reported, drove out the devil;
but, from the account given me by more intelligent
obfervers, it appears that thofe poffeffed are no other
than perfons afflicted with idiotly, madnefs, and epi-
lepfies; and it is worth remarking, that *poffeffion* and
epilepfy are denoted by the fame Arabic word.*

The court of Rome, in affiliating the Maronites,
has granted them an Hofpitium, at Rome, to which
they may fend feveral of their youth, to receive a
gratuitous education. It fhould feem that this inftitu-
tion might introduce among them the ideas and arts
of Europe; but the pupils of this fchool, limited to
an education purely monaftic, bring home nothing
but the Italian language, which is of no ufe, and a
ftock of theological learning, from which as little
advantage can be derived; they accordingly foon affi-
milate with the reft. Nor has a greater change been
operated by the three or four miffionaries maintained
by the French capuchins at Gazir, Tripoli, and Bairout. Their labours confift in preaching in their
church, in inftructing children in the catechifm, Thomas a Kempis, and the Pfalms, and in teaching them
to read and write. Formerly the Jefuits had two

* *Kabal* and *Kabat.* The *K* here is the *Spanifh jota.*

miſſionaries at their houſe at Antoura, and the Lazarites have now ſucceeded them in their miſſion. The
moſt valuable advantage that has reſulted from theſe
apoſtolical labours is, that the art of writing has become more common among the Maronites, and rendered them in this country, what the Copts are in
Egypt, I mean, they are in poſſeſſion of all the poſts
of writers, intendants, and kiayas among the Turks,
and eſpecially of thoſe among their allies and neighbours, the Druzes.

S E C T. III.

Of the Druzes.

THE Druzes, or Derouz, who engaged the attention of Europe about the end of the ſixteenth century, are an inconſiderable people, who in their mode
of life, form of government, language, and cuſtoms,
bear a ſtriking reſemblance to the Maronites. Religion conſtitutes the principal difference between them.
That of the Druzes was long a problem; but the
myſtery is at length unveiled, and it is now not difficult to give a tolerably accurate account of it, as well
as of their origin, with which it is connected. To
gain a proper idea of their hiſtory, it will be neceſſary to trace facts up to their firſt ſources.

Twenty-three years after the death of Mahomet,
the diſputes between Ali, his ſon-in-law, and Moaouia,
Governor of Syria, occaſioned the firſt ſchiſm in the
empire of the Arabs, and the two ſects ſubſiſt to this
day; but, in reality, this difference related only to
power; and the Mahometans, however divided in
opinion reſpecting the rightful ſucceſſor of the pro-
phét, were agreed with reſpect to their dogmas.* It

* The radical cauſe of this great difference was the averſion
conceived againſt Ali, by Ayeſha, wife of Mahomet, becauſe,

was not until the following century that the perufal of
Greek books introduced among the Arabs a fpirit of
difcuffion and controverfy, to which, till then, they
were utter ftrangers. The confequence was, as might
be expected, by reafoning on matters not fufceptible
of demonftration, and guided by the abftract principles of an unintelligible logic, they divided into a multitude of fects and opinions. At this period, too the
civil power loft its authority, and religion, which
from that derives the means of preferving its unity,
fhared the fame fate, and the Mahometans now experienced what had before befallen the Chriftians. The
nations which had received the religion of Mahomet,
mixed with it their former abfurd notions ; and the
errors which had anciently prevailed over Afia, again
made their appearance, though altered in their forms.
The Metempfychofis, the doctrine of a good and evil
principle, and the renovation after fix thoufand years,

as it is faid, he had difcovered her infidelity to the Prophet.
She never could pardon him this indifcretion, and, after getting him three times excluded from the Califat, finding that by
his intrigues he was likely to fucceed in the fourth attempt, fhe
refolved to deftroy him by open violence. For this purpofe fhe
excited againft him feveral Arab chiefs, and, among others,
Amrou, Governor of Egypt, and *Moaouia*, Governor of Syria.
The latter procured himfelf to be proclaimed *Calif*, or *Succeffor*,
in the city of Damafcus. *Ali*, in order to difpoffefs him, declared war ; but the impropriety of his conduct ruined his affairs. After fome hoftilities, in which the advantages were
equal on both fides, he perifhed at Koufa by the hand of an
Affaffin or *Batenian*. His partizans elected his fon Hofain in
his place ; but this young man, ill adapted to fuch difficult circumftances, was flain in a rencounter by the partizans of Moaouia. His death rendered the two factions ftill more irreconcileable. Their hatred, prevented their agreeing in the expofi-
tion of the Koran. The doctors of the refpective parties took
a pleafure in contradicting each other ; and hence arofe the divifion of the Mahometans into two fects, who confider each
other as heretics. The Turks follow that of Omar and Moaouia, whom they hold to be the legitimate fucceffors of the
Prophet : the Perfians are followers of *Ali.*

as it had been taught by Zoroafter, were again revived
among the Mahometans. In this political and religious confufion, every enthufiaft became an apoftle,
and every apoftle the head of a feƈt. No lefs than
fixty of thefe were reckoned, remarkable for the numbers of their followers, all differing in fome points of
faith, and all difavowing herefy and error. Such was
the ftate of thefe countries, when at the commencement of the eleventh century, Egypt became the theatre of one of the moft extravagant fcenes of enthufiafm
and abfurdity ever recorded in hiftory. The following account is extraƈted from the eaftern writers. In
the year of the Hejira, 386 (A. D. 996) the third
Calif, of the race of the Fatmites, called *Hakem-b'amr-
ellah*, fucceded to the throne of Egypt, at the age of
eleven years. He was one of the moft extraordinary
princes of whom hiftory has preferved the memory.
He caufed the firft Califs, the companions of Mahomet,
to be curfed in the mofques, and afterwards revoked
the anathema: He compelled the Jews and Chriftians to abjure their religion, and then permitted them
to refume it. He prohibited the making flippers for
women, to prevent them from coming out of their
houfes. He burnt one half of the city of Cairo for
his diverfion, while his foldiers pillaged the other.
Not contented with thefe extravagant aƈtions, he forbad
the pilgrimage to Mecca, fafting and the five prayers;
and at length carried his madnefs fo far as to defire
to pafs for God himfelf. He ordered a regifter of
thofe who acknowledged him to be fo, and the number amounted to fixteen thoufand. This impious pre-
tenfion was fupported by a falfe prophet, who came
from Perfia into Egypt; which impoftor, named Mohammad-ben-Ifmael, taught that it was not neceffary
to faft or pray, to praƈtife circumcifion, to make the
pilgrimage to Mecca, or obferve feftivals; that the
prohibition of pork and wine was abfurd; and that
marriage between brothers and fifters fathers and

children was lawful. To ingratiate himfelf with Hakem, he maintained that this Calif was God himfelf
incarnate ; and, inftead of his name *Hakem-b'amr-el-
lah*, which fignifies, governing by the order of God, he
called him *Hakem-b'amr-eh*, governing by his own
order. Unluckily for the prophet, his new god had
not the power to protect him from the fury of his
enemies, who flew him in a tumult, almoft in the arms
of the Calif, who was himfelf maffacred foon after on
Mount *Mokattam*, where he, as he faid, had held converfation with angels.*

The death of thefe two chiefs did not ftop the progrefs of their opinions : A difciple of Mohammad-
ben-Ifmael, named Hamza-ben-Ahmud, propagated
them with an indefatigable zeal in Egypt, in Paleftine, and along the coaft of Syria, as far as Sidon
and Berytus. His profelytes, it feems, underwent
the fame fate as the Maronites ; for being perfecuted
by the fect in power, they took refuge in the mountains of Lebanon, where they were better able to
defend themfelves ; at leaft it is certain, that, fhortly
after this era, we find them eftablifhed there, and
forming an independent fociety like their neighbours.

The difference of their opinions difpofes them to
be enemies, but the urgent intereft of their common
fafety forces them to allow mutual toleration, and
they have always appeared united, and have jointly
oppofed, at different times, the Crufaders, the Sultans
of Aleppo, the Mamlouks, and the Ottomans. The
conqueft of Syria by the latter, made no change in
their fituation. Selim I. on his return from Egypt,
meditating no lefs than the conqueft of Europe, dif-
dained to wafte his time before the rocks of Lebanon.
Soliman II. his fucceffor, inceffantly engaged in important wars, either with the Knights of Rhodes, the
Perfians, the kingdom of Yemen, the Hungarians,

* Vide El-Makin. Hift. Saracen. Lib. I.

the Germans, or the Emperor Charles V. had no time to think of the Druzes. Emboldened by this inattention, and not content with their independence, they frequently defcended from their mountains to pillage the Turks. The Pachas in vain attempted to repel their inroads; their troops were invariably routed or repulfed. And it was not till the year 1588 that Amurath III. wearied with the complaints made to him, refolved, at all events, to reduce thefe rebels, and had the good fortune to fucceed. His general, Ibrahim Pacha, marched from Cairo, and attacked the Druzes and Maronites with fo much addrefs and vigour as to force them into their ftrong holds, the mountains. Diffenfion took place among their chiefs, of which he availed himfelf to exact a contribution of upwards of one million of piafters, and to impofe a tribute which has continued to the prefent time.

It appears that this expedition was the Epocha of a confiderable change in the conftitution of the Druzes. Till that they had lived in a fort of anarchy, under the command of different Shaiks, or Lords. The nation was likewife divided into two factions, fuch as is to be found in all the Arab tribes, and which are diftinguifhed into the party *Kaifi*, and the party *Yamani*.* To fimplify the adminiftration, Ibrahim permitted them only one Chief, who fhould be refponfible for the tribute, and execute the office of civil magiftrate; and this governor, from the nature of his fituation, acquiring great authority, became almoft the king of the republic; but as he was always chofen from among the Druzes, a confequence followed which the Turks had not forefeen, and which was nearly fatal to their power. For the Chief thus chofen, having at his difpofal the whole ftrength of the nation, was able to give it unanimity and energy, and it naturally

---

* Thefe factions diftinguifh themfelves by the colour of their flags; that of the Kaifis is red, that of the Yamanis white.

turned againſt the Turks; ſince the Druzes, by becoming their ſubjects, had not ceaſed to be their enemies. They took care, however, that their attacks
ſhould be indirect, ſo as to ſave appearances, and
only engaged in ſecret hoſtilities, more dangerous,
perhaps, than open war.

About this time, that is, the beginning of the
ſeventeenth century, the power of the Druzes attained its greateſt height; which it owed to the talents
and ambition of the celebrated Emir Fakr-el-din,
commonly called Fakardin. No ſooner was this prince
advanced to be Chief of that people than he turned
his whole attention to humble the Ottoman power,
and aggrandize himſelf at its expenſe; in this enterprize he diſplayed an addreſs ſeldom ſeen among the
Turks. He firſt gained the confidence of the Porte,
by every demonſtration of loyalty and fidelity; and
as the Arabs, at that time, infeſted the plain of Balbek, and the countries of Sour and Acre; he made
war upon them, freed the inhabitants from their depredations, and thus rendered them deſirous of living under his government.

The city of Bairout was ſituated advantageouſly
for his deſigns, as it opened a communication with
foreign countries, and, among others, with the Venetians, the natural enemies of the Turks. Fakr-el-
din availed himſelf of the miſconduct of the Aga,
expelled him, ſeized on the city, and even had the
art to make a merit of this hoſtility with the Divan,
by paying a more confiderable tribute. He proceeded in the ſame manner at Saide, Balbek, and Sour,
and, at length, about the year 1613, ſaw himſelf
maſter of all the country, as far as Adjaloun and
Safad. The Pachas of Tripoli and Damaſcus could
not ſee theſe encroachments with indifference; ſometimes they oppoſed him with open force, though ineffectually, and ſometimes endeavoured to ruin him
at the Porte, by ſecret inſinuations; but the Emir,

who maintained there his fpies and defenders, defeated every attempt.

At length, however, the Divan began to be alarmed at the progrefs of the Druzes, and made preparations for an expedition capable of crufhing them. Whether from policy or fear, Fakr-el-din did not think proper to wait this ftorm. He had formed connections in Italy, on which he built great hopes, and determined to go in perfon to folicit the fuccours they had promifed him ; perfuaded that his prefence would encreafe the zeal of his friends, while his abfence might appeafe the refentment of his enemies. He therefore embarked at Bairout, and, after refigning the adminiftration to his fon Ali, repaired to the court of the Medici, at Florence. The arrival of an Oriental prince in Italy, did not fail to attract the public attention. Enquiry was made into his nation, and the origin of the Druzes became a popular topic of refearch. Their hiftory and religion were found to be fo little known as to leave it a matter of doubt whether they fhould be claffed with the Mahometans or Chriftians. The Crufades were called to mind, and it was foon fuggefted that a people who had taken refuge in the mountains, and were enemies to the natives, could be no other than the off-fpring of the Crufaders.

This idle conceit was too favourable to Fakr-el-din for him to endeavour to difprove it : he was artful enough, on the contrary, to pretend he was related to the houfe of Lorraine ; and the miffionaries and merchants, who promifed themfelves a new opening for converfions and commerce, encouraged his pretenfions. When an opinion is in vogue, every one difcovers new proofs of its certainty. The learned in etymology, ftruck with the refemblance of the names, infifted, that *Druzes* and *Dreux* muft be the fame word, and, on this foundation, formed the fyftem of a pretended colony of French Crufaders, who,

under the conduct of a Comte *de Dreux*, had formed
a fettlement in Lebanon. This hypothefis, however,
was completely overthrown, by the remark that the
name of the Druzes is to be found in the Itinerary of
Benjamin of Tudela, who travelled before the time
of the Crufades. Indeed the futility of it ought to
have been fufficiently apparent, at firft, from the fingle confideration, that had they been defcended from
any nation of the Franks, they muft have retained,
at leaft, the traces of fome European language; for
a people, retired into a feparate diftrict, and living
diftinct from the natives of the country, do not lofe
their language. That of the Druzes, however, is
very pure Arabic, without a fingle word of European
origin. The real derivation of the name of this
people has been long in our poffeffion, without our
knowing it. It originates from the founder of the
fect of Mohammad-ben-Ifmael, who was furnamed
El-Dorzi, and not *El Darari*, as it is ufually printed:
the confufion of thefe two words, fo different in our
writing, arifes from the figure of the two Arabian
letters *r* and *z*, which have only this difference, that
the *z* has a point over it, frequently omitted, or effaced in the manufcripts.*

After a ftay of nine years in Italy, *Fakr-el-din* returned to refume the government of his country.
During his abfence, his fon Ali had repulfed the

---

* This difcovery is due to M. Mitchel, Dragoman, *Baratairet*
of France, at Saide, of which place he was a native: he has
written a memoir on the Druzes, of which he gave one of the
two copies he had to the Chevalier de Taules, Conful at Saide,
and the other to the Baron de Tott, when he was there, in
1777, to infpect that factory.

† *Barataire*, is a fubject of the Turkifh government, privileged by one of the European Minifters, in amity with the
Porte, and by that means placed upon a footing with the Franks,
with refpect to the payment of duties, &c. Each Minifter
poffeffes a certain number of thefe *Barats* at his difpofal, which
he cannot exceed. T.

Turks, appeafed difcontents, and maintained affairs in tolerable good order. Nothing remained for the Emir, but to employ the knowledge he could not but have acquired, in perfecting the internal adminif-tration of government, and promoting the welfare of the nation ; but inftead of the ufeful and valuable arts, he wholly abandoned himfelf to the frivolous and expenfive, for which he had imbibed a paffion while in Italy. He built numerous villas ; conftruct-ed baths, and planted gardens ; he even prefumed, without refpect to the prejudices of his country, to employ the ornaments of painting and fculpture, not-withftanding thefe are prohibited by the Koran.

The confequences of this conduct foon manifefted themfelves : the Druzes, who paid the fame tribute as in time of war, became diffatisfied. The Yamani faction were roufed ; the people murmured at the expenfes of the prince ; and the luxury he difplayed renewed the jealoufy of the Pachas. They attempted to levy greater tribute : hoftilities again commenced, and *Fakr-el-din* repulfed the forces of the Pachas, who took occafion, from this refiftance, to render him fufpected by the Sultan himfelf. Amurath III. incenfed that one of his fubjects fhould dare to enter into a competition with him, refolved on his deftruc-tion ; and the Pacha of Damafcus received orders to march, with all his forces, againft Bairout, the ufual refidence of Fakr-el-din ; while forty galleys invefted it by fea, and cut off all communication.

The Emir, who depended on his good fortune, and fuccours from Italy, determined at firft to brave the ftorm. His fon, Ali, who commanded at Safad, was ordered to oppofe the progrefs of the Turkifh army, and in fact he bravely refifted them, notwithftanding the great difparity of his forces ; but, after two en-gagements, in which he had the advantage, being flain in a third attack, the face of affairs were greatly changed, and every thing went to ruin. Fakr-el-din, terrified at the lofs of his troops, afflicted at the death of his fon, and enfeebled by age and a voluptuous life, loft both courage and prefence of mind. He no longer faw any refource but in a peace, which he fent his fecond fon to folicit of the Turkifh Admiral, whom he attempted to feduce by prefents; but the Admiral, detaining both the prefents and the Envoy, declared he would have the prince himfelf. Fakr-el-din, intimidated, took to flight, and was purfued by the Turks, now mafters of the country. He took refuge on the fteep eminence of Niha, where they befieged him ineffectually for a whole year, when they left him at liberty: but, fhortly after, the companions of his adverfity, wearied with their fufferings, betrayed and delivered him up to the Turks. Fakr-el-din, though in the hands of his enemies, conceived hopes of pardon, and fuffered himfelf to be carried to Conftantinople, where Amurath, pleafed to behold at his feet a prince fo celebrated, at firft treated him with that benevolence which arifes from the pride of fuperiority; but foon returning to his former jealoufies, yielded to the inftigations of his courtiers, and, in one of his violent fits of paffion, ordered him to be ftrangled, about the year 1631.

After the death of *Fakr-el-din*, the pofterity of that prince ftill continued in poffeffion of the Government, though at the pleafure, and as vaffals, of the Turks. This family failing in the male-line at the beginning of the prefent century, the authority devolved, by the election of the Shaiks, on the houfe of Shelah, in which it ftill continues. The only Emir of that houfe, whofe name deferves to be preferved, is the Emir Melhem, who reigned from 1640 to 1759; in which interval he retrieved the loffes of the Druzes, and reftored them to that confequence which they had loft by the defeat of Fakr-el-din. Towards the end of his life, about the year 1754, Melhem, wearied with the cares of government, abdicated his authority, to live in religious retirement, after the manner of the Ok-kals; but the troubles that fucceeded occafioned him once more to refume the the reins of government, which he held till 1759, when he died, univerfally regretted.

He left three fons, minors: the eldeft of whom ought, according to the cuftom of the country to have fucceeded him; but, being only eleven years of age, the authority devolved upon his uncle, Manfour, agreeably to a law very general in Afia, which wills the people to be governed by a fovereign who has arrived at years of maturity. The young prince was but little fitted to maintain his pretenfions; but a Maronite, named Sad-el-Kouri, to whom Melhem had entrufted his education, took this upon himfelf. Af-piring to fee his pupil a powerful prince, that he might himfelf become a powerful vifir, he made every exertion to advance his fortune. He firft retired with him to Djebail, in the Kefraouan, where the Emir Youfef poffeffed large domains, and there undertook to conciliate the Maronites, by embracing every op-portunity to ferve both individuals and the nation. The great revenues of his pupil, and the moderation of his expenditure, amply furnifhed him with the means. The farm of the Kefraouan was divided be-tween feveral Shaiks, with whom the Porte was not very well fatisfied. Sad treated for the whole with the Pacha of Tripoli, and got himfelf appointed fole Receiver. The Motoualis of the valley of Balbek had, for fome years before, made feveral encroach-ments on Lebanon, and the Maronites began to be alarmed at the near approach of thefe intolerant Ma-hometans. Sad purchafed of the Pacha of Damafcus a permiffion to make war upon them, and, in 1763, drove them out of the country. The Druzes were at that time divided into two factions: Sad united his intereft with thofe who oppofed Manfour, and fecretly prepared the plot which was to raife the nephew on the ruin of the uncle.

At this period the Arab Daher, who had made himfelf mafter of Galilee, and fixed his refidence at Acre, difquieted the Porte by his progrefs and pretenfions: To oppofe him, the Divan had juft united the Pachalics of Damafcus, Saide, and Tripoli, in the hands of Ofman and his children; and it was evident, that an open war was not very remote. Manfour, who dreaded the Turks too much to refift them, made ufe of the policy ufual on fuch occafions, pretending a zeal for their fervice, while he fecretly favoured their enemy. This was a fufficient motive for Sad to purfue meafures directly oppofite. He fupported the Turks againft the faction of Manfour, and manœuvered with fo much good fortune or addrefs as to depofe that Emir, in 1770, and place Youfef in his government.

In the following year, Ali Bey declared war, and attacked Damafcus. Youfef, called on by the Turks, took part in the quarrel, but without being able to draw the Druzes from their mountains, to enter into the army of the Ottomans. Befides their natural repugnance, at all times, to make war out of their country, they were, on this occafion, too much divided at home to quit their habitations, and they had reafon to congratulate themfelves on the event. The battle of Damafcus enfued, and the Turks, as we have already feen, were completely routed. The Pacha of Saide, efcaping from this defeat, and not thinking himfelf in fafety in that town, fought an afylum even in the houfe of Emir Youfef. The moment was unfavourable, but the face of affairs foon changed, by the flight of Mohammad Bey. The Emir, concluding that Ali Bey was dead, and not imagining that Daher was powerful enough fingly to maintain the quarrel, declared openly againft him. Saide was threatened with a fiege, and he detached fifteen hundred men of his faction to its defence; while himself, in person, prevailing on the Druzes and Maronites to follow him, made an incursion with twenty-five thousand peasants into the valley of Bekaa, and, in the absence of the Motoualis, who had joined the army of Daher, laid the whole country waste, with fire and sword, from Belbek to Tyre.

. While the Druzes, proud of this exploit, were marching in disorder towards the latter city, five hundred Motoualis, informed of what had happened, flew from Acre, enflamed with rage and despair, and fell with such impetuosity on their army, as to give them a complete overthrow. Such was the surprise and confusion of the Druzes, that imagining themselves attacked by Daher himself, and betrayed by their companions, they turned their swords on each other as they fled. The steep declivities of Djezin, and the pine-woods which were in the route of the fugitives, were strewed with dead, but few of whom perished by the hands of the Motoualis.

The Emir Youfef, ashamed of this defeat, escaped to Dair-el-Kamar, and, shortly after, attempted to take revenge; but, being again defeated in the plain between Said and Sour, (Tyre,) he was constrained to resign, to his uncle Manfour, the ring, which, among the Druzes, is the symbol of command. In 1773, he was restored by a new revolution; but he could not support his power but at the expense of a civil war. In order, therefore, to prevent Bairout falling into the hands of the adverse faction, he requested the assistance of the Turks, and demanded, of the Pacha of Damascus, a man of sufficient abilities to defend that city. The choice fell on an adventurer, who, from his subsequent fortune, and the part he is now acting, merits to be made known.

This man, named Ahmad, is a native of Bosnia, and speaks the Sclavonian as his mother tongue, as the Ragusan captains, with whom he converses in preference to thofe of every nation, affert. It is faid, that flying from his country at the age of fixteen, to efcape the confequences of an attempt to violate his fifter-in-law, he repaired to Conftantinople, where, deftitute of the means of procuring a fubfiftence, he fold himfelf to the flave-merchants, to be conveyed to Egypt; and, on his arrival at Cairo, was pur-chafed by Ali Bey who placed him among his Mam-louks.

Ahmad was not long in diftinguifhing himfelf by his courage and addrefs. His patron employed him on feveral occafions, in dangerous coups de main, fuch as the affaffination of fuch Beys and Cachefs as he fufpeded; of which commiffions he acquitted himfelf fo well as to acquire the name of *Djezzar,* which fignifies *Cut-throat.** With this claim to his friendfhip, he enjoyed the favour of Ali, until it was difturbed by an accident.

This jealous Bey having profcribed one of his be-nefactors, called Saleh Bey, commanded Djezzar to cut off his head. Either from humanity or fome fe-cret friendfhip for the devoted victim, Djezzar hefi-tated, and even remonftrated againft the order. But learning the next day that Mohammad Bey had exe-cuted the commiffion, and that Ali had fpoken of him not very favourably, he thought himfelf a loft man, and, to avoid the fate of Saleh Bey, efcaped unobferved, and reached Conftantinople. He there folicited employments fuitable to his former rank, but meeting, as is ufual in capitals, with a great number of rivals, he purfued another plan, and went to feek his fortune in Syria, as a private foldier. Chance conducted him among the Druzes, where he was hof-

---

* This Djezzar *is the monfter fo well defcribed by Baron de Tott, in Part* IV. *of his Memoirs. The Baron tranflates the word Djezzar,* Butcher.—*He was in the beginning of* 1787 *in open re-volt againft the Porte.*

pitably entertained, even in the houfe of the Kiaya
of the Emir Youfef. From thence he repaired to
Damafcus, where he foon obtained the title of Aga,
with a command of five *pair of colours*, that is to fay,
of fifty men; and he was thus fituated when fortune
deftined him to the government of Bairout.

Djezzar was no fooner eftablifhed there, than he
took poffeffion of it for the Turks. Youfef was confounded at this proceeding. He demanded juftice at
Damafcus; but finding his complaints treated with
contempt, entered into a treaty with Daher, and concluded an offenfive and defenfive alliance with him,
at Ras-el-aen, near to Sour. No fooner was Daher
united with the Druzes than he laid fiege to Bairout,
by land, whilft two Ruffian frigates, whofe fervice
was purchafed by fix hundred purfes, cannonaded it
by fea. Djezzar was compelled to fubmit to force,
and, after a vigorous refiftance, gave up the city,
and furrendered himfelf prifoner. Shaik Daher,
charmed with his courage, and flattered with the
preference he had given him in the furrender, conducted him to Acre, and fhewed him every mark of
kindnefs. He even ventured to truft him with a
fmall expedition into Paleftine; but Djezzar, on approaching Jerufalem, went over to the Turks, and
returned to Damafcus.

The war of Mohammad Bey breaking out, Djezzar offered his fervice to the Captain Pacha, and
gained his confidence. He accompanied him to the
fiege of Acre, and that admiral having deftroyed
Daher, and finding no perfon more proper than
Djezzar to accomplifh the defigns of the Porte in
that country, named him Pacha of Saide.

Being now, in confequence of this revolution, fuperior Lord to the Emir Youfef, Djezzar is mindful
of injuries in proportion as he had reafon to accufe
himfelf of ingratitude. By a conduct truly Turkifh,
feigning alternately gratitude and refentment, he is

alternately on terms of difpute and reconciliation with
him, continually exacting money as the price of
peace, or as indemnity for war. His artifices have
fucceeded in well that, within the fpace of five years,
he has extorted from the Emir four millions of French
money, (above a hundred and fixty thoufand pounds),
a fum the more aftonifhing as the farm of the country of the Druzes did not then amount to one hundred thoufand livres, (four thoufand pounds.)

In 1784, he made war on him, depofed him, and
beftowed the government on the Emir of the country
of Hafbeya, named Ifmael. Youfef, having once
more purchafed his favor, returned, towards the end
of the fame year, to Dair-el-Kamar, and even courted his confidence fo far as to wait on him at Acre,
from whence nobody expected him to return, but
Djezzar is too cunning to fhed blood while there are
any hopes of getting money : he releafed the prince,
and fent him back with every mark of friendfhip.
Since that period, the Porte has named him Pacha
of Damafcus, where he now refides. There, ftill
retaining the fovereignty of the Pachalic of Acre,
and of the country of the Druzes, he has feized on
Sad, the Kiaya of the Emir, and, under pretext of
his being the author of the troubles, has threatened
to ftrike off his head. The Maronites, alarmed for
the fafety of this man, whom they revere, have offered nine hundred purfes for his ranfom. The Pacha
demands a thoufand ; and if, as will probably be the
cafe, their money be exhaufted by thefe repeated
contributions, woe to the prince and his minifter !
on their fate depends that of many others ; and, indeed, they may be faid to have deferved it, for it was
the unfkilfulnefs of the one, and the ambition of the
other, which, by inviting the Turks to interfere in
the affairs of the Druzes, has given fo fatal a blow
to the fafety and tranquility of the nation that, in
the ordinary courfe of things, it will be long before

it can poffibly recover its former profperity and power.

Let us return to the religion of the Druzes. What has been already faid of the opinions of Mohammad-ben-Ifmael may be regarded as the fubftance of it. They practife neither circumcifion, nor prayers, nor fafting; they obferve neither feftivals, nor prohibitions. They drink wine, eat pork, and allow marriage between brothers and fifters, though not between fathers and children. From this we may conclude, with reafon, that the Druzes have no religion: yet, one clafs of them muft be expected, whofe religious cuftoms are very peculiar. Thofe who compofe it are to the reft of the nation what the *initiated* were to the *profane*; they affume the name of *Okkals*, which means fpiritualifts, and beftow on the vulgar the epithet of *Djahel*, or ignorant; they have various degrees of initiation, the higheft orders of which require celibacy. Thefe are diftinguifhable by the White Turban they affect to wear, as a fymbol of their purity; and fo proud are they of this fuppofed purity, that they think themfelves fullied by even touching a profane perfon. If you eat out of their plate, or drink out of their cup, they break them; and hence the cuftom, fo general in this country, of ufing vafes, with a fort of cock, which may be drank out of without touching them with the lips. All their practices are enveloped in myfteries: their Oratories always ftand alone, and are conftantly fituated on eminences: in thefe they hold their fecret affemblies, to which women are admitted. It is pretended they perform ceremonies there in prefence of a fmall ftatue refembling an ox or a calf; whence fome have pretended to prove that they are defcended from the Samaritans. But, befides that the fact is not well afcertained, the worfhip of the ox may be deduced from other fources.

They have one or two books which they conceal
with the greateſt care : but chance has deceived their
jealouſy ; for, in a civil war, which happened ſix or
ſeven years ago, the Emir Youſef, who is *Djahel*, or
ignorant, found one among the pillage of one of their
oratories. I am aſſured, by perſons who have read
it, that it contains only a myſtic jargon, the obſcurity
of which, doubtleſs, renders it valuable to adepts.
Hakem Bamr-ellah is there ſpoken of, by whom they
mean God, incarnated in the perſon of the Calif. It
likewiſe treats of another life, of a place of puniſhment, and a place of happineſs, where the Okkals
ſhall, of courſe, be moſt diſtinguiſhed. Several degrees of perfection are mentioned, to which they arrive by ſucceſſive trials. In other reſpects, theſe ſec-
taries have all the inſolence, and all the fears, of ſuperſtition : they are not communicative, becauſe they
are weak ; but it is probable that, were they powerful,
they would be promulgators and intolerant.

The reſt of the Druzes, ſtrangers to this ſpirit,
are wholly indifferent about religious matters. The
Chriſtians who live in their country, pretend that ſeveral of them believe in the Metempſychoſis ; that
others worſhip the ſun, moon, and ſtars, all which is
poſſible ; for, as among the Anſaria, every one left
to his own fancy, follows the opinion that pleaſes him
moſt ; and theſe opinions are thoſe which preſent
themſelves moſt naturally to unenlightened minds.
When among the Turks, they affect the exterior of
Mahometans, frequently the Moſques, and perform
their ablutions and prayers. Among the Maronites,
they accompany them to church, and, like them,
make uſe of the holy water. Many of them, impor-
tuned by the miſſionaries, ſuffer themſelves to be
baptized ; and if ſolicited by the Turks, receive cir-
cumciſion, and conclude by dying neither Chriſtians

nor Mahometans; but they are not fo indifferent in matters of civil policy*.

Of the Government of the Druzes.

THE Druzes, as well as the Maronites, may be divided into two claffes, the common people, and the people of eminence and property, diftinguifhed by the title of Shaiks, and Emirs, or defcendants of princes. The greater part are cultivators, either as farmers or proprietors; every man lives on his inheritance, improving his mulberry-trees and vineyards; in fome diftricts they grow tobacco, cotton, and fome grain, but the quantity of thefe is inconfiderable. It appears that at firft, all the lands were, as formerly in Europe in the hands of a fmall number of families. But to render them productive, the great proprietors were forced to fell part of them, and let leafes, which fubdivifion is become the chief fource of the power of the ftate, by multiplying the number of perfons interefted in the public weal: there ftill exift, however, fome traces of the original inequality, which even to

---

* The above accounts of the *Druzes* correfponds exactly with the *Hiftorical Memoire* on that people, tranflated from the manufcript of M. *Venture de Parardis*, which contains *extracts* from their *facred books, a catechifm*, &c. The Memoir in queftion, confirms the accuracy of our Author, who had never feen it, nor was acquainted with M. Venture. The latter gentleman and M. Sugufte, a moft amiable man, and a well informed traveller in the eaft, who had juft done the tranflator the honour of a vifit, concur in beftowing the higheft commendations on the prefent work, and do not hefitate to pronounce it the moft accurate modern book that has appeared refpecting Syria and Egypt. To their elogium may be added the diftinguifhed approbation of M. de St. Prieft, the late Ambaffador of the Court of France at Conftantinople, which he has expreffed in the ftrongeft terms. T.

this day produces pernicious effects. The great property possessed by some families give them too much influence in all the measures of the nation; and their private interests have too great weight in every public transaction. Their history, for some years back, affords sufficient proofs of this; since all the civil or foreign wars in which they have been engaged have originated in the ambition and personal views of some of the principal families, such as the the Lesbeks, the Djambelats, the Ismaels of Solyma, &c. The Shaiks of these houses, who alone possess one tenth part of the country, procured creatures by their money, and at last, involved all the Druzes in their dissensions. It must be owned, however, that possibly, to this conflict between contending parties the whole nation owes the good fortune of never having been enslaved by its chief.

This chief, called *Hakem*, or governor, also Emir, or Prince, is a sort of king, or general, who unites in his own person the civil and military powers. His dignity is sometimes transmitted from father to son, sometimes from one brother to another, and the succession is determined rather by force than any certain laws. Females can in no case pretend to this inheritance. They are already excluded from succession in civil affairs, and consequently, can still less expect it in political: in general, the Asiatic governments are too turbulent, and their administration renders military talents too necessary to admit of the sovereignty of women. Among the Druzes, the male line of any family being extinguished, the government devolves to him who is in possession of the greatest number of suffrages and resources. But the first step is to obtain the approbation of the Turks, of whom he becomes the vassal and tributary. It even happens, that, not unfrequently to assert their supremacy, they name the *Hakem*, contrary to the wishes of the nation, as in the case of Ismael Hasbeya, raised to that dignity by Djezzar; but this conſtraint laſts no longer than it is maintained by that violence which gave it birth. The office of the government is to watch over the good order of the ſtate, and to pre- vent the Emirs, Shaiks, and villages, from making war on each other; in caſe of diſobedience, he may employ force. He is alſo at the head of the civil power, and names the Cadis, only, always reſerving to himſelf the power of life and death. He collects the tribute, from which, he annually pays to the Pa- cha a ſtated ſum. This tribute varies, in proportion as the nation renders itſelf more or leſs formidable: at the beginning of this century, it amounted to one hundred and ſixty purſes, (eight thouſand three hun- dred and thirty pounds,) but Melhem forced the Turks to reduce it to ſixty. In 1784, Emir Youſef paid eighty and promiſed ninety. This tribute, which is called *Miri*, is impoſed on the mulberry-trees, vine- yards, cotton, and grain. All ſown land, pays in proportion to its extent; every foot of mulberries is taxed at three Medins, or three Sols, nine Deniers, (not quite two-pence.) A hundred feet of vineyard, pays a Piaſter, or forty Medins, and freſh meaſurements are often made, to preſerve a juſt proportion. The Shaiks and Emirs have no exemption in this reſpect, and it may be truly ſaid, they contribute to the public ſtock in proportion to their fortune. The col- lection is made almoſt without expence. Each man pays his contingent at Dair-el-Kamer, if he pleaſes, or to the collectors of the prince, who make a circuit round the country, after the crop of ſilks. The ſur- plus of this tribute is for the prince, ſo that it is his intereſt to reduce the demands of the Turks, as it would be likewiſe to augment the impoſt; but this meaſure requires the ſanction of the Shaiks, who have the privilege of oppoſing it. Their conſent is necef- ſary, likewiſe, for peace and war. In theſe caſes, the Emir muſt convoke general aſſemblies, and lay before them the ſtate of his affairs. There, every Shaik, and every Peaſant, who has any reputation for courage or underſtanding, is entitled to give his ſuffrage, ſo that this government may be conſidered as a well-proportioned mixture of monarchy, ariſtocracy, and democracy. Every thing depends on circumſtances: if the governor be a man of ability, he is abſolute; if weak, a cypher. This proceeds from the want of fixed laws; a want common to all Aſia, and the radical cauſe of all the diſorders in the governments of the Aſiatic nations.

Neither the chief nor the individual Emirs maintain troops; they have only perſons attached to the domeſtic ſervice of their houſes, and a few black ſlaves. When the nation makes war, every man, whether Shaik or Peaſant, able to bear arms, is called upon to march. He takes with him a little bag of flour, a muſket, ſome bullets, a ſmall quantity of powder, made in his village, and repairs to the rendezvous appointed by the governor. If it be a civil war, as ſometimes happens, the ſervants, the farmers, and their friends, take up arms for their patron, or the chief of their family, and repair to his ſtandard. In ſuch caſes, the parties irritated, frequently ſeem on the point of proceeding to the laſt extremities; but they ſeldom have recourſe to acts of violence, or attempt the death of each other; mediators always interpoſe, and the quarrel is appeaſed the more readily as each patron is obliged to provide his followers with proviſions and amunition. This ſyſtem, which produces happy effects in civil troubles, is attended with great inconvenience in foreign wars, as ſufficiently appeared in that of 1784. Djezzar, who knew that the whole army lived at the expence of the Emir Youſef, aimed at nothing but delay, and the Druzes, who were not diſpleaſed at being fed for doing nothing, prolonged the operations; but the Emir, wearied of paying, concluded a treaty, the terms of which were not a little rigorous for him, and eventually for the whole nation, since nothing is more certain than that the interests of a prince and his subjects are always inseparable.

The ceremonies to which I have been a witness on these occasions, bear a striking resemblance to the customs of ancient times. When the Emir and the Shaiks had determined on war, at Dair-el-Kamar, cryers in the evening, ascended the summits of the mountain ; and there began to cry with a loud voice : *To war, to war ; take your guns, take your pistols : noble Shaiks, mount your horses ; arm yourselves with the lance and sabre ; rendezvous to-morrow at Dair-el-Kamar. Zeal of God ! zeal of combats !* This summons heard from the neighbouring villages, was repeated there, and, as the whole country is nothing but a chain of lofty mountains, and deep vallies, the proclamation passed in a few hours to the frontiers. These voices, from the stillness of the night, the long surrounding echoes, and the nature of the subject, had something awful and terrible in their effect. Three days after, fifteen thousand armed men rendezvoused at Dair-el-Kamar, and operations might have been immediately commenced.

We may easily imagine that troops of this kind no way resemble our European soldiers ; they have neither uniforms, nor discipline, nor order. They are a crowd of peasants with short coats, naked legs, and muskets in their hands differing from the Turks and Mamlouks, in that they are all foot ; the Shaiks and Emirs alone have horses, which are of little use from the rugged nature of the country. War there, can only be a war of posts. The Druzes never risk themselves in the plain, and with reason, for they would be unable to stand the shock of cavalry, having no bayonets to their muskets. Their whole art consists in climbing rocks, creeping among the bushes and blocks of stone, from whence their fire is the more dangerous; as they are covered, fire at their eafe, and by hunting, and military fports, have acquired the habit of hitting a mark with great dexterity. They are accuftomed to fudden inroads, attacks by night, ambufcades, and all thofe *coups de main,* which require to fall fuddenly on, and come to clofe fight with the enemy. Ardent in improving their fuccefs, eafily difpirited, and prompt to refume their courage, daring even to temerity, and fometimes ferocious, they poffefs above all, two qualities effential to the excellency of any troops; they ftrictly obey their leaders, and are endowed with a temperance and vigour of health at this day unknown to moft civilized nations. In the campaign of 1784, they paffed three months in the open air, without tents, or any other covering than a fheep-fkin; yet were there not more deaths and maladies than if they had remained in their houfes. Their provifions confifted, as at other times, of fmall loaves baked on the afhes, or on a brick, raw onions, cheefe, olives, fruits, and a little wine. The table of the chiefs was almoft as frugal, and we may affirm, that they fubfifted a hundred days, on what the fame number of Englifhmen or Frenchmen would not have lived ten. They have no knowledge of the fcience of fortification, the management of artillery, or encampments, nor, in a word, any thing which conftitutes the art of war. But, had they among them a few perfons verfed in military fcience, they would readily acquire its principles, and become a formidable foldiery. This would be the more eafily effected, as their mulberry plantations and vineyards do not occupy them all the year, and they could afford much time for military exercifes.*

* In this leifure time, when the crop of filk is over in Lebanon, a great many Peafants like our inhabitants of the Limoufin leave the mountains to get in the harvefts in the plains.

By the laſt eſtimate, it appears the number of men able to bear arms was forty thouſand, which ſuppoſes a total population of a hundred and twenty thouſand : no addition is to be made to this calculation, ſince there are no Druzes in the cities or on the coaſt. As the whole country contains only one hundred and ten ſquare leagues, there reſults for every league one thouſand and ninety perſons ; which is equal to the population of our richeſt provinces. To render this more remarkable, it muſt be obſerved that the ſoil is not fertile, that a great many eminences remain un-cultivated, that they do not grow corn enough to ſupport themſelves three months in the year, that they have no manufactures, and that all their exportations are confined to ſilks and cottons, the balance of which exceeds very little the importation of corn from the Hauran, the oils of Paleſtine, and the rice and coffee they procure from Bairout.—Whence ariſes then ſuch a number of inhabitants, within ſo ſmall a ſpace ? I can diſcover no other cauſe than that ray of liberty which glimmers in this country. Unlike the Turks, every man lives in a perfect ſecurity of his life and property. The peaſant is not richer than in other countries ; but he is free, " he fears not," as I have often heard them ſay, " that the Aga, the Kaimma-" kam, or the Pacha, ſhould ſend their Djendis,* to " pillage his houſe, carry off his family, or give him " the baſtinado." Such oppreſſions are unknown among theſe mountains. Security, therefore, has been the original cauſe of population, from that in-herent deſire which all men have to multiply them-ſelves wherever they find an eaſy ſubſiſtence. The frugality of the nation, which is content with little, has been a ſecondary, and not leſs powerful reaſon ; and a third, is the emigration of a number of Chriſ-tian families, who daily deſert the Turkiſh provinces

* Soldiers.

to settle in Mount Lebanon, where they are received with open arms by the Maronites, from similarity of religion, and by the Druzes from principles of toleration, and a conviction how much it is the interest of every country to multiply the number of its cultivators, consumers, and allies. They all live quietly together; but I cannot help adding, that the Christians frequently display an indiscreet and meddling zeal, too well calculated to disturb this tranquility.

The comparison, which the Druzes often have an opportunity of making between their situation and that of other subjects of the Turkish government has given them an advantageous opinion of their superiority, which, by a natural effect, has an influence on their personal character. Exempt from the violence and insults of despotism, they consider themselves as more perfect than their neighbours, because they have the good fortune not to be equally debased. Hence they acquire a character more elevated, energetic, and active ; in short, a genuine republican spirit. They are considered throughout the Levant as restless, enterprising, hardy, and brave even to temerity. Only three hundred of them have been seen to enter Damascus in open day, and spread around them terror and carnage. It is remarkable, that though their form of Government is nearly similar, the Maronites do not possess these qualities to the same degree. Enquiring the reason, one day, in a company where this observation was made, in consequence of some recent events, an old Maronite, after a moment's silence, taking his pipe from his mouth, and curling his beard round his finger, made answer, " Perhaps " the Druzes would be more afraid of death, did " they believe in a future state." Nor are they great preachers of that morality which consists in pardoning injuries. No people are more nice than they with respect to the point of honour : Any offence of that kind, or open insult, is instantly punished by

blows of the kandjur or the mufket; while among
the inhabitants of the towns, it only excites injurious retorts. This delicacy has occafioned in their
manners and difcourfe, a referve, or, if you will, a
politenefs, which one is aftonifhed to difcover among
peafants. It is carried even to diffimulation and falfehood, efpecially among the chiefs, whofe greater interefts demand greater attentions. Circumfpection is
neceffary to all, from the formidable confequences of
that retaliation of which I have fpoken. Thefe cuftoms may appear barbarous to us; but they have the
merit of fupplying the deficiency of regular juftice,
which is neceffarily tedious and uncertain in thefe dif-
orderly and almoft anarchial governments.

The Druzes have another point of honour: that
of hofpitality. Whoever prefents himfelf at their door
in the quality of a fuppliant or paffenger, is fure to
be entertained with lodging and food, in the moft
generous and unaffected manner. I have often feen
the loweft peafants give the laft morfel of bread they
had in their houfes to the hungry traveller; and
when I obferved to them that they wanted prudence,
their anfwer was: " God is liberal and great, and all
men are brethren." There are, therefore, no inns
in this country, any more than in the reft of Turkey.
When they have once contracted with their gueft,
the facred engagement of *bread* and *falt*, no fubfequent event can make them violate it: various inftances of this are related, which do honour to their
character. A few years ago, an Aga of the Janiffa-
ries, having been engaged in a rebellion, fled from
Damafcus, and retired among the Druzes. The
Pacha was informed of this, and demanded him of
the Emir, threatening to make war on him in cafe of
refufal. The Emir demanded him of the Shaik Talhouk, who had received him; but the indignant
Shaik replied, " When have you known the Druzes
" deliver up their guefts? Tell the Emir, that, as

" long as Talhouk fhall preferve his beard, not a hair
" of the head of his fuppliant fhall fall!" The
Emir threatened him with force; Talhouk armed his
family. The Emir, dreading a revolt, adopted a
method practifed as juridical in that country. He
declared to the Shaik, that he would cut down fifty
mulberry-trees a day, until he fhould give up the
Aga. He proceeded as far as a thoufand, and Talhouk ftill remained inflexible. At length, the other
Shaiks, enraged, took up the quarrel, and the commotion was about to become general, when the Aga,
reproaching himfelf with being the caufe of fo much
mifchief, made his efcape, without the knowledge
even of Talhouk.*

* I have found in an Arabic manufcript, another anecdote,
which, though foreign to my prefent fubject, I think too excellent to be omitted.

' In the time of the Califs, fays the author, when Abdalah,
' the *fhedder of blood*, had murdered every defcendant of Om-
' miah, within his reach, one of that family, named Ibrahim,
' the fon of Soliman, fon of Abd-el-Malek, had the good for-
' tune to efcape, and reach Koufa, which he entered in dif-
' guife. Knowing no perfon in whom he could confide, he
' fat down under the portico of a large houfe. Soon after the
' mafter, arriving, followed by feveral fervants, alighted from
' his horfe, entered, and, feeing the ftranger, afked him who
' he was. I am an unfortunate man, replied Ibrahim, and re-
' queft from thee an afylum. God protect thee, faid the rich
' man; enter, and remain in peace. Ibrahim lived feveral
' months in this houfe, without being queftioned by his hoft.
' But, aftonifhed to fee him every day go out on horfeback, and
' return, at the fame hour, he ventured one day to enquire the
' reafon—I have been informed, replied the rich man, that a
' perfon named Ibrahim, the fon of Soliman, is concealed in
' this town; he has flain my father, and I am fearching for him
' to retaliate.—Then I knew, faid Ibrahim, that God had pur-
' pofely conducted me to that place; I adored his decree, and,
' refigning myfelf to death, I anfwered,—God has determined
' to avenge thee, offended man; thy victim is at thy feet. The
' rich man, aftonifhed, replied,—O! ftranger! I fee thy mif-
' fortunes have made thee weary of life; thou feekeft to lofe
' it, but my hand cannot commit fuch a crime.—I do not de-

The Druzes have alſo the prejudices of the Bedouins reſpecting birth; like them, they pay great reſpect to the antiquity of families; but this produces no eſſential inconveniencies. The nobility of the Emirs and Shaiks does not exempt them from paying tribute, in proportion to their revenues. It confers on them no prerogatives, either in attainment of landed property, or public employments. In. this country, no more than in all Turkey, are they acquainted with game-laws, or glebes, or ſeigniorial, or eccleſiaſtical tithes, franc fiefs or alienation fines; every thing is held, as I have ſaid, in freehold: every man, after paying in his miri and his rent, is maſter of his property. In ſhort, by a particular privilege, the Druzes and Maronites pay no fine for their ſucceſſion; nor does the Emir, like the Sultan, arrogate to himſelf original and univerſal property: there exiſts, neverthelefs, in the law of inheritance, an imperfection which produces diſagreeable effects. Fathers have, as in the Roman law, the power of preferring ſuch of their children as they think proper; hence it has happened, in ſeveral families of the Shaiks, that the whole property has centered in the ſame perſon, who has preverted it to the purpoſe of intriguing and caballing, while his relations remain, as they well expreſs it, *princes of olives and cheeſe;* that is to ſay, poor as peaſants.

' ceive thee, ſaid Ibrahim; thy father was ſuch a one; we met
' each other in ſuch a place, and the affair happened in ſuch a
' manner." A violent trembling then ſeized the rich man; his
teeth chattered as if from intenſe cold; his eyes alternately
ſparkled with fury, and overflowed with tears. In this agitation, he remained a long time; at length, turning to Ibrahim—
To-morrow, ſaid he, deſtiny ſhall join thee to my father, and
God will have retaliated. But as for me how can I violate the
aſylum of my houſe? Wretched ſtranger, fly from my preſence! There, take theſe hundred ſequins: Begone quickly,
and let me never behold thee more!

In confequence of their prejudices, the Druzes do not choofe to make alliances out of their own families. They invariably prefer their relation, though poor, to a rich ftranger; and poor peafants have been known to refufe their daughters to merchants of Saidè and Bairout, who poffeffed from twelve to fifteen thoufand piafters. They obferve alfo, to a certain degree, the cuftom of the Hebrews, which directed that a brother fhould efpoufe his brother's widow; but this is not peculiar to them, for they retain that as well as feveral other cuftoms of that ancient people, in common with other inhabitants of Syria, and all the Arab tribes.

In fhort, the proper and diftinctive character of the Druzes, is, as I have faid, a fort of republican fpirit, which gives them more energy than any other fubjects of the Turkifh government, and an indifference for religion, which forms a ftriking contraft with the zeal of the Mahometans and Chriftians. In other refpects, their private life, their cuftoms and prejudices, are the fame with other Orientals. They may marry feveral wives, and repudiate them when they chufe; but, except by the Émir and a few men of eminence, that is rarely practifed. Occupied with their rural labours, they experience neither artificial wants, nor thofe inordinate paffions, which are produced by the idlenefs of the inhabitants of cities and towns. The veil, worn by their women, is of itfelf a prefervative againft thofe defires which are the occafion of fo many evils in fociety. No man knows the face of any other woman than his wife, his mother, his fifter, and fifters-in-law. Every man lives in the bofom of his own family, and goes little abroad. The women, thofe even of the Shaiks, make the bread, roaft the coffee, wafh the linen, cook the victuals, and perform all domeftic offices. The men cultivate their lands and vineyards, and dig canals for watering them. In the evening they fometimes affemble

in the court, the area, or houſe of the chief of the
village or family. There, ſeated in a circle, with
legs croſſed, pipes in their mouths, and poniards at
their belts, they diſcourſe of their various labours,
the ſcarcity or plenty of their harveſts, peace or war,
the conduct of the Emir, or the amount of the taxes;
they relate paſt tranſactions, diſcuſs preſent intereſts,
and form conjectures on the future.   Their children,
tired with play, come frequently to liſten; and a
ſtranger is ſurpriſed to hear them, at ten or twelve
years old, recounting, with a ſerious air, why Djezzar declared war againſt the Emir Youſef, how many
purſes it coſt that prince, what augmentation there
will be of the miri, how many muſkets there were in
the camp, and who had the beſt mare.   This is their
only education.   They are neither taught to read the
Pſalms, as among the Maronites, nor the Koran, like
the Mahometans; hardly do the Shaiks know how to
write a letter.   But if their mind be deſtitute of uſeful or agreeable information, at leaſt, it is not pre-
occupied by falſe or hurtful ideas; and, without doubt,
ſuch natural ignorance is well worth all our artificial
folly.   This advantage reſults from it, that their un-
derſtandings being nearly on a level, the inequality of
conditions is leſs perceptible.   For, in fact, we do not
perceive among the Druzes that great diſtance which,
in moſt other ſocieties, degrades the inferior, without contributing to the advantage of the great.   All,
whether Shaiks or peaſants, treat each other with that
rational formality, which is equally remote from rude-
neſs and ſervility.   The Grand Emir, himſelf, is not
a different man from the reſt; he is a good country
gentleman, who does not diſdain admitting to his table
the meaneſt farmer.   In a word, their manners are
thoſe of ancient times, and that ruſtic life, which
marks the origin of every nation; and prove the
people among whom they are ſtill found are, as yet,
only in the infancy of the ſocial ſtate.

SECT. V.

Of the Motoualis.

To the eaft of the country of the Druzes, in the deep valley which feparates their mountains from thofe of Damafcus, we find another fmall nation, known in Syria by the name of Motoualis. The charaƈteriſtic diſtinƈtion between them and the other inhabitants of Syria, is, that they, like the Perfians, are of the feƈt of Ali, while all the Turks follow that of Omar or Moaouia. This diſtinƈtion, occafioned by the fchifm, which, in the thirty-fixth year of the Hejira, arofe among the Arabs, refpeƈting the fucceffors of Mahomet, is the caufe, as I have already obferved, of an irreconcileable hatred between the two parties. The feƈtaries of Omar, who confider themfelves as the only orthodox, affume the title of *Sonnites,* which has that fignification, and term their adverfaries *Shiites,* that is *Seƈtaries,* (of Ali.) The word *Motouali* has the fame meaning in the dialeƈt of Syria. The followers of Ali, diffatisfied with this name, fubſtitute that of *Adlia,* which means afferters of *Juſtice,* literally *Juſticiarians,* a denomination which they have affumed in confequence of a doƈtrinal point they advance in oppofition to the Sonnite faith. A fmall Arabic treatife, entitled, *Theological Fragments concerning the feƈts and Religions of the world,** has the following paffage.

" Thofe feƈtaries who pretend that God aƈts only
" on principles of Juſtice, conformable to human rea-
" fon, are called Adlia, or Juſticiarians. God can-
" not, fay they, command an impraƈticable worſhip,
" nor ordain impoffible aƈtions, nor enjoin men to

* Abarat el Motkallamim fi mazaheb oua Dianat el Donia.

" perform what is beyond their ability ; but wherever
" he requires obedience, will beftow the power to
" obey. He removes the caufe of evil, he allows us
" to reafon, and impofes only what is eafy, not what
" is difficult; he makes no man refponfible for the
" actions of another, nor punifhes him for that in
" which he has no part ; he imputes not as a crime
" what himfelf has created in man ; nor does he re-
" quire him to avoid what deftiny has decreed. This
" would be injuftice and tyranny, of which God is
" incapable from the perfection of his being." To
this doctrine, which diametrically oppofes the fyftem
of the Sonnites, the Motoualis add certain ceremonies
which increafe their mutual averfion. They curfe
Omar and Moaouia as rebels and ufurpers ; and celebrate Ali and Hofain as faints and martyrs. They
begin their ablutions at the elbow, inftead of the end
of the finger, as is cuftomary with the Turks ; they
think themfelves defiled by the touch of ftrangers, and
contrary to the general practice of the Eaft, neither
eat nor drink out of a veffel which has been ufed by
a perfon not of their fect, nor will they even fit with
fuch at the fame table.

Thefe doctrines and cuftoms, by feparating the
Motoualis from their neighbours, have rendered them
a diftinct fociety. It is faid, they have long exifted
as a nation, in this country, though their name has
never been mentioned by any European writer before
the prefent century ; it is not even to be found in the
maps of Danville : La Roque, who left their country
not a hundred years ago, gives them the name of
Amédiens. Be this as it may, in later times, their
wars, robberies, fuccefs, and various changes of fortune, have rendered them of confequence in Syria.
Till about the middle of this century, they only poffeffed Balbek, their capital, and a few places in the
valley, and Anti Lebanon, which feems to have been
their original country. At that period, we find them

under a like government with the Druzes, that is to say, under a number of Shaiks, with one principal chief, of the family of Harfoufh. After the year 1750, they eftablifhed themfelves among the heights of Bekaa, and got footing in Lebanon, where they obtained lands belonging to the Maronites, almoft as far as Befharrai. They even incommoded them fo much by their ravages, as to oblige the Emir Youfef to attack them with open force, and expel them ; but on the other fide, they advanced along the river, even to the neighbourhood of Sour, (Tyre.) In this fituation, Shaik Daher had the addrefs, in 1760, to attach them to his party. The Pachas of Saide and Damafcus claimed tributes, which they had neglected paying, and complained of feveral robberies committed on their fubjects by the Motoualis ; they were defirous of chaftifing them, but this vengeance was neither certain nor eafy. Daher interpofed, and, by becoming fecurity for the tribute, and promifing to prevent any depredations, acquired allies who were able, as it is faid, to arm ten thoufand horfemen, all refolute and formidable troops. Shortly after, they took poffeffion of Sour, and made this village their principal fea-port. In 1771, they were of great fervice to Ali Bey and Daher, againft the Ottomans. But Emir Youfef, having, in their abfence, armed the Druzes, ravaged their country. He was befieging the caftle of Djezen, when the Motoualis, returning from Damafcus, received intelligence of this invafion. At the relation of the barbarities committed by the Druzes, an advanced corps, of only five hundred men, were fo enraged, that they immediately rufhed forward againft the enemy, determined to perifh in taking vengeance. But the furprize and confufion they occafioned, and the difcord which reigned between the two factions of Manfour and Youfef, fo much favoured this defperate attack, that the whole army, con-fitting of twenty five thoufand men, was completely overthrown.

In the following year, the affairs of Daher taking a favourable turn, the zeal of the Motoualis cooled towards him, and they finally abandoned him in the cataftrophe in which he loft his life. But they have fuffered for their imprudence, under the adminiftration of the Pacha who fucceeded him. Since the year 1777, Djezzar, mafter of Acre and Saide, has inceffantly laboured to deftroy them. His perfecution forced them, in 1784, to a reconciliation with the Druzes, and to enter into an alliance with the Emir Youfef. Though reduced to lefs than feven hundred armed men, they did more in that campaign than fifteen or twenty thoufand Druzes and Maronites, affembled at Dair-el-Kamar. They alone took the ftrong fortrefs of Mar-Djebaa, and put to the fword fifty or fixty Arnauts,* who defended it. But the mifunderftanding which prevailed among the chiefs of the Druzes having rendered abortive all their operations, the Pacha has obtained poffeffion of the whole valley, and the city of Balbek itfelf. At this period, not more than five hundred families of the Motoualis remained, who took refuge in Anti-Lebanon, and the Lebanon of the Maronites; and driven as they now are from their native foil, as it is probable they will be totally annihilated, and even their very name become extinct.

Such are the different people comprifed within the limits of Syria. The remainder of the inhabitants, who are confiderably the moft numerous, are, as I have faid, compofed of Turks, Greeks, and Arabs. It now remains for me to give a fketch of the divifions of the country, under the Turkifh adminiftration, and to add a few general reflections on its forces

---

* The name given by the Turks to the Macedonian and Epirot foldiers.

and revenues, its form of government, and the characters and manners of its inhabitants.

But before I proceed to thefe particulars, it may be proper to give fome idea of the commotions, which, in our days, were on the point of producing an important revolution, and erecting an independent power in Syria; I mean the infurrection of Shaik Daher, who for many years attracted the attention of Politicians. A fuccinct narrative of his hiftory muft be the more interefting as it is new, and as the accounts we have feen in the Gazettes of Europe are ill calculated to furnifh a juft idea of the real ftate of affairs in thefe diftant countries.

CHAP. VI.

Summary of the hiftory of Daher, fon of Omar, who governed at Acre from 1750 to 1776.

SHAIK Daher, who, in our time, has given fo much trouble to the Porte, was an Arabian by birth, defcended from one of thofe tribes of Bedouins who ufually encamp on the banks of the Jordan, and the environs of Lake Tabaria, (the ancient Tiberias). His enemies are fond of reminding us that in his youth he was a camel driver; but this circumftance, which does honour to his abilities, by fuggefting the difficulties he muft have encountered in his rife, has befides in this country nothing incompatible with a diftinguifhed birth: it is now, and always will be, ufual with the Arab princes, to employ themfelves in occupations which appear to us mean. Thus I have already obferved that the Shaiks themfelves guide their camels, and look after their horfes, while their wives and daughters grind the corn, bake the bread,

wash the linen, and fetch water, as in the times of
Abraham, and Homer ; and this simple and laborious life, possibly contributes more to happiness than
that lifeless inactivity, and satiating luxury which surround the great in polished nations. As for Daher,
it is certain that he was one of the most powerful
families of the country. After the death of his father Omar, about the beginning of the present century, he divided the government with his uncle and
two brothers. His domain was Safad, a small town
and stronghold in the mountains, to the north-west
of the Lake of Tabaria, to which he shortly after
added Tabaria itself. There Pococke* found him in
1737, occupied in fortifying himself against the Pacha
of Damascus, who not long before had strangled one
of his brothers. In 1742, another Pacha, named
Soliman-el-adm, besieged him there, and bombarded
the place, to the great astonishment of all Syria,
where bombs are but little know, even at present†.
In spite of his courage, Daher was reduced to the
last extremity ; when a fortunate, and, as it is alledged, premeditated incident, relieved him from his em-
barrassment. A violent and sudden cholic carried off
Soliman in two days. Asad-el-adm, his brother and
successor, wanted either the same motives, or the
same inclinations, to continue the war, and Daher
was unmolested on the part of the Ottomans. But
his activity, and the intrigues of his neighbours, soon
gave him other employment. Reasons of interest
embroiled him with his uncle and brother, recourse
was had to arms more than once, and Daher, always
victorious, thought it best to conclude these disputes
by the death of his competitors.

* Pococke's Travels, vol. ii. p. 69.

† I have seen letters of M. Jean Joseph Blanc, a merchant of
Acre, who was in Soliman's camp at this time, in which a cir-
cumstantial account is given of this affair.

Invefted then with the whole power of his family, and abfolute mafter of its force, new profpects opened to his ambition. The commerce in which he engaged, according to the cuftom of all the Afiatic princes and governors, made him fenfible of the advantage of an immediate communication with the fea. He conceived that a port in his hands would become a public market, to which ftrangers reforting, a competition would arife favourable to the fale of his commodities. Acre, fituated in his neighbourhood, and under his eye, was fuited to his defigns, fince for feveral years he had tranfacted bufinefs there with the French factors. This town was in reality but a heap of ruins, a miferable open village, without defence. The Pacha of Saide maintained there an Aga, and a few foldiers who dared not fhew themfelves in the field; while the Bedouins really governed, and were mafters of all the country, up to its very gates. The plain, fo fertile in former times, was nothing but an extenfive wafte, on which the waters ftagnated, and infected the environs by their vapours. The ancient harbour was choaked up, but the road of Haifa, which is dependant on it, was fo advantageoufly fituated that Daher determined to gain poffeffion of it. A pretext was neceffary, which was foon furnifhed by the conduct of the Aga.

One day, while fome warlike ftores, intended to be employed againft the Shaik, were landing, Daher marched brifkly towards Acre, fent a menacing letter to the Aga, which made him take to flight, and entered the town, where he eftablifhed himfelf, without refiftance: this happened about the year 1749. He was then fixty-three years old. This age feems rather too advanced for fuch enterprizes; but when we recollect, that, in 1776, at near ninety, he ftill boldly mounted a fiery fteed, it is evident he was much younger than that age ufually implies. So bold a meafure could not pafs unnoticed; this he forefaw, therefore inflantly difpatched a letter to the Pacha of Saide, reprefenting to him that the affair was entirely perfonal between him and the Aga, and protefting that he was not lefs the very fubmiffive fubject of the Sultan, and the Pacha; that he would pay the tribute of the diftrict he now occupied, as had been done heretofore by the Aga; and would undertake befides to reftrain the Arabs, and do every thing in his power to reftore this ruined country. This application, backed by a few thoufand Sequins, produced its effect in the Divans of Saide, and Conftantinople: his reafons were acknowledged juft, and all his demands granted.

Not that the Porte was the dupe of the proteftations of Daher; it is too much accuftomed to fuch proceedings to miftake them; but it is a maxim with the Turks, not to keep their vaffals in too ftrict an obedience; they have long been convinced, that were they to make war with all rebels, it would be an endlefs labour, and occafion a vaft confumption of men and money: without reckoning the rifk of frequent defeats, and the confequent encouragement to revolt. Their plan therefore, is to be patient; temporize*; and excite the neighbours, relations, and the children of the revolters againft them: and, fooner, or later, the rebels, who uniformly follow the fame fteps, fuffer the fame fate, and end by enriching the Sultan with their fpoils.

Daher, on his part, well knew the real value of this apparent friendfhip. Acre, which he intended for his refidence, was deftitute of defence, and might eafily be furprized, either by fea or land; he determined therefore to fortify it. In the year 1750, under pretext of building himfelf a houfe, he erected, on

---

* The Arabs, in reference to this, have a fingular proverb, which admirably paints this conduct; "The Ofmanli, fay they, "catch hares with waggons."

the northern angle towards the fea, a palace, which
he provided with cannon. He then built feveral towers for the defence of the fort, and enclofed the town
by a wall, in which he left only two gates. Thefe by
the Turks were imagined very formidable works,
though they would be laughed at in Europe. The
palace of Daher, with its lofty and flight walls, its
narrow ditch, and antique turrets, is incapable of
the fmalleft refiftance : four field pieces would demo-
lifh, in two difcharges, both the walls and the wretched cannon mounted on them, at the height of fifty
feet. The wall of the town is ftill more feeble; it
has neither foffe, nor rampart, and is not three feet
thick. Through all this part of Afia, baftions, lines
of defence, covered ways, ramparts, and, in fhort,
every thing relative to modern fortification, are utterly
unknown. A fingle thirty gun frigate would, without difficulty, bombard and lay in ruins the whole
coaft : but, as this ignorance is common both to the
affailants and defendants, the balance remains equal.

After thefe precautions, Daher occupied himfelf in
effecting fuch a reformation in the country as fhould
augment his power. The Arabs of Saker, Muzaina,
and other neighbouring tribes, had caufed a defertion
of the Peafants, by their inroads and devaftations : he
undertook to repel them ; and by alternately employ-
ing prayers and menaces, prefents and arms, he reftored fecurity to the hufbandman, who might now
fow his corn, without fear of feeing the harveft deftroyed, or carried off by robbers. The excellence of
the foil attracted cultivators, but the certainty of fecurity, that bleffing fo precious to thofe who have
lived in a ftate of continual alarm, was a ftill ftronger
inducement. The fame of Daher fpread through
Syria, and Mahometan and Chriftian farmers, every
where defpoiled and harraffed, took refuge, in great
numbers, with a prince under whom they were fure
to find both civil and religious toleration. A colony

of Greeks emigrated from Cyprus, now nearly defolated, by the oppreffions of the governor, the infur-
rections they produced, and the cruelty with which
Kior Pacha expiated fuch offences*. To thefe, Daher affigned a fpot of ground, under the walls of
Acre, which they laid out into gardens. The Europeans, who found a ready fale for their merchandize,
formed numerous fettlements; the lands were cleared,
the waters drained, the air became purer, and the
country at once falubrious and pleafant.

To ftrengthen himfelf ftill more, Daher renewed
his alliances with the great tribes of the defert, among
whom he had difpofed of his children in marriage.
This policy had feveral advantages; for, in them, he
fecured an inviolable afylum, in cafe of accidents;
by this means, alfo, he kept in check the Pacha of
Damafcus, and procured excellent horfes, of which
he was always paffionately fond. He courted, therefore, the Shaiks of Anaza, of Sardia, and Saker.
Then, for the firft time, were feen in Acre, thofe
little dry and parched men, unufual, even to the
Syrians. He furnifhed them with arms and cloathing: and the defert, alfo, for the firft time, beheld
men in clofe dreffes, and armed with mufkets and
piftols, inftead of bows and match-lock guns.

For fome years, the Pachas of Said and Damafcus
had been incommoded by the Motoualis, who pillaged their lands, and refufed their tribute. Daher,
fenfible of the advantage to be made of thefe allies,
firft interpofed as mediator, and, afterwards, in order
to accommodate the parties, offered to become fecurity for the Motoualis, and pay their tribute. The
Pachas accepted this propofal, which rendered their

---

* When Kior Pacha came to Cyprus, he precipitated a number of the revolters, from the tops of the walls, upon iron
hooks, where they remained fufpended, till they expired in
dreadful torments.

revenues certain, and Daher was content with the
bargain he had made, fince he had fecured the friendfhip of a people who could bring ten thoufand horfe
into the field.

The Shaik, however, did not peaceably enjoy the
fruit of his labours; fince he ftill had to fear the attacks of a jealous fuperior, and his power was fhaken
at home, by domeftic enemies, almoft as dangerous.
Agreeable to the wretched policy of the eaft, he had
beftowed feparate governments on his fons, and placed them at a diftance from him, in countries which
were fufficient for their maintenance. From this ar-
rangement it followed, that thefe Shaiks, feeing themfelves the children of a great prince, wifhed to fupport
a fuitable ftate, fo that their revenues foon fell fhort
of their expences. Their fubjects were oppreffed by
them and their agents, and complaints were made to
Daher, who reprimanded them; and court flatterers
irritating both parties, a quarrel was the confequence,
and war broke out between the father and his children. The brothers, too, frequently quarrelled with
each other, which was another caufe of war. Befides,
the Shaik was growing old, and his fons, who confidered him as having arrived at the ufual limits of
human life, longed to anticipate the fucceffion. He
muft neceffarily leave a principal heir to his titles and
power; each thought himfelf entitled to the preference, and this competition furnifhed a frefh fubject
of jealoufy and diffention. From motives of narrow
and contemptible policy, Daher fomented the difcord;
this might indeed produce the effect of keeping his
foldiery in exercife, and inured them to war; but,
befides that it was productive of numberlefs diforders, it had the farther inconvenience of chufing a
diffipation of treafure, which obliged him to have
recourfe to ruinous expedients; the cuftom-houfe
duties were augmented, and commerce, oppreffed,
loft its activity. Thefe civil wars, befides, were de-

ftructive to agriculture, which cannot be injured, without the confequences being always fenfibly felt, in a ftate fo limited as the fmall territories of Daher.

Nor did the Divan of Conftantinople behold, without chagrin, the increafing power of Daher; and his ambitious views, which were now become apparent, increafed its jealoufy. Its jealoufy was ftill more increafed by a requeft he prefented. Till that time he had only held his domains under the title of a renter, and by annual leafe. His vanity was wearied of this reftriction; and as he had poffeffed all the effentials of power, he afpired to its titles: nay, perhaps, he thought them neceffary, more effectually to eftablifh his authority over his children and his fubjects. About the year 1768, he therefore folicited a permanent inveftiture of his government, for himfelf and his fucceffor, and demanded to be proclaimed; *Shaik of Acre, Prince of Princes, Governor of Nazareth, Tabaria, and Safad, and Shaik of all Galilee.* The Porte conceded every thing to fear and money: but this proof of vanity, awakened more and more her jealoufy and difpleafure.

There were, befides, too many caufes of complaint, which, though palliated by Daher, could not but increafe this diftruft, and roufe a defire of vengeance. Such was the adventure of the celebrated pillage of the caravan of Mecca, in 1757. Sixty thoufand pilgrims plundered and difperfed over the defert, a great number deftroyed by fword or famine, women reduced to flavery, the lofs of immenfe riches, and above all, the facrilegious violation of fo folemn an act of religion, produced a commotion in the empire, which is not yet forgotten. The plundering Arabs were the allies of Daher, who received them at Acre, and there permitted them to fell their booty. The Porte loaded him with the bittereft reproaches, but he endeavoured to exculpate himfelf, and to appeafe the Divan, by

fending the white banner of the prophet to Conftantinople.

Such was alfo the affair of the Maltefe Corfairs.
For fome years they had infefted the coafts of Syria,
and, under the falfe pretext of a neutral flag, were
received into the road of Acre : where they unloaded
their fpoils, and fold the prizes they had taken from
the Turks. No fooner were thefe abufes divulged,
than the Mahometans exclaimed againft the facrilege,
and the Porte thundered vengeance. Daher pleaded
ignorance of the fact, and, to prove he no way favoured
a commerce fo difgraceful to the ftate and to religion,
armed two galliots, and fent them to fea, with oftenfible orders to drive off the Maltefe. But the fact is,
that thefe galliots committed no hoftilities againft the
Maltefe, but ferved, on the contrary, to correfpond
with them at fea, remote from all witneffes. Daher
did more : he pretended the road of Haifa was unpro-
tected ; that the enemy might take fhelter there in
fpite of him, and required the Porte to build a fortrefs
there, and provide it with cannon, at the expence of
the Sultan : his demand was complied with, and Daher fhortly after, procured the fort to be adjudged
ufelefs, demolifhed it, and tranfported the brafs cannon from thence to Acre.

Thefe things kept alive the difcontent and alarms
of the Divan, and though thefe were diminifhed by
the great age of Daher ; the turbulent fpirit of his
fons, and the military talents of Ali, the eldeft of
them, ftill gave the Porte much uneafinefs : fhe dreaded to fee an independent power perpetuate itfelf, and
even become formidable. But fteady to her ordinary
fyftem, refrained from open hoftilities, and proceeded
by fecret means ; fhe fent Capidjis, excited domeftic
quarrels, and oppofed agents, capable at leaft of preventing, for a time, the confequences fhe feared.

The moft perfevering of thefe was that Ofman, Pacha of Damafcus, whom we have feen act a leading

part in the war of Ali Bey.   He had merited the favour of the Porte, by discovering the treasures of Soliman Pacha, whose Mamlouk he was.   The personal hatred he bore to Daher, and the known activity of his character, were still greater recommendations. He was considered as a proper counterpoise to Daher, and was accordingly named Pacha of Damascus in 1760.   To give him still additional weight, his two sons were appointed to the pachalics of Tripoli and Saide ; and, to complete his power, in 1765, Jerusalem and all Palestine were added to his apanage.

Osman perfectly seconded the views of the Porte : As soon as he had taken possession of his government, he greatly annoyed Daher.   He augmented the tribute of the lands he held under the Pachalic of Damascus : the Shaik resisted, the Pacha menaced, and it was evident the quarrel would come to a speedy issue.   Osman watched the opportunity to strike a blow which should bring the matter to a decision : this at length presented itself, and war broke out.

Every year the Pacha of Damascus makes what is called the circuit* of his government, the object of which is to levy the miri or impost on the lands.   On this occasion he always takes with him a body of troops, strong enough to support his authority.   He thought to avail himself of this opportunity to surprise Daher ; and, followed by a numerous body of troops, took his route, as usual, towards the country of Nablous.   Daher was then besieging a castle defended by two of his sons : his danger was the greater as he relied on a truce with the Pacha, and he owed his deliverance to his good fortune.

One evening, at the moment he least expected it, a Tartar courier† brought him some letters from

---

* This is practised in almost all the great pachalics, where the vassals are but in little subjection.

† The Tartars perform the office of couriers in Turkey.

Conftantinople. Daher opened them, and, immediately fufpending all hoftilities, difpatched a horfeman
to his children, and defired them to prepare a fupper
for him and three of his attendants, for that he had
affairs to communicate of the laft importance to them
all. The character of Daher was known; his fons
obey him; he arrives at the appointed hour; they
fup chearfully together; and at the end of the repaft,
he produces his letters and reads them; they were
from his fpies at Conftantinople, and to the following purport:—" That the Sultan had deceived him
" in the laft pardon he had fent him; that he had
" at the fame inftant delivered a *kat-sherif* * againft
" his head and property; that every thing was con-
" certed between the three Pachas, Ofman, and his
" fons, to furround and deftroy him and his family;
" and that the Pacha was marching in force towards
" Nablous to furprife him." The aftonifhment this
intelligence excited, may eafily be imagined; a council was immediately held, in which the opinions were
divided. The greateft number were for marching
with all their forces againft the Pacha; but the eldeft
of Daher's fons, Ali, who has rendered himfelf illuf-
trious in Syria, by his exploits, reprefented, that a
large army could not march quick enough to furprife
the Pacha; that he would have time to provide for
his defence, and the difgrace of violating the truce
fall on them; that nothing could be effected but by a
coup de main, which he would take upon himfelf. He
demanded five hundred horfe; his courage was
known, and his demand acceded to. He fet off immediately, marching all night, and concealing himfelf during the day; and the following night was fo

---

* Kat-fherif, which words fignify, *Noble Signature*, is a letter of profcription conceived in thefe terms: " *Such a one, who
" art the flave, of my Sublime Porte, go to fuch a one, my flave,
" and bring back his head to my feet, at the peril of thy own.*"

expeditious, as to reach the enemy early in the morning of the fecond day. The Turks, according to
cuftom, were afleep in their camp, without order and
without centinels ; Ali and his cavalry fell upon them,
fabre in hand, cutting to pieces every thing that came
in their way. All was panic and tumult ; the very
name of Ali fpread terror throughout the camp, and
the Turks fled in the utmoft confufion. The Pacha
had not even time to put on his peliffe : fcarcely was
he out of his tent, before Ali arrived, who made
himfelf mafter of his coffer, his fhawls, his peliffes,
his poniard, his nerkeel,* and, to complete his fuccefs, the kat-fherif of the Sultan. From this moment there was open war, which was carried on, according to the cuftom of the country, by inroads and
fkirmifhes, in which the Turks but rarely gained the
advantage.

The expences it occafioned foon drained the coffers
of the Pacha ; and, to reimburfe them, he had recourfe to the grand expedient of the Turks. He
levied contributions on the towns, villages, and individuals ; whoever was fufpected of having money,
was fummoned, baftinadoed, and plundered. Thefe
oppreffions had occafioned a revolt at Ramla in Paleftine the very firft year he obtained the government,
which he fuppreffed by ftill more odious cruelties.
Two years after, in 1767, fimilar conduct occafioned
a revolt at Gaza ; he renewed thefe proceedings at
Yafa, in 1769, where among other acts of defpotifm,
he violated the law of nations, in the perfon of the
Refident of Venice, John Damiâni, a refpectable old
man, whom he put to the torture, by five hundred
ftrokes on the foles of his feet, and, who could only
preferve the feeble remains of life, by collecting from

---

* A pipe, in the Perfian manner, confifting of a large flafk
filled with water, through which the fmoke paffes, and is puri-
fied before it reaches the mouth.

his own fortune, and the purses of all his friends, a sum of near sixty thousand livres, (twenty-five hundred pounds), for the Pacha. This tyranny is common in Turkey; but as it is not usually either so violent, or so general, such cruelties drove the oppressed to despair. The people began to murmur on every side, and Palestine, emboldened by the vicinity of Egypt, now in a state of rebellion, threatened to call in a foreign protector.

Under these circumstances, Ali Bey, the conqueror of Mecca and the Said, turned his projects of aggrandizement towards Syria. The alliance of Daher, the war with the Russians, which entirely occupied the Turks, and the discontents of the people, all conspired to favour his ambition. He accordingly published a manifesto in 1770, in which he declared, that God having bestowed a signal benediction on his arms, he thought himself bound, in duty, to make use of them for the relief of the people, and to repress the tyranny of Osman in Syria. He immediately dispatched a body of Mamlouks to Gaza, who seized on Ramla and Loud. Their appearance divided the adjacent town of Yafa into two factions, one of which was desirous of submitting to the Egyptians; while the other was for calling in Osman, who flew thither immediately, and encamped near the town. Two days after, Daher was announced, who had likewise hastened thither for the same purpose. The inhabitants of Yafa, then imagining themselves secure, shut their gates against the Pacha; but, in the night, while he was preparing to escape, a party of his troops, passing along the sea-shore, entered, by an opening in the wall, and sacked the city. The next day Daher appeared, and, not finding the Turks, took possession of Yafa, Ramla, and Loud, without resistance, in which towns he placed garrisons.

Things thus prepared, Mohammad Bey arrived in Palestine, with the grand army, in the month of February 1771, and followed the Shaik along the sea

coaft to Acre. There, having been joined by twelve
or thirteen hundred Motoualis, under the command
of Nafif, and fifteen hundred Safadians, led by Ali,
fon of Daher, he marched in April towards Damafcus. We have already feen in what manner this
combined army beat the united forces of the Pachas,
and how Mohammad, mafter of Damafcus, and on
the point of taking poffeffion of the caftle, on a fudden changed his defign, and again took the road to
Cairo. On this occafion, Ibrahim Sabbar, Minifter
of Daher, receiving no other explanation from Mohammad than menaces, wrote to him in the name
of the Shaik, a letter filled with reproaches, which
proved eventually the caufe, or, at leaft, the pretext
of a frefh quarrel. Ofman, however, on his return
to Damafcus, recommenced his oppreffions and hoftilities ; and imagining that Daher, chagrined by the
unexpected news he had received, would not be prepared for defence, he formed the project of furprizing him even in Acre. But fcarcely was he on his
march, when Ali, Daher, and Nafif, informed of his
intentions, propofed to turn the tables on him ; they,
therefore, fecretly left Acre, and learning he was encamped on the weftern bank of Lake Houla, arrived
there at break of day, took poffeffion of the bridge
of Yakoub, which they found negligently guarded,
and fell on him fabre in hand, in his camp, where
they made a dreadful carnage. This, like the affair
of Nablous, was a total defeat ; the Turks, preffed
on the land fide, threw themfelves into the lake, hoping to fwim acrofs it ; but the terror and confufion of
this multitude of men and horfes, which mutually embarraffed each other, was fuch that the enemy made a
prodigious flaughter, while ftill greater numbers perifhed in the water and mud of the lake. The Pacha was
thought to be among the number of the latter, but he
had the good fortune to efcape, being faved by two
negroes, who fwam acrofs with him on their fhoulders.

In the interim, Darouifh, fon of Ofmond, Pacha of
Saide, had engaged the Druzes in his caufe, and fifteen hundred Okkals had arrived, under the command
of Ali-Djambalat, to reinforce the garrifon; while the
Emir Youfef, defcending into the valley of the Motoualis with twenty-five thoufand men, laid every thing
wafte with fire and fword. Ali, Daher and Nafif, on
this intelligence, directed their courfe inftantly on
that fide, and, on the 21ft of October, 1771, happened the action in which the advanced corps of five
hundred Motoualis entirely defeated the whole army
of the Druzes, whofe flight fpread terror through
Saide, whither they were clofely purfued by the Safadians. Ali-Djambalat, defpairing to defend the town,
evacuated it without delay; but not before his Okkals had pillaged it in their retreat. The Motoualis,
finding it without defence, entered and plundered it
in their turn. At length, the chiefs put an end to
the pillage, and took poffeffion in the name of Daher,
who appointed Deguizla, a native of Barbary, renowned for his bravery, to be his *Motfallam*, or governor.

The Porte, terrified at the defeats fhe had met with,
both from the Ruffians, and her rebellious fubjects,
now offered peace to Daher, on very advantageous
conditions. To induce him to confent, fhe removed
the Pachas of Damafcus, Saide, and Tripoli; difavowed their conduct, and folicited a reconciliation
with the Shaik. Daher, now eighty-five or eighty-
fix years old, was willing to accept this offer, that
he might terminate his days in peace; but he was di-
verted from this intention by his minifter, Ibrahim;
who did not doubt, but Ali Bey would, the enfuing
winter, proceed to the conqueft of Syria, and that
this Mamlouk would cede a confiderable portion of
that country to Daher, and in the future aggrandizement of his mafters power, he hoped the advance-
ment of his own private fortune, and the means of

adding frefh treafures to thofe he had already amaffed
by his infatiable avarice. Seduced by this brilliant
profpect, he rejected the propofitions of the Porte,
and prepared to carry on the war with redoubled activity.

Such was the ftate of affairs, when, in the month of
February of the following year, Mohammad Bey
reared the ftandard of rebellion againft his patron
Ali. Ibrahim, at firft, flattered himfelf this revolt
would have no ferious confequences; but he was foon
undeceived, by the news of Ali's expulfion, and his
fubfequent arrival at Acre, as a fugitive and fuppliant.
This ftroke revived the courage of all the enemies of
Daher, and the Turkifh faction in Yafa availed themfelves of it to regain their afcendency. They appropriated to themfelves, the effects left there by the little fleet of Rodoan; and, aided by a Shaik of Nablous, began a revolt in the city, and oppofed the paffage of the Mamlouks. Circumftances now became
very critical, as the fpeedy arrival of a large army of
Turks was announced, which was affembled near
Aleppo: Daher, it may be, ought to have remained
in the vicinity of Acre; but imagining his diligence
would fecure him from every attack, he marched towards Nablous, chaftifing the rebels as he paffed, and
joining Ali Bey, below Yafa, conducted him without
oppofition to Acre.

After a reception fuitable to Arabian hofpitality,
they marched together againft the Turks, who, under
the command of feven Pachas, and in concert with
the Druzes, were befieging Saide. In the road of
Haifa were fome Ruffian veffels, which, profiting by
the revolt of Daher, were taking in provifions: the
Shaik negociated with them, and, for a prefent of
fix hundred purfes, engaged them to fecond his operations by fea. His army, at this time, might confift
of five or fix thoufand Safadian and Motouali cavalry,
eight hundred of Ali's Mamlouks, and about one

thoufand Mograbian infantry. The Turks, on the contrary, united with the Druzes, amounted to ten thoufand cavalry, and twenty thoufand peafants, who, as foon as they received intelligence of the approach of the enemy, raifed the fiege, and retreated to the north of the town, not intending flight, but to wait for Daher, and give him battle ; and the armies engaged the next day, in better order than had hitherto been ufual.

The Turkifh army, extending from the fea to the foot of the mountains, was drawn up in platoons, nearly in the fame line. The Okkals, on foot, were pofted on the fea-fhore, behind fome hedges of Nopals, and in trenches they had dug, to prevent a fally from the town, while the cavalry occupied the plain in no little confufion. Towards the centre, and advanced a little in the front, were eight cannon, twelve and twenty-four pounders, the only artillery hitherto made ufe. of in the open field. At the foot of the mountains, and on their declivity, was the militia of the Druzes, armed with mufkets, without entrenchments, and without cannon. On the fide of Daher, the Motoualis and the Safadians, ranged themfelves, fo as to prefent the greateft front poffible, and endeavoured to occupy as much of the plain as the Turks. The right wing, commanded by Nafif, confifted of the Motoualis, and the thoufand Mograbian infantry, intended to oppofe the peafant Druzes. The other, led on by Aii Daher, was left without fupport againft the Okkals; but he relied on the Ruffian boats and veffels, which, keeping clofe in with the fhore, advanced in a line parallel to the army. In the centre, were the eight hundred Mamlouks, and behind them, Ali Bey, with the aged Daher, who ftill animated his people, both by his words and his example.

The action was begun by the Ruffian veffels ; and no fooner had they fired a few broadfides on the Okkals, than they retreated in confufion ; the fquadrons of cavalry now advancing, nearly in a line, came within cannon-fhot of the Turks. Inftantly the Mamlouks, anxious to juftify the general opinion of their bravery, galloped full fpeed towards the enemy. The gunners, intimidated by their intrepidity, and feeing themfelves on foot, between two lines of cavalry, unfupported, either by redoubts or infantry, fired their pieces with precipitation, and took to flight. The Mamlouks, who fuffered but little from this volley, rufhed in an inftant amid the cannon, and fell headlong upon the cavalry of the enemy. They met but a feeble refiftance, and, in the confufion which enfued, every one not knowing what to do, or what was paffing around him, was more difpofed to fly than fight. The Pachas firft fet the example, and in an inftant the flight became general. The Druzes, who never engage with good-will on the fide of the Turks, prefently left the field, and hid themfelves in their mountains, and in lefs than an hour the plain was cleared. The allies, fatisfied with their victory would not rifk a purfuit, in a country which would become more difficult the nearer they approached Bairout; but the Ruffian fhips, to punifh the Druzes, proceeded to cannonade that town, where they made a defcent, and burnt three hundred houfes.

Ali Bey and Daher, on their return to Acre, determined to take vengeance for the treachery of the people of Nablous and Yafa, and, in the beginning of July 1772, appeared before the latter city. The firft propofed an accommodation, but the Turkifh faction rejecting every propofition, they were compelled to have recourfe to arms. This fiege, properly fpeaking, was only a blockade, nor muft we imagine the affailants made their approaches after the European method. They had no other artillery, on either fide, than a few large cannon, badly mounted, ill fituated, and ftill worfe ferved. The attacks were carried on neither by trenches, nor mines; and, it

muſt be owned, that ſuch means were not neceſſary
againſt a ſlight wall, without ditch or rampart. A
breach was ſoon made, but the cavalry of Daher and
Ali Bey ſhewed no great eagerneſs to paſs it; the beſieged having defended the inſide with ſtones, ſtakes
and deep holes which they had dug. The whole attack was made with ſmall arms, which killed very
few, and eight months were waſted in this manner,
in ſpite of the impatience of Ali Bey, who had alone
the conduct of the ſiege. At length the beſieged,
exhauſted with fatigue, and being in want of proviſions, ſurrendered by capitulation. In the month
of February 1773, Ali Bey placed a governor in the
town, for Daher, and haſtened to join the Shaik at
Acre, where he found him occupied in preparations
to enable him to return to Egypt, to accelerate which
event, Ali contributed all in his power.

They waited only for a ſuccour of ſix hundred men
promiſed by the Ruſſians, but the impatience of Ali
Bey determined him to depart without them. Daher
made uſe of every argument to detain him a few days
longer. But finding nothing could alter his reſolu-
tion, he ſent fifteen hundred cavalry to accompany
him, commanded by Otman, one of his ſons. Not
many days after (in April 1773), the Ruſſians arrived with the reinforcement which though leſs conſiderable than was expected, he greatly regretted he could
not employ; but this regret was ſeverely aggravated,
when Daher ſaw his ſon and his cavalry return as fugitives, to announce to him their own diſaſter, and
the fate of Ali Bey. He was the more affected at
this event, as, inſtead of a uſeful ally, powerful in
reſources, he acquired an enemy formidable from his
hatred and activity. This, at his age, was a moſt
afflicting proſpect, and it is highly to his honor, that
he bore it with proper fortitude.

A fortunate event combined at this juncture, with
his natural firmneſs, to conſole him, and divert his

attention. The Emir Youfef, thwarted by a powerful faction, had been obliged to folicit the affiftance of the Pacha of Damafcus, to maintain himfelf in poffeffion of Bairout. He had placed there a creature of the Turks, the Bey, Ahmed-el-Djezzar, of whom I have fpoken before. No fooner was this man invefted with the command of the town, than he determined to feize it for himfelf. He began by converting to his own ufe, fifty thoufand piafters belonging to the prince, and openly declared he acknowledged no mafter but the Sultan; the Emir, aftonifhed at this perfidy, in vain demanded juftice of the Pacha of Damafcus. Djezzar was difavowed, but not ordered to reftore the town. Piqued at this refufal, the Emir complied at length with the general wifh of the Druzes, and contracted an alliance with Daher. The treaty was concluded near Sour, and the Shaik, charmed with acquiring fuch powerful friends, went immediately to reduce the rebel. The Ruffian fhips, which for fome time paft, had never quitted the coaft, now joined the Druzes, and, for a fecond fum of fix hundred purfes, agreed to cannonade Bairout. This double attack had the defired fuccefs. Djezzar, notwithftanding his vigorous refiftance, was obliged to capitulate; he furrendered himfelf to Daher alone, and followed him to Acre, from whence, as I have related, he efcaped foon after.

The defection of the Druzes did not difcourage the Turks: the Porte expecting great fuccefs in the intrigues fhe was then carrying on in Egypt, ftill entertained hopes of overcoming all her enemies; fhe again placed Ofman at Damafcus, and gave him an unlimited power over all Syria. The firft ufe he made of this, was to affemble under his orders fix Pachas, whom he led through the vale of Bekaa, to the village of Zahla, with intention to penetrate into the mountainous country. The ftrength of this army, and the rapidity of its march, fpread confternation on every fide, and the Emir Youfef, always timid and irrefolute, already repented his alliance with Daher; but this aged man, folicitous for the fafety of his allies, took care to provide for their defence. The Turks had hardly been encamped fix days, at the foot of the mountains, before they learnt that Ali, the fon of Daher, was approaching to give them battle. Nothing more was neceffary to intimidate them. In vain were they told the enemy had but five hundred horfe, while they were upwards of five thoufand ftrong : the name of Ali Daher fo terrified them that this whole army fled, in one night, and left their camp, full of fpoils and baggage, to the inhabitants of Zahla.

After this fuccefs, it might be fuppofed Daher would have allowed himfelf time to breathe, and have turned his attention to preparations for his defence, which was become every day more neceffary; but fortune had determined he fhould no longer enjoy any repofe. For feveral years paft, domeftic troubles had accompanied foreign wars : and it was only by means of the latter, he had been able to appeafe the former. His children, who were themfelves old men, were wearied of waiting fo long for their inheritance; and, befides this conftant difpofition to revolt, had real grievances to complain of, which by giving too much reafon for their difcontents, rendered them more dangerous. For feveral years, the Chriftian Ibrahim, minifter of the Shaik, had engroffed all his confidence, which he fhamefully abufed to gratify his own avarice. He dared not openly exercife the tyranny of the Turks; but he neglected no means, however unjuft, by which he could amafs money. He monopolized every article of commerce; he alone had the fale of corn, cotton, and other articles of exportation; and he alone purchafed cloths, indigo, fugars, and other merchandize,

His avarice had frequently invaded the fuppofed privileges, and even the real rights of the Shaiks; they
did not pardon him this abufe of power, and every
day, furnifhing frefh objeƈts of complaint, was pro-
duƈtive of new difturbances. Daher, whofe underftanding began to be impaired by his extreme old age,
did not adopt meafures calculated to appeafe them.
He called his children rebels and ungrateful, and
imagined he had no faithful and difinterefted fervant
but Ibrahim: this infatuation ferved only to deftroy
all refpeƈt for his perfon, and to inflame and juftify
their difcontents.

The unhappy effeƈts of this conduƈt fully difplayed
themfelves in 1774. Since the death of Ali Bey,
Ibrahim, finding he had more to fear than hope, had
abated fomething of his haughtinefs. He no longer
faw the fame certainty of amaffing money by making
war. His allies, the Ruffians, in whom all his confidence was placed, began themfelves to talk of peace;
and thefe motives determined him likewife to conclude it, for which purpofe he entered into a Treaty
with a Capidji whom the Porte maintained at Acre.
It was agreed that Daher and his fons fhould lay
down their arms, but retain the government of the
country, by receiving the *Tails*, which are the fym-
bols of this power. But it was likewife ftipulated,
that Saide fhould be reftored, and the Shaik pay the
miri, as he had done formerly. Thefe conditions
were extremely diffatisfaƈtory to the fons of Daher,
and the more fo becaufe they were concluded without
their participation. They deemed it difgraceful again
to become tributaries, and were ftill more offended
that the Porte had granted to none of them the title
of their father; they therefore all revolted. Ali repaired to Paleftine, and took up his quarters at
Habroun; Ahmad and Seid retired to Nablous, Otman among the Arabs of Saker, and the remainder
of the year paffed in thefe diffenfions.

Such was the fituation of affairs, when, at the beginning of 1775, Mohammad Bey appeared in Paleftine, with all the forces he was able to collect. Gaza, deftitute of ammunition, did not venture to refift. Yafa, proud of the part fhe had acted in former difputes, had more courage; the inhabitants took arms, and their refiftance had nearly difappointed the vengeance of the Mamlouk; but every thing confpired to the deftruction of Daher. The Druzes dared not ftir; the Motoualis were difcontented: Ibrahim fummoned affiftance from every quarter, but he offered no money, and his folicitations had no effect; he had not even the prudence to fend provifions to the befieged. They were compelled to furrender, and the rout to Acre was laid open to the enemy. As foon as the taking of Yafa was known, Ibrahim and Daher fled, and took refuge in the mountains of Safad. Ali Daher, confiding in the treaty between himfelf and Mohammad, took the place of his father; but foon perceiving he had been deceived, he took to flight likewife in his turn, and Acre remained in the poffeffion of the Mamlouks.

It would have been difficult to forefee the confequences of this revolution, but the unexpected death of its author rendered it, of a fudden, of no effect. The flight of the Egyptians, leaving free the country and capital of Daher, he loft no time in returning; but the ftorm was by no means appeafed. He foon learnt that a Turkifh fleet, under the command of Haffan, the celebrated Captain Pacha, was laying fiege to Saide. He then difcovered too late the perfidy of the Porte, which had lulled his vigilance by profeffions of friendfhip, while fhe was concerting with Mohammad Bey the means of his deftruction. During a whole year that the Turks had been difengaged from the Ruffians, it was not difficult to forefee their intentions from their motions. Still, however, it was in his power to endeavour to prevent the consequences of this error; but, unfortunately, even this he neglected. Degnizla, bombarded in Saide without hope of succour, was constrained to evacuate the town; and the Captain Pacha appeared instantly before Acre. At sight of the enemy, a consultation was held how to escape the danger, and this led to a quarrel, which decided the fate of Daher.

In a general council, Ibrahim gave his opinion to repel force by force: his reasons were, that the Captain Pacha had but three large vessels; that he could neither make an attack by land, nor remain at anchor, without danger, before the castle; that there was a sufficient force of cavalry and Mograbian infantry to hinder a descent, and that it was almost certain the Turks would relinquish the enterprize without attempting any thing. In opposition to him, Degnizla declared for peace, because resistance could only prolong the war; he maintained it was unreasonable to expose the lives of so many brave men, when the same object might be effected by less valuable means, that is by money; that he was sufficiently acquainted with the avidity of the Captain Pacha, to assert he would suffer himself to be corrupted; and was certain not only that he could procure his departure, but even make him a friend, for the sum of two thousand purses. This was precisely what Ibrahim dreaded; he therefore exclaimed against the measure, protesting there was not a medin in the Treasury. Daher supported his assertion. "The Shaik is in the right," replied Degnizla; "his servants have long known that " his generosity does not suffer his money to stagnate " in his coffers; but does not the money they obtain " from him belong to him? And can it be believed " that thus entitled to them we know not where to " find two thousand purses?" At these words Ibrahim interrupted him, exclaimed, that as for himself, no man could be poorer. "Say baser," resumed Dig-

nizla, tranfported with rage. " Who is ignorant,
" that for the laft fourteen years, you have been
" heaping up enormous treafures ? that you have mo-
" nopolized all the trade of the country ; that you
" fell all the lands, and keep back the payments that
" are due ; that in the war of Mohammad Bey, you
" plundered the whole territory of Gaza, carried
" away all the corn, and left the inhabitants of
" Yafa without the neceffaries of life ?" He was
proceeding, when the Shaik, commanding filence,
protefted the innocence of his Minifter, and accufed
Degnizla of envy and treachery. Degnizla inftantly
quitted the council, and affembling his countrymen,
the Mograbians or Barbary Arabs, who compofed
the chief ftrength of the place, forbid them to fire
upon the Captain Pacha.

Daher however, determined to ftand the attack,
made every neceffary preparation ; and, the next day,
Haffan, approaching the caftle, began to cannonade.
Daher anfwered with the few pieces near him ; but in
fpite of his reiterated orders, the others did not fire.
Finding himfelf betrayed, he mounted his horfe ; and,
leaving the town by the gate which opens towards the
gardens on the North, attempted to gain the country ; but, while he was paffing along the walls of
thefe gardens, a Mograbian foldier fhot him with a
mufquet in the loins, and he fell from his horfe,
when the Barbary Arabs, inftantly furrounded his
body, cut off his head, which they carried to the
Captain Pacha, who, according to the odious cuftom
of the Turks, loaded it with infults while he furvey-
ed it, and had it pickled, in order to carry it to Conftantinople, as a prefent to the Sultan, and a fpectacle
to the people.

Such was the tragical end of a man, in many refpects, worthy of a better fate. It is long fince Syria
has beheld among her chiefs fo great a character. In
military affairs, no man poffeffed more courage, acti-

vity, coolnefs, or refources. In politics, the noble
franknefs of his mind was not diminifhed even by his
ambition.   He was fond only of brave and open meafures ; and heroically prefered the dangers of the
field to the wily intrigues of the cabinet ; nor was it
till he had taken Ibrahim for his minifter that his conduct was blemifhed with a fort of duplicity which that
Chriftian called Prudence.   The reputation of his
juftice had eftablifhed throughout his eftates, a fecurity unknown in Turkey ; difference in religion occafioned no difputes on this head : he poffeffed the toleration, or, perhaps, the indifference of the Bedouin
Arabs.   He had alfo preferved the fimplicity of their
cuftoms and manners.   His table was not different
from that of a rich farmer ; the luxury of his drefs
never exceeded a few Peliffes, and he never wore any
trinkets.   The greateft expence he incured was in
blood mares, for fome of which he even paid as high
as twenty thoufand livres, (eight hundred and twenty-five pounds).   He likewife loved women ; but was
fo jealous of decency and decorum, that he ordered
that every one taken in an act of gallantry, or offering infult to a woman, fhould fuffer death ; he had,
in fhort, attained the difficult medium between pro-
digality and avarice, and was at once generous and
œconomical.   Whence was it, then, that with fuch
great qualities, he did not further extend, and more
firmly eftablifh his power ?   To this queftion a minute
knowledge of his adminiftration would furnifh an eafy
anfwer, but I fhall content myfelf with affigning the
three principal caufes.

. Firft, His government wanted that internal good
order, and juftnefs of principle, without which all
improvement muft be flow and irregular.

· Secondly, The early conceffions he made to his
children introduced a multitude of diforders, which
prevented the improvement of agriculture, impover-

iſhed his finances, divided his forces, and prepared the downfall of himſelf and his government.

A third and more efficacious cauſe than all the reſt, was the avarice of Ibrahim Sabbar. This man, abuſing the confidence of his maſter, and the weakneſs incident to age, by his rapacity, alienated from him, his children, ſervants, and allies. His extortions even lay ſo heavy on the people, towards the end of his life, as to render them indifferent whether they returned under the Turkiſh yoke. His paſſion for money was ſo ſordid that, amid the wealth he was amaſſing, he lived only on cheeſe and olives; and, ſo great was his parſimony, that he frequently ſtopped at the ſhops of the pooreſt merchants, and partook of their frugal repaſt. He never wore any think but dirty and ragged garments. To behold this meagre, one-eyed wretch, one would have taken him rather for a beggar than the miniſter of a conſiderable ſtate. By theſe vile practices, he amaſſed about twenty millions of French money, (eight hundred and twenty-five thouſand pounds), which fell to the Turks. No ſooner was the death of Daher known in Acre than, the public indignation breaking out againſt Ibrahim, he was ſeized, and given up to the Captain Pacha, to whom no preſent could be more acceptable. The report of this man's treaſures was general thoughout Turkey; it had contributed to animate the reſentment of Mohammad Bey, and was the principal motive of the meaſures of the Captain Pacha. He no ſooner had him in his power than he endeavoured to extort from him a declaration of the ſums he poſſeſſed, and the place where they were concealed; but Ibrahim firmly denied any ſuch treaſures exiſted. In vain did the Pacha employ careſſes, menaces, and the torture, all were ineffectual; and it was by other indications Haſſan at length diſcovered, among the Fathers of the Holy Land, and at the houſes of two French merchants, ſeveral cheſts, ſo large, and ſo full of gold, that the biggeſt required eight men to carry it. With this gold were found alſo ſeveral trinkets, ſuch as pearls and diamonds, and, among others, the Kandjar of Ali Bey, the handle of which was eſtimated at upwards of two hundred thouſand livres, (about eight thouſand pounds). All this was conveyed to Conſtantinople with Ibrahim, who was loaded with chains. The Turks, ferocious and inſatiable, ſtill hoping to diſcover new treaſures, inflicted on him the moſt cruel tortures, to force him to confeſſion, but, it is aſſerted, he invariably maintained the firmneſs of his character, and periſhed with a courage worthy of a better cauſe.

After the death of Daher, the Captain Pacha confirmed Djezzar Pacha of Acre and Saide, and committed to him the care of completing the deſtruction of the rebels. Faithful to his inſtructions, Djezzar alternately attacked them by ſtratagem and force, and ſo far ſucceeded, as, to induce Otman, Seid, and Ahmad, to deliver themſelves into his hands. Ali Daher alone refuſed, and him they wiſhed for moſt. In the following year (1776), the Captain Pacha returned, and, in concert with Djezzar, beſieged Ali in Dair-Hanna, a ſtrong hold, about a day's journey from Acre, but he eſcaped them. To free themſelves from their fears, they employed a ſtratagem worthy of their character. They ſuborned ſome Barbary Arabs, who, pretending to have been diſmiſſed from Damaſcus, came into the country where Ali was encamped. After relating their hiſtory to his attendants, they applied to the hoſpitality of the Shaik. Ali received them as became an Arab, and a brave man; but theſe wretches falling on him in the night, maſſacred him, and haſtened to demand their reward, though they were not able to bring with them his head. The Captain Pacha, having no longer any thing to fear from Ali, murdered his brothers, Seid, Ahmad, and their children. Otman alone, on ac-

count of his extraordinary talents for poetry, was
spared, and carried to Conftantinople. Degnizla,
who was fent from that capital to Gaza, with the
title of governor, perifhed on the road, not without
fufpicions of poifon. The Emir Youfef, terrified at
thefe events, made his peace with Djezzar, and, from
that time, Galilee, again fubjected to the Turks, only
retains an unprofitable remembrance of the power
of Daher.

———◆———

CHAP. VII.

*The diftribution of Syria into Pachalics, under the
Turkifh government.*

AFTER Sultan Selim I. had taken Syria from the
Mamlouks, he fubjected that province, like the reft
of the empire, to the government of Viceroys, or
Pachas*, invefted with unlimited power. The more
effectually to fecure his authority, he divided the
country into five governments, or *Pachalics*, which
divifion ftill remains. Thefe Pachalics are thofe of
Aleppo, Tripoli, and Saide, lately removed to Acre,
that of Damafcus, and laftly, that of Paleftine, the
feat of which is fometimes at Gaza, and fometimes
at Jerufalem. Since the time of Selim, the limits
of thefe Pachalics have often varied, but their general extent has always been nearly the fame. I fhall
now proceed to give a more circumftantial detail of
the moft interefting particulars of their prefent ftate,
fuch as the revenues, productions, forces, and moft
remarkable places.

---

* The Turkifh word *Pacha*, is formed of the two Perfian
words *Pa-fhah*, which literally fignify *Viceroy*.

CHAP. VIII.

Of the Pachalic of Aleppo.

THE Pachalic of Aleppo comprehends the country extending from the Euphrates to the Mediterranean, between two lines, one drawn from Scandaroon to Beer, along the mountains; the other from
Beles to the fea, by Mara, and the bridge of Shoger.
This fpace principally confifts of two plains; that of
Antioch to the weft, and that of Aleppo to the eaft:
the north and the fea-coaft are occupied by confiderably high mountains, known to the ancients by the
names of Amanus, and of Rhofus. In general, the
foil of this government is fat and loamy. The lofty
and vigorous plants, which fhoot up every where
after the winter rains, prove its fertility, but its actual
fruitfulnefs is but little. The greateft part of the
lands lie wafte; fcarcely can we trace any marks of
cultivation, in the environs of the towns and villages.
Its principal produce confifts in wheat, barley, and,
cotton, which are found efpecially in the flat country. In the mountains, they rather chufe to cultivate
the vine, mulberry, olive, and fig-trees. The fides
of the hills towards the fea-coaft are appropriated to
tobacco, and the territory of Aleppo, to Piftachios.
The pafturage is not to be reckoned, becaufe, that
is abandoned to the wandering Hordes of the Turkmen and Curds.

In the greater part of the Pachalics the Pacha is,
as his title imports, at once the Viceroy and Farmer-
general of the country; but in that of Aleppo, he
does not poffefs the latter office. This the Porte has
beftowed on a *Mehaffel*, or Collector, who is immediately accountable for what he receives. His leafe
is only for a year. The prefent rent of his farm is

eight hundred purfes, which make a million of French money, (above forty thoufand pounds); but to this muft be added, the *price of the babouches**, or a pre-fent of eighty or one hundred thoufand livres, (three or four thoufand pounds), to purchafe the favour of the Vifir, and men in office. For thefe two fums, the farmer receives all the duties of the government, which are; Firft, The produce of import and export duties on merchandize coming from Europe, India, and Conftantinople, and on that exported in ex-change. Secondly, The taxes paid by the herds of cattle brought every year by the Turkmen and Curds, from Armenia and the Diarbekar, to be fold in Syria. Thirdly, The fifth of the falt works of Djeboul. And, laftly, The Miri, or land-tax. Thefe united may produce from fifteen to fixteen hundred thou-fand livres, (above fixty thoufand pounds)

The Pacha, deprived of this lucrative branch of the adminiftration, receives a fixed allowance of eighty thoufand piaftres, (eight thoufand three hundred and thirty pounds.) This revenue has always been in-adequate to the expences; for befides the troops he is obliged to maintain, and the reparation of the high-ways and fortreffes, the expences of which he is obli-ged to defray, he is under the neceffity of making large prefents to the minifters, in order to keep his place; but the Porte adds to the account, the contri-butions he may levy on the Curds and Turkmen, and his extortions from the villages and individuals; nor do the Pachas come fhort of this calculation. Abdi Pacha, who governed twelve or thirteen years ago, carried off, at the end of fifteen months, upwards of four millions of livres, (one hundred and fixty thou-fand pounds) by laying under contribution every trade, even the very cleaners of tobacco pipes; and, very lately, another of the fame name has been obliged to

* Turkifh Slippers.

fly for fimilar oppreffions. The former was rewarded
by the Divan with the command of an army againft
the Ruffians : but if the latter has not enriched himfelf, he will be ftrangled as an extortioner. Such is
the ordinary progrefs of affairs in Turkey !

Cuftom requires that the commiffion of the Pacha
fhould be only for three months ; but it is frequently
extended to fix, and even to a year. His office is to
retain the province in obedience, and provide for the
fecurity of his country againft every foreign and domeftic enemy. For this purpofe he maintains five or
fix hundred horfe, and about the fame number of
infantry. Befides thefe, he has the command of the
Janifaries who are a fort of enrolled national malitia.
As this corps is founded throughout Syria, it will be
proper to fay a few words concerning its conftitution.

The Janifaries I have mentioned confift, in each
Pachalic of a certain number of enrolled men, who
muft hold themfelves ready to march whenever they
are required. As there are certain privileges and
exemptions attached to their body, there is a competition to obtain admiffion into it. Formerly they were
fubjeft to regular exercife and difcipline ; but all ob-
fervance of this has fo declined, within the laft fixty or
eighty years, that there no longer remains the flighteft
trace of their ancient good order. Thefe pretended
foldiers are only a croud of artizans and peafants, as
ignorant as the reft of that clafs, but infinitely lefs
tractable. When a Pacha abufes his authority, they
are always the firft to erect the ftandard of fedition.
They depofed and expelled Abdi Pacha from Aleppo,
and compelled the Porte to fend another in his ftead.
The Turkifh government revenges itfelf, it is true,
by ordering the moft active mutineers to be ftrangled ;
but on the firft opportunity, the Janifaries create other
chiefs, and affairs return to their ufual courfe. The
Pachas, feeing themfelves thwarted by this national
militia, have had recourfe to the expedient made ufe

of in similar cases; they have taken foreign soldiers
into their service, who have neither friends nor families in the country. These are of two sorts cavalry
and infantry.

The cavalry who alone merit the name of soldiers,
for this reason assume the appellation of *Daoula* or
Deleti, and likewise *Delibashes* and *Laouend*, from
whence we have formed *Leventi*. Their arms are
short sabres, pistols, muskets, and lances. Their head
dress is a long cylinder of black felt, without edges,
nine or ten inches high, extremely inconvenient, as
it does not shade the eyes, and easily falls off their
bald heads. Their saddles are made in the English
manner, of a single skin stretched upon a wooden tree:
they are bare, but not the less incommodious for this,
as they shift the horseman so as to prevent him from
clinging; in the rest of their accoutrements and cloathing, they resemble the Mamlouks; with this difference, that they are not provided with so good.
Their ragged cloaths, their rusty arms, and their
horses of different sizes, make them resemble banditti
more than soldiers; and, in fact, the greatest part of
them have first distinguished themselves in the former
capacity, nor have they greatly changed in adopting
their second occupation.

Almost all the cavalry in Syria are Turkmen,
Curds, or Caramanians; who, after exercising the
trade of robbers, in their own country, seek employment and asylum near the person of the Pacha.
Throughout the empire, these troops are, in like manner, formed of plunderers, who roam from place to
place. From want of discipline, they retain their
former manners, and are the scourge of the country
which they lay waste, and of the peasants, whom they
often pillage by open force.

The infantry are a corps still inferior in every respect. Formerly they were procured from the inhabitants of the country by forced inlistments; but,

within the laft fifty or fixty years the peafants of Tu-
nis, Algiers, and Morocco, have thought proper to
feek in Syria and in Egypt, that refpect which is denied them in their own country. They alone, under
the name of *Magarba*, *Mograbians*, or *Men of the
Weft*, compofe the infantry of the Pachas. So that,
by a whimfical exchange, it happens, that the foldiery
of the Barbary States confift of Turks, while that of
the Turks is compofed of the natives of Barbary. It
is impoffible for troops to be lefs encumbered than
thefe ; for their whole accoutrements and baggage
are confined to a rufty firelock, a large knife, a leathern bag, a cotton fhirt, a pair of drawers, a red cap,
and fometimes flippers. Their pay is five piafters
(about ten fhillings and ten-pence) per month, out of
which they are obliged to furnifh themfelves with
arms and cloathing. They are maintained at the
expence of the Pacha ; which, altogether, may be
efteemed tolerable encouragement ; the pay of the
cavalry is double, and each horfeman has, befides
this, his horfe and his ration, which is a meafure of
chopped ftraw, and fifteen pounds of barley a day.
Thefe troops are divided in the ancient Tartar manner,
by *bairaks*, or colours ; each bairak is reckoned ten
men, but they rarely confift of above fix effectives :
the reafon of which is, that the *Agas*, or commanders
of colours, being entrufted with the pay of the foldiers,
maintain as few as poffible, to profit by the deficiency.
The fuperior Agas tolerate thefe abufes, and partake
of the fpoils ; nay, the Pachas themfelves difregard
them, and, in order to avoid the payment of the complete number, connive at the rapacity and want of
difcipline of their troops.

In confequence of fuch wretched government, the
greater part of the Pachalics in the empire are impoverifhed and laid wafte. This is the cafe in particular
with that of Aleppo ; In the ancient *deftars*, or regifters of impofts upwards of three thoufand two hund-

dred villages were reckoned; but at prefent the collector can fcarcely find four hundred. Such of our merchants as have refided there twenty years have themfelves feen the greater part of the environs of Aleppo become depopulated. The traveller meets with nothing but houfes in ruins, cifterns rendered ufelefs and the fields abandoned. Thofe who culti-vated them are fled into the towns, where the popula-tion is abforbed, but where at leaft the individual conceals himfelf among the crowd from the rapa-cious hand of defpotifm.

The places which merit moft attention in this Pachalic are, firft, the city of Aleppo, called by the Arabs *Halab**. This city is the capital of the pro-vince, and the ordinary refidence of the Pacha. It is fituated in the vaft plain which extends from the Orontes to the Euphrates, and which, towards the fouth, terminates in the defert. The fituation of Aleppo, befide the advantage of a rich and fruitful foil, poffeffes alfo that of a ftream of frefh water, which never becomes dry. This rivulet, which is about as large as that of the *Gobelins* at Paris, or the New River near London, rifes in the mountains of Aentab, and terminates fix leagues below Aleppo, in a morafs full of wild boars and pelicans. Near Aleppo, its banks, inftead of the naked rocks which line them in the upper part of its courfe, are covered with a fertile earth, and laid out in gardens, or rather orchards, which, in a hot country, and efpe-cially in Turkey, cannot but be delightful. The city is in itfelf one of the moft agreeable in Syria, and is perhaps the cleaneft and beft built of any in Turkey.

---

* This is the name of which the ancient geographers made *Chalybon :* the *ch* reprefents here the Spanifh *jota ;* and it is remarkable, that the modern Greeks ftill render the Arabic *ha* by the fame found of *jota ;* which occafions a thoufand double meanings in their converfation, as the Arabs have the *jota* in another letter.

On whatever fide it is approached, its numerous
minarets and domes prefent an agreeable profpect to
the eye, fatigued with the continued famenefs of the
brown and parched plains. In the center is an artificial mountain furrounded by a dry ditch, on which
is a ruinous fortrefs. From hence we have a fine
profpect of the whole city, and to the north difcover
the fnowy tops of the mountains of Bailan ; and on
the weft, thofe which feparate the Orontes from the
fea ; while to the fouth and eaft, the eye can difcern
as far as the Euphrates. In the time of Omar, this
caftle ftopped the progrefs of the Arabs for feveral
months, and was at laft taken by treachery, but at
prefent would not be able to refift the feebleft affault.
Its flight wall, low, and without a buttrefs, is in
ruins ; its little old towers are in no better condition ;
and it has not four cannon fit for fervice, not excepting a culverine nine feet long, taken from the Perfians at the fiege of Bafra (Baffora). Three hundred
and fifty Janifaries, who fhould form the garrifon,
are bufy in their fhops, and the Aga fcarcely finds
room in it to lodge his retinue. It is remarkable that
this Aga is named immediately by the Porte, which,
ever fufpicious, divides as much as poffible, the different offices. Within the walls of the caftle is a
well, which, by means of a fubterraneous communication, derives its water from a fpring a league and ·
a quarter diftant. In the environs of the city, we
find a number of large fquare ftones, on the top of
which is a turban of ftone, which are fo many tombs.
There are many rifing grounds round it, which, in
cafe of a fiege, would greatly facilitate the approaches
of the affailants. Such, among others, is that on
which the houfe of the Derviches ftands, and which
commands the canal and the rivulet : Aleppo, therefore, cannot be efteemed a place of importance in
war, though it be the key of Syria to the north ;
but, confidered as a commercial city, it has a differ-

ent appearance. It is the emporium of Armenia and the Diarbekar; fends caravans to Bagdad, and into Perfia; and communicates with the Perfian Gulph and India, by Bafra; with Egypt and Mecca by Damafcus; and with Europe by Scandaroon (Alexandretta) and Latakia. Commerce is there principally carried on by barter. The chief commodities are raw or fpun cottons, clumfy linens fabricated in the villages; filk ftuffs manufactured in the city, copper, *bourres* (coarfe cloths) like thofe of Rouen, goats hair brought from Natolia; the gall nuts of the Kourdeftan, the merchandize of India, fuch as fhawls* and muflins; and piftachio nuts of the growth of the neighbourhood. The articles fupplied by Europe, are the Languedoc cloths, cochineal, indigo, fugar, and fome other groceries. The coffee of America, though prohibited, is introduced, and ferves to mix with that of Moka. The French have at Aleppo a conful, and feven counting-houfes; the Englifh and the Venetians two, and the merchants of Leghorn and Holland one. The Emperor appointed a conful there, in 1784, in the perfon of a rich Jew merchant, who fhaved his beard to affume the uniform and the fword. Ruffia has alfo fent one very lately. Aleppo is not exceeded in extent by any city in Turkey, except Conftantinople and Cairo, and perhaps Smyrna. The number of inhabitants has been computed at two hundred thoufand; but, in thefe calculations, certainty is impoffible. However, if we obferve, that this city is not larger than Nantes or Marfeilles, and that the houfes confift only of one

---

* Shawls are woollen handkerchiefs, an ell wide, and near two long. The wool is fo fine and filky, that the whole handkerchief may be contained in the two hands clofed: it is faid that no wool is employed but that of lambs torn from the belly of their mother before the time of birth. The moft beautiful fhawls come from Cafhmire: their price is from 150 livres (about fix guineas,) to 1200 livres (or 50l. fterling.)

ftory, we fhall, perhaps, not think it probable they exceed a hundred thoufand. The people of this city, both Turks and Chriftians, are, with reafon, efteemed the moft civilized in all Turkey; and the European merchants no where enjoy fo much liberty, or are treated with fo much refpect.

The air of Aleppo is very dry and piercing, but, at the fame time, very falubrious for all who are not troubled with afthmatic complaints. The city, however, and the environs, are fubject to a fingular endemial diforder, which is called the ringworm or pimple of Aleppo; it is in fact a pimple which is at firft inflammatory, and at length becomes an ulcer of the fize of the nail. The ufual duration of this ulcer is one year; it commonly fixes on the face, and leaves a fcar which disfigures almoft all the inhabitants. It is alledged that every ftranger, who refides there three months, is attacked with it; experience has taught that the beft mode of treatment is to make ufe of no remedy. No reafon is affigned for this malady; but I fufpect it proceeds from the quality of the water, as it is likewife frequent in the neighbouring villages, in fome parts of the Diarbekar, and even in certain diftricts near Damafcus, where the foil and the water have the fame appearances.

Every body has heard of the pigeons of Aleppo, which ferve as couriers at Alexandretta and Bagdad. This ufe of them, which is not fabulous, has been laid afide for the laft thirty or forty years, becaufe the Curd robbers killed the pigeons. The manner of fending advice by them was this: they took pairs which had young ones, and carried them on horfeback to the place from whence they wifhed them to return, taking care to let them have a full view. When the news arrived, the correfpondent tied a billet to the pigeon's foot, and let her loofe. The bird, impatient to fee its young, flew off like lightning, and arrived at Aleppo in ten hours from Alexandretta, and in two days from Bagdad. It was not difficult for them to find their way back, since Aleppo may be difcovered at an immenfe diftance. This pigeon has nothing peculiar in its form, except its noftrils, which, inftead of being fmooth and even are fwelled and rough.

The confpicuous fituation of Aleppo brings numbers of fea birds thither, and affords the curious a fingular amufement: if you go after dinner on the terraces of the houfes, and make a motion as if throwing bread, numerous flocks of birds will inftantly fly round you, though at firft you cannot difcover one; but they are floating aloft in the air, and defcending in a moment to feize, in their flight, the morfels of bread, which the inhabitants frequently amufe themfelves with throwing to them.

Next to Aleppo, Antioch, called by the Arabs Antakia, claims our attention. This city, anciently renowned for the luxury of its inhabitants, is now no more than a ruinous town, whofe houfes, built with mud and ftraw, and narrow and miry ftreets, exhibit every appearance of mifery and wretchednefs. Thefe houfes are fituated on the fouthern bank of the Orontes, at the extremity of an old decayed bridge: they are covered to the fouth by a mountain, upon the flope of which is a wall, built by the Crufaders. The diftance between the prefent town and this mountain may be about four hundred yards, which fpace is occupied by gardens and heaps of rubbifh, but prefents nothing interefting.

Notwithftanding the unpolifhed manners of its inhabitants, Antioch, was better calculated than Aleppo to be the emporium of the Europeans. By clearing the mouth of the Orontes, which is fix leagues lower down, boats might have been towed up that river, though they could not have *failed* up, as Pococke has afferted; its current is too rapid. The natives, who never knew the name of Orontes, call it, on account of the swiftness of its stream, Elaasi,* that is the Rebel. Its breadth, at Antioch, is about forty paces. Seven leagues above that town it passes by a lake abounding in fish, and especially in eels. A great quantity of these are salted every year, but not sufficient for the numerous fasts of the Greek Christians. It is to be remembered, we no longer hear at Antioch, either of the Grove of Daphne, or of the voluptuous scenes of which it was the theatre.

The plain of Antioch, though the soil of it is excellent, is uncultivated and abandoned to the Turkmen; but the hills on the side of the Orontes, particularly opposite Serkin, abound in plantations of figs and olives, vines, and mulberry trees, which, a thing uncommon in Turkey, are planted in quincunx,† and exhibit a landscape worthy our finest provinces.

The Macedonian king, Seleucus Nicator, who founded Antioch, built, also, at the mouth of the Orontes, on the northern bank, a large and well fortified city, which bore his name, but of which at present not a single habitation remains: nothing is to be seen but heaps of rubbish, and works in the adjacent rock, which prove that this was once a place of very considerable importance. In the sea also may be perceived the traces of two piers, which are indications of an ancient port, now choaked up. The inhabitants of the country go thither to fish, and call the name of the place Souaidia. From thence, as we proceed to the north, the sea coast is shut up by a chain of high mountains, known to the ancient geographers by the name of *Rhosus :* which name was probably derived from the Syriac, and still subsists in

* This is the name which the Greek Geographers have rendered by *Axius.*

† This mode of planting in *Quincunx,* is likewise in use among the Druzes, and is particularly mentioned by Baron de Tott.

that of *Ras-el-Kanzir*, or Cape of the Wild Boar, a head land on this coaft.

The Gulph towards the north-eaft, is remarkable for the town of Alexandretta, or Skandaroon, of which it bears the name. This town fituated on the fea fhore, is, properly fpeaking, nothing but a village, without walls, in which the tombs are more numerous than the houfes, and whch entirely owes its exiftence to the road which it commands. This is the only road in all Syria, where veffels anchor on a folid bottom, without their cables being liable to chafe: but in other refpects, it has fo many ferious inconveniences, that neceffity alone can prevent the merchants from abandoning it.

Firft, It is infefted, during winter, by a wind, peculiar to this place, called by the French failors *le Raguier*, which, rufhing from the fnowy fummits of the mountains, frequently forces fhips to drag their anchors feveral leagues.

Secondly, When the fnow begins to cover the mountains which furround the Gulph, tempeftuous winds arife which prevent veffels from entering for three or four months together.

Thirdly, The road from Alexandretta to Aleppo, by the plain, is infefted by Curd robbers, who conceal themfelves in the neighbouring rocks,* and frequently attack and plunder the ftrongeft caravans.

Another reafon, more forcible than thefe is the unwholefomenefs of the air of Alexandretta, which is extreme. It may be affirmed that it every year carries off one third of the crews of the veffels which remain there during the fummer; nay, fhips frequently lofe all their men in two months. The feafon for this epidemic diforder is principally from May to the

---

* The place they are found in exactly correfponds with the Caftle of Gyndarus, which, in the time of Strabo was a haunt of robbers.

end of September : it is an intermitting fever of the
moft malignant kind, and is accompanied with ob-
ftructions of the liver, which terminate in a dropfy.
The cities of Tripoli, Acre, and Larneca in Cyprus,
are fubject to the fame diforder, though in a lefs degree. In all thefe places the fame local circumftances
feem to have given birth to the contagion ; the caufe
of it in all is to be afcribed to the adjoining moraffes,
ftagnant waters, and confequent vapours and mephitic
exhalations ; a convincing proof of this is, that this
diforder does not prevail in feafons when no rain has
fallen. But, unfortunately, Alexandretta is condemned, from its fituation to be never wholly exempt
from it ; for the plain on which the town is built is
fo low and flat* that the rivulets, finding no declivity,
can never reach the fea. When they are fwelled by
the winter rains, the fea, fwelled likewife by tempefts,
hinders their difcharging themfelves into it ; hence
their waters, forced to fpread themfelves, form lakes
in the plain. On the approach of the fummer, the
waters become corrupted by the heat, and exhale
vapours equally corrupt, which cannot difperfe, being
confined by the mountains that encircle the gulph.
The entrance of the bay befides lies to the weft,
which, in thofe countries, is the moft unhealthy ex-
pofure when it correfponds with the fea. The labour
neceffary to remedy this would be immenfe, and after
all infufficient ; and, indeed fuch an undertaking
would be abfolutely impoffible, under a government
like that of the Turks. A few years ago, the merchants of Aleppo, difgufted with the numerous inconveniences of Alexandretta, wifhed to abandon that
port and carry the trade to Latakia. They propofed
to the Pacha of Tripoli to repair the harbour at

---

* This plain which is about a league in breadth, and lies at the
foot of the mountains, has been formed by the earth, brought
down by torrents and rain.

their own expence, provided he would grant them
an exemption from all duties for ten years. To induce him to comply with their requeſt, the agent they
employed talked much of the advantage which would
in time, reſult to the whole country: " But what
" ſignifies it to me what may happen *in time*, replied
" the Pacha? I was yeſterday at Marach, to-morrow,
" perhaps, I ſhall be at Djedda; Why ſhould I de-
" prive myſelf of preſent advantages, which are cer-
" tain, for future benefits I cannot hope to partake?"
The European factors were obliged therefore to remain at Skandaroon. There are three of theſe factors, two for the French, and one for the Engliſh
and Venetians. The only curioſity which they have
to amuſe ſtrangers with, conſiſts in ſix or ſeven marble monuments, ſent from England, on which you
read: *Here lies ſuch a one, carried off in the flower
of his age, by the fatal effects of a contagious air.* The
ſight of theſe is the more diſtreſſing, as the languid
air, yellow complexion, livid eyes, and dropſical bel-
lies of thoſe who ſhew them, make it but too probable
they cannot long eſcape the ſame fate. It is true,
they have ſome reſource in the village of Bailan, the
pure air and excellent waters of which ſurprizingly
reſtore the ſick. This village, ſituated among the
mountains, three leagues from Alexandretta, on the
road to Aleppo, preſents the moſt beautiful picturesque
appearance. It is built among the precipices in a
narrow and deep valley, from whence the Gulph of
Skandaroon is ſeen as through a tube. The houſes,
leaning againſt the ſteep declivities of the two mountains, are ſo diſpoſed, that the terraces of the lower
ſerve as ſtreets and courts to thoſe above. In winter, caſcades pour down on every ſide, which ſtun the
inhabitants with their noiſe, and, in their fall, ſometimes rend off large pieces of the rocks, and even
throw down the houſes. The cold is very ſevere
there, during that ſeaſon, but the ſummer delightful;

the inhabitants, who fpeak only Turkifh, live on their goats and buffaloes, and the produce of a few gardens which they cultivate. The Aga, for fome years paft, has applied the duties of the cuftom-houfe of Alexandretta to his own ufe, and rendered himfelf almoft independent of the Pacha of Aleppo. The Turkifh empire is full of fuch rebels, who frequently die in peaceable poffeffion of their ufurpations.

On the road from Alexandretta to Aleppo, at the laft place travellers fleep at, is the village of Martawan, celebrated among the Turks and Europeans, on account of an extraordinary practice of the inhabitants who let out their wives and daughters for a trifling fum.* This proftitution, held in abhorrence by the Arabs, feems to me to have originated in fome religious cuftom, which ought perhaps to be fought for in the ancient worfhip of the goddefs Venus, or to be attributed to the community of women permitted by the Anfarians, to which tribe the inhabitants of Martawan belong. The Franks pretend that the women are pretty. But it is probable that long abftinence at fea, and the vanity of intrigue, conftitute all their merit ; for their exterior announces nothing but the difgufting uncleanlinefs of mifery.

In the mountains which terminate the Pachalic of Aleppo to the north, we find Kles and Aentah, two confiderable villages. They are inhabited by Armenian Chriftians, Curds, and Mahometans, who, notwithftanding the difference of their religions, live in friendfhip, and, by their union, are enabled to refift the Pacha, whom they often brave, and enjoy in tranquility the produce of their flocks, bees, and a

---

* See Baron de Tott's Memoirs. M. du Rocher now refident of the king of France with the Emperor of Morocco, has furnifhed me with many entertaining anecdotes refpecting this whimfical cuftom, but too indelicate for the prefs. T.

few cultivated fpots on which they grow corn and
tobacco.*

Two days journey to the north-eaft of Aleppo is
the town of Mambedj, fo celebrated in ancient times,
under the names of Bambyce, and Hierapolis†. No
traces remain of the temple of that great goddefs
with whofe worfhip Lucian has made us acquainted.
The only remarkable monument is a fubterraneous
canal, which conducts the water from the mountains
of the north for the diftance of four leagues. All
this country was formerly full of fuch aqueducts:
the Affyrians, Medes, and Perfians, efteemed it a
religious duty to convey the water to the defert, in
order to multiply, according to the precepts of Zoroafter, *the principles of life and of abundance :* we therefore, at every ftep, meet with aftonifhing proofs of
ancient population. Along the whole road from
Aleppo to Hama, we difcover the ruins of ancient
villages, cifterns fallen in, and the remains of fortreffes, nay even of temples. I particularly remarked
a quantity of oval and round hillocks, which, from
the nature of the earth and their fteep afcent on this
even plain, evidently appear to have been the work
of man. The reader may form fome idea of the
labour they muft have coft, from the dimenfions of
that of Kan-Shaikoun, which I found to be feven
hundred and twenty paces, or fourteen hundred
French feet in circumference, and near a hundred
feet high. Thefe hillocks, fcattered at regular intervals of nearly a league from each other, are covered with the ruins of citadels, and, probably, were
alfo places facred to the adoration of fome deity,
according to the well known practice of the ancients,

---

* Thefe towns fuccefsfully revolted in 1780, againft the
tyranny of the Second Abdi Pacha, mentioned by our author. T.

† The name of Hierapolis ftill fubfifts in that of another village, called *Yeraboles*, and fituated on the Euphrates.

of worſhipping " on high places." Theſe conjectures
ſeem confirmed by the tradition of the inhabitants,
who attribute all theſe works to the infidels. At preſent, inſtead of that cultivation which might be expected, we meet with nothing but waſte and deſolate
lands : yet the ſoil is of a good quality, and the ſmall
quantity of grain, cotton, and ſeſamum it produces,
is excellent. But all the frontiers of the Deſert are
deſtitute of ſprings and running water. That of the
wells is brackiſh ; and the winter rains, on which the
inhabitants place their principal dependance, ſometimes fail. For this reaſon, nothing can be conceived
more melancholy than theſe parched and duſty plains,
without trees, and without verdure ; or more miſera-
ble than the appearance of the ſtraw and earthen
huts which form their villages ; nor can any greater
wretchedneſs be imagined than that of the peaſants,
expoſed at once to the oppreſſion of the Turks, and
the robberies of the Bedouin Arabs. The tribes
which encamp in theſe plains are called the Mawalis ;
they are the moſt powerful, and the richeſt among
the Arabs, as they pay ſome attention to agriculture,
and partake in the trade of the caravans which go
from Aleppo, either to Baſſora or Damaſcus, or to
Tripoli by the way of Hama.

CHAP. IX.

Of the Pachalic of Tripoli.

THE Pachalic of Tripoli comprehends the country which ſtretches along the Mediterranean, from
Latakia to the Narh-el-Kelb, and is bounded on the
weſt by that torrent, and the chain of mountains
which overlook the Orontes.

The principal part of this government is hilly; the sea-coast alone, between Tripoli and Latakia, is a level country. The numerous rivulets which water it contribute greatly to its fertility; but, notwithstanding this advantage, this plain is much less cultivated than the mountains, without even excepting Lebanon, with its numerous rocks and pine-trees. Its chief productions are corn, barley, and cotton. In the territory of Latakia tobacco and olives are principally cultivated: but in Lebanon, and the Kesraouan, white mulberry-trees and vineyards.

This Pachalic contains several different tribes and religions. From Lebanon to above Latakia, the mountains are peopled by the Ansarians of whom I have before spoken; Lebanon and the Kefraouan are inhabited entirely by the Maronites, and the sea-coast and cities, by Schismatic Greeks, and Latins, Turks, and descendants of the Arabs.

The Pacha of Tripoli enjoys all the privileges of his place. The military and finances are in his hands; he holds the government in quality of a farm from the Porte, on a lease of one year only, at the annual rent of seven hundred and fifty purses, (thirty-nine thousand pounds;) besides this, he is obliged to supply the Caravan of Mecca with corn, barley, rice, and other provisions, the expenses of which are estimated at seven hundred and fifty purses more. He is himself obliged to conduct this convoy into the Desert, to meet the pilgrims. To indemnify him for these expenses he receives the Miri, the customs, the farms of the Ansarians and the Kefraouan, and adds to all these numerous annual extortions and exactions; indeed had he no more than this last article, his profits would be considerable. He maintains about five hundred cavalry, as ill provided as those of Aleppo, and a few Mograbian infantry.

The Pacha of Tripoli has always been desirous of personally governing the country of the Ansarians,

and the Maronites; but thefe people having invariably oppofed by force the entrance of the Turks into
their mountains, he has been conftrained to abandon
the collection of the tribute to under farmers, approved of by the inhabitants. Their office is not like
his, held only for a year, but is difpofed of by auc-
tion; whence arifes a competition of wealthy perfons, who perpetually afford him the means of exciting or fomenting troubles in the tributary nation:
this adminiftration is the fame we find in hiftory to
have been ufual with the ancient Perfians and Affyrians, and which appears to have been frequent in all
ages in the eaftern world.

The farm of the Anfarians is at this day divided
between three chiefs or *Mokaddamin;* that of the
Maronites is wholly in the hands of the Youfef, who
pays thirty purfes (fifteen hundred and fixty pounds)
for it. Among the remarkable places in this Pachalic we muft firft mention Tripoli,* in Arabic *Tarabolos,*
the refidence of the Pacha. It is fituated on the river
Kadifha, at the diftance of a quarter of a league from
its mouth, and precifely at the foot of Mount Lebanon, which overlooks and furrounds it with its
branches to the eaft, the fouth, and even a little to the
north-weft. It is feparated from the fea by a fmall
triangular plain, half a league in breadth, at the point
of which is the village where the veffels land their goods.
The Franks call this village *la Marine,*† the general
name given by them to thefe places in the Levant.
There is no harbour but a fimple road, which extends from the fhore to the fhoals called *the Rabbit
and Pigeon Iflands.* The bottom is rocky, and ma-
riners are not fond of remaining here, as the cabals

---

* A Greek name, fignifying *three cities,* it having been built
by three colonies, from Sidon, Tyre, and Aradus, who each of
them formed fettlements fo near each other, that they were foon
united into one.

† Such maritime places were by the ancients called *Majuma.*

are foon worn out, and the veffels expofed to the north-weft winds, which are frequent and violent on all this coaft. In the time of the Franks, this road was defended by towers, feven of which are ftill fubfifting, from the mouth of the river to the village. They are ftrong built, but now ferve only as a place of refort for birds of prey.

All the environs of Tripoli are laid out in orchards, where the nopal grows fpontaneoufly, and the white mulberry is cultivated for the filk worm; and the pomegranate, the orange, and the lemon tree, for their fruit, which is of the greateft beauty. But thefe places, though delightful to the eye, are unhealthy. Every year, from July to September, epidemic fevers like thofe of Skandaroon and Cyprus, rage here: thefe are owing to the artificial inundations with which the mulberry-trees are watered, in order that they may throw out their fecond leaves. Befides, as the city is open only to the weft, the air does not circulate, and the fpirits are in a conftant ftate of oppreffion, which makes health at beft but a kind of convalefcence.* The air, though more humid, is more falubrious at *la Marine*, doubtlefs becaufe it has room to circulate. It is ftill more fo in the iflands ; and were the place in the hands of an enlightened government, the inhabitants fhould be invited to live there. Nothing more would be neceffary to induce them, than to convey water to the village by conduits, as feems formerly to have been done. It is worthy

---

* Since my return from France, I have received accounts that in the fpring, 1785, there raged an epidemical diforder, which defolated Tripoli and the Kefraouan. It was a violent fever, accompanied with blue fpots, which made it fufpected to have an affinity with the plague. What may be efteemed fin-gular, it was obferved to attack very few Mahometans, but made its chief ravages among the Chriftians ; whence it may be concluded it was in a great meafure occafioned by the unwhole-fome food and meagre diet they live on during Lent.

of obfervation, alfo, that foutbern fhore of the fmall
plain is full of the ruins of habitations, and columns
broken and buried in the earth, or in the fea fands.
The Franks had employed a great number of them in
the building their walls, in the remains, of which they
are ftill to be feen laid croffways.

The commerce of Tripoli confifts almoft wholly in
indifferent coarfe filks, which are made ufe of for
laces. It is obferved, that they are every day lofing
their quality. The reafon affigned for which, by well
informed perfons, is the decay of the muiberry-tree,
of which fcarcely any thing now remains but fome
hallow trunks. A ftranger inftantly replies why not
plant new ones? But I anfwer, that is an European
obfervation. Here they never plant; becaufe, were
they to build or plant, the Pacha, would fay this man
has money. He would fend for him, and demand it
of him: fhould he deny that he has any, he muft fuffer the baftinado; and fhould he confefs, he muft
ftill receive it to extort from him the acknowledgment
that he has ftill more. Not that the Tripolitans are
remarkable for their patience; they are on the contrary, confidered as extremely mutinous. Their title
of Janifaries, and the green turban they wear, in
quality of *Sherifs*, infpire them with the fpirit of revolt. Ten or twelve years ago, the extortions of a
Pacha drove them to extremities; they expelled him,
and remained eight months independent; but the
Porte fent a man well verfed in her maxims, who, by
dint of promifes, oaths, and pardons, gained and
difperfed them, and concluded by putting to death
eight hundred in one day; their heads are ftill to
be feen in a cave near Kadifha. Such is the government of the Turks! The commerce of Tripoli is in
the hands of the French alone. They have a conful here, and three commercial houfes. They export
filks, and fpunges fifhed up in the road; thefe they
exchange for cloths, cochineal, fugar and Weft-India

coffee; but this factory, both with respect to imports and exports, is inferior to its fubordinate town Latakia.

The town of Latakia, founded by Seleucus Nicator, under the name of *Laodicea*, is fituated at the bafe, and on the fouthern fide of a fmall peninfula, which projects half a league into the fea. Its port, like all the others on this coaft, is a fort of bafon, environed by a mole, the entrance of which is very narrow. It might contain five and twenty or thirty veffels; but the Turks have fuffered it fo to be choaked up, as fcarcely to admit four. Ships of above four hundred tons cannot ride there; and hardly a year paffes, that one is not ftranded in the entrance. Notwithstanding this, Latakia carries on a very great commerce, confisting chiefly of tobacco, of which upwards of twenty cargoes are annually fent to Damietta: the returns from thence are rice, which is bartered in Upper Syria for oils and cottons. In the time of Strabo, inftead of tobacco, the exports confifted in its famous wines, the produce of the hill fides. Even then, Egypt was the market by way of Alexandria. Have the ancients or the moderns gained by this exchange? Neither Latakia nor Tripoli can be mentioned as places of ftrength. They have neither cannon nor foldiers; a fingle privateer would make a conqueft of them both. They are each fuppofed to contain from four to five thoufand inhabitants.

On the coaft, between thefe towns, we meet with feveral inhabited villages, which formerly were large cities: fuch are Djebila, Merkab, fituated on a fteep declivity, and Tartoufa; but we find ftill more places which have only the half-deftroyed remains of ancient habitations. Among the latter, one of the principal is the rock, or ifland of Rouad, formerly a powerful city and republic, known by the name of *Aradus*. Not a fingle wall is remaining of all that

VOL. II.   O

multitude of houfes, which, according to Strabo, were
built with more ftories than even thofe of Rome.
The liberty enjoyed by the inhabitants had rendered
it very populous, and it fubfifted by naval commerce,
manufactures, and arts.   At prefent the ifland is deferted; nor has tradition even retained the memory
of a fpring of frefh water in its environs, which the
people of Aradus difcovered at the bottom of the fea,
and from which they drew water, in time of war, by
means of a leaden bell, and a leathern pipe fitted to
its bottom.   To the fouth of Tripoli is the country
of the Kefraouan, which extends from Nahr-el-Kelb,
paffing by Lebanon, as far as Tripoli.   Djebail, the
ancient Byblos, is the moft confiderable town in this
territory: it has not, however, above fix thoufand
inhabitants.   Its ancient port, which refembles that
of Latakia, is in a ftill worfe fituation; fcarcely any
traces of it remain.   The river Ibrahim, the ancient
Adonis, which is two leagues to the fouthward, has
the only bridge to be feen, that of Tripoli excepted,
from thence to Antioch.   It is of a fingle arch, fifty
feet wide, and upwards of thirty high; of a very
light architecture, and appears to have been a work
of the Arabs.

Among the mountains, the places moft frequented
by the Europeans, are the villages of Eden and
Befharrai, where the miffionaries have a houfe.   During the winter, many of the inhabitants defcend to
the coaft, and leave their houfes under the fnow,
with fomebody to guard them.   Befharrai is in the
road to the Cedars, to which it is a journey of feven
hours, though the diftance be but three leagues.
Thefe Cedars, fo boafted, refemble many other wonders; they fupport their reputation very indifferently
on a near infpection; the fight of four or five large
trees, which are all that remain, and have nothing
remarkable in their appearance, is not worth the trou-

ble it cofts the traveller to climb the precipices that lead to them.

On the frontiers of the Kefraouan, a league to the northward of Nahr-el-kelb, is the little village of Antoura, where the Jefuits were eftablifhed in a houfe, which, though it has not the fplendor of thofe in Europe, is a neat and fimple manfion. Its fituation on the fide of the hill, the limpid waters which refrefh its vineyards and mulberry-trees, the profpect it commands over the valley, and the diftant view it has of the fea, render it a moft agreeable hermitage. The Jefuits attempted to annex to it a convent of young women, fituated at a quarter of a league's diftance in front; but the Greek Chriftians having difpoffeffed them, they built one clofe to them, under the name of the *Vifitation*. They had alfo built two hundred paces higher, a feminary, which they wifhed to fill with Maronite and Latin-Greek ftudents; but it has remained deferted. The Lazarites, who have fucceeded them, maintain a fuperior curate, and a lay-brother at Antoura, who do the duties of the miffion with equal charity, politenefs, and decency.

CHAP. X.

Of the Pachalic of Saide, called likewife the Pachalic of Acre.

TO the fouth of the Pachalic of Tripoli, and on the fame coaft, is a third Pachalic, that, till now, has borne the name of the city of Saide, its capital, but may henceforward affume that of Acre, to which place the Pacha has of late years transferred his refidence. The extent of this government has greatly varied at different times. Before Shaik Daher, it was compofed of the country of the Druzes, and the whole coaft from Nahr-el-kelb, as far as Mount Carmel. In proportion as Daher obtained power, he infringed on the territories of the Pacha, and reduced him to the city of Saide, from which he was at laft expelled; but after the ruin of Daher, the government refumed its ancient limits. Djezzar, who fucceeded that chief in quality of Pacha for the Turks, has annexed to the Pachalic the countries of Safad, Tabaria, and Balbek, formerly tributary to Damafcus, and the territory of Kaifaria, (the ancient Cefarea) inhabited by the Arabs of Saker. This Pacha, perceiving the advantage of the works erected by Daher at Acre, transferred his refidence to that city, which is now become the capital of that province.

By thefe different augmentations, the Pachalic of Acre at prefent includes all the country from the Nahr-el-kelb, to the fouth of Kaifaria, between the Mediterranean to the weft, and Anti-Lebanon, and the upper part of the courfe of Jordan, to the eaft. It derives the more importance from this extent as it unites the valuable advantages of fituation and foil. The plains of Acre, Efdrelon, Sour, Havula, and the Lower Bekaa, are juftly boafted for their fertility. Corn, barley, maize, cotton, and fefamum, produce, notwithftanding the imperfection of the culture, twenty and twenty-five for one. The country of Kaifaria poffeffes a foreft of oaks, the only one in Syria. Safad furnifhes cottons, which, from their whitenefs, are held in as high eftimation as thofe of Cyprus. The neighbouring mountains of Sour produce as good tobacco as that of Latakia, and in a part of them is produced a perfume of cloves, which is referved exclufively for the ufe of the Sultan and his women. The country of the Druzes abounds in wines and filks, in fhort, from the fituation of the coaft, and the number of its creeks, this Pachalic neceffarily

becomes the emporium of Damafcus and all the interior parts of Syria.

The Pacha enjoys all the privileges of his office;
he is defpotic governor, and farmer general. He re-
mits to the Port annually the fixed fum of feven hundred and fifty purfes; but he, as well as the Pacha
of Tripoli, is obliged to furnifh the *Djerde* or provifions for the pilgrims of .Mecca. His expences for
this article are eftimated likewife at feven hundred
and fifty purfes, in rice, corn, barley, &c. The time
limited for his government is a year, but is frequently
prolonged. His revenues are, the Miri; the farms
of the tributaries, as the Druzes, the Motoualis and
fome Arab tribes; the numerous fees from fucceffions
and extortions; and the produce of the cuftoms on the
exports, imports, and the conveyance of merchandize;
which article alone amounted to one thoufand purfes
(above fifty thoufand pounds,) when Djezzar farmed
all the harbours and creeks in 1784. This Pacha
likewife, as is ufual with the Turkifh governors in
Afia, cultivates lands on his own account, enters into
partnerfhip with merchants and manufacturers, and
lends out money for intereft to hufbandmen and traders; the total from thefe various emoluments is
eftimated at between nine and ten millions of French
money, (about four hundred thoufand pounds.) If we
compare with this his tribute, which, with the fupply
of the caravan, amounts only to fifteen hundred
purfes, or one million, eight hundred and feventy-five
thoufand livres, (feventy-eight thoufand one hundred
and twenty-five pounds), we muft be aftonifhed that
the Porte allows him fuch enormous profits; but this
alfo is a part of the policy of the Divan. The tribute
once fettled never varies, only, if the Pacha becomes
rich, he is fqueezed by extraordinary demands. He
is often left to accumulate in peace; but when he
has once amaffed great wealth, fome expedient is

always contrived to bring to Conftantinople his coffers or his head.

At prefent, the Porte is on good terms with Djezzar, on account, it is faid, of his former fervices; in fact, he greatly contributed to the ruin of Daher: he deftroyed the family of that prince, reftrained the Bedouins of Sakar, humbled the Druzes, and nearly annihilated the Motoualis. Thefe fucceffes have caufed him to be continued in his government for ten years. He has lately received the three tails, and the title of *Wazir* (Vifir), which accompanies them;* but the Porte, as ufual, begins to take umbrage at his good fortune. She is alarmed at his enterprizing fpirit, and he, on his fide, is apprehenfive of the duplicity of the Divan: fo that a mutual diftruft prevails, from which fome important confequences may well be expected. He maintains a greater number of foldiers, and in better condition than any other Pacha, and takes care to enroll none but thofe of his own country; that is to fay, Bofhnaks and Arnauts; their number is about nine hundred horfemen. Added to thefe, he has nine thoufand Mograbian infantry. The gates of his frontier towns have regular guards, which is ufual in the reft of Syria.

By fea, he has one frigate, two galliots, and a xebeck, which he has lately taken from the Maltefe. By thefe precautions, apparently intended to fecure him from foreign enemies, he has put himfelf on his guard againft the ftratagems of the Divan. More than one attempt has been made to deftroy him by Capidjis; but he has watched them fo narrowly, that they have not been able to effect any thing; and the *cholic*, of which two or three of them have fuddenly died, has cooled the zeal of thofe who take upon them fo tickiifh an employment. Befides, he conftantly maintains fpies in pay, in the *Serai*, or palace of the

---

* Every Pacha of three tails is ftiled *Vifir.*

Sultan; and his money procures him plenty of pro-
tectors.   By thefe means he has juft obtained the Pachalic of Damafcus, to which he had long afpired, and
which is, in fact, the moft important in all Syria.
He has refigned that of Acre to a Mamlouk, named
Selim, his friend, and the companion of his fortune ;
but this man is fo devoted to him, that Djezzar may
be confidered as in poffeffion of both the governments.   It is faid, he is foliciting that of Aleppo ;
which if he procures, he will poffefs nearly the whole
of Syria, and the Porte poffibly may find in him a
rebel more dangerous than Daher ; but, as conjectures
concerning fuch events are of little ufe, I fhall pafs,
without, purfuing them any further, to give fome
defcription of the moft remarkable places of this Pachalic.*

The firft that prefents itfelf, as we proceed along
the coaft, is the town of Berytus, which the Arabs
pronounce *Bairout*, like the ancient Greeks.   It is
fituated in a plain, which from the foot of Lebanon,
runs out into the fea, narrowing to a point, about
two leagues from the ordinary line of the fhore, and
on the north fide forms a pretty long road, which
receives the river of Nahr-el-Salib, called alfo Nahr-
Bairout.   This river has fuch frequent floods in winter, as to have occafioned the building of a confiderable
bridge ; but it is in fo ruinous a ftate as to be impaf-
fable : the bottom of the road is rock, which chafes
the cables, and renders it very infecure.   From
hence, as we proceed weftward towards the point, we
reach, after an hour's journey, the town of Bairout.
This, till lately, belonged to the Druzes ; but Djez-

---

* It is afferted on good authority, that Djezzar, dreading a
vifit from his *old friend*, the *Captain Pacha*, now employed in
quelling the revolt in Egypt, has quitted his government, and
prudently fled with all his ill-gotten wealth, it is fuppofed, into
Bofhnia, his native country, at the commencement of the year
1787.   T.

zar thought proper, as we have feen, to take it from
them, and place in it a Turkifh garrifon. It ftill
continues, however, to be the emporium of the Maronites and the Druzes, where they export their cottons and filks, almoft all of which are deftined for
Cairo. In return, they receive rice, tobacco, coffee,
and fpecie, which, they exchange again for the corn
of Bekaa, and the Hauran. This commerce maintains near fix thoufand perfons. The dialect of the
inhabitants is juftly cenfured as the moft corrupt of
any in the country ; it unites in itfelf the twelve faults
enumerated by the Arabian grammarians.

The port of Bairout, formed like all the others of
the coaft, by a pier, is, like them, choaked up with
fands and ruins. The town is furrounded by a wall,
the foft and fandy ftone of which may be pierced by
a cannon ball, without breaking or crumbling ; which
was unfavourable to the Ruffians in their attack ;
but in other refpects this wall and its old towers,
are defencelefs. Two inconveniencies will prevent
Bairout from ever becoming a place of ftrength ; for
it is commanded by a chain of hills to the fouth-eaft,
and is entirely deftitute of water, which the women
are obliged to fetch from a well at the diftance of
half a quarter of a league, though what they find
there is but indifferent. Djezzar has undertaken
to conftruct a public fountain, as he has done at Acre ;
but the canal which I faw dug, will foon become
ufelefs. By digging, in order to form refervoirs,
fubterraneous ruins have been difcovered, from which
it appears, that the modern town is built on the
ancient one. The fame may be obferved of Latakia,
Antioch, Tripoli, Saide, and the greater part of the
towns on the coaft, which has been occafioned by
earthquakes, that have deftroyed them at different
periods. We find likewife without the walls to the
weft, heaps of rubbifh, and fome fhafts of columns,
which indicate that Bairout has been formerly much

larger than at prefent. The plain around it is entirely
planted with white mulberry-trees, which, unlike
thofe of Tripoli, are young and flourifhing; becaufe,
in the territories of the Druzes, there is no danger
in renewing them. The filk, therefore, produced
here, is of the very fineft quality. As we defcend
from the mountains, no profpect can be more delightful than to behold, from their fummits or declivities,
the rich carpet of verdure, formed by the tops of
thefe ufeful trees in the diftant bottom of the valley.

In fummer, it is inconvenient to refide at Bairout,
on account of the heat, and the warmth of the water;
the town, however is not unhealthy, though it is
faid to have been fo formerly. It has ceafed to be
unhealthy fince the Emir Fakr-el-din planted a wood
of fir trees, which is ftill ftanding, a league to the
fouthward of the town. The monks of Mahr-Hanna,
who are not fyftematical philofophers, have made the
fame obfervation refpecting feveral convents; they
even affert, that fince the heights have been covered
with pines, the waters of feveral fprings have become
more abundant, and more falubrious; which agrees
with other known facts.*

The country of the Druzes affords few interefting
places. The moft remarkable is *Dair-el-Kamar*, or
Houfe of the Moon, which is the capital and refidence
of the Emirs. It is not a city, but a large town ill
built, and very dirty. It is fituated on the back of
a mountain, at the foot of which flows one of the
branches of the ancient river Tamyras, at prefent the
rivulet of Damour. It is inhabited by Greek Catho-

---

* Dr. Franklin, to whom mankind are indebted for fo much,
in every branch of knowledge, has given very fatisfactory reafons for this falutary effect of trees, particularly pines; the fubject
has been well treated too by feveral Englifh and French philofophers; among others by the *Marquis de Caftellun,* in his
North America, under the article *Virginia.* T.

lics and Schifmatics, Maronites and Druzes, to the
number of fifteen or eighteen hundred. The *Serai*,
or palace of the prince, is only a large wretched houfe
falling to ruin.

I muft alfo mention Zahla, a village at the foot of
the mountains in the valley of *Bekaa ;* for the laft
twenty years this place is become the centre of cor-
refpondence between Balbek, Damafcus, Bairout,
and the interior of the Mountains. It is even faid
that the counterfeit money is made here ; but the
clumfy artifts, though they can imitate the Turkifh
piafters, have not been able to approach the workmanfhip of the German Dahlers.

I neglect to obferve that the country of the Druzes
is divided into *Katas,* fections, or diftricts, which.
have each of them a diftinct character. The *Matra,*
which is to the north, is the moft ftoney, and abounds
moft in iron. The *Garb* affords the moft beautiful
pines. The *Sahel* or *flat* Country, which lies next
the fea, produces mulberry-trees and vineyards.
The *Shouf* in which Dair-el-Kamar is fituated, has
the greateft number of Okkals, and produces the fineft
filks. The *Tefah,* or diftrict of Apples, which is to
the fouth, abounds in that fpecies of fruit. The
Shakif grows the beft tobacco, and the name of *Djourd*
is given to all the higher country and the coldeft
of the mountains : to this diftrict in fummer the
fhepherds retire with their flocks.

I have already faid that the Druzes had received
among them the Greek Chriftians and Maronites,
and granted them lands to build convents on. The
Greek Catholics, availing themfelves of this permiffion, have founded twelve within the laft feventy
years. The principal is Mar-Hanna : this monaftery
is fituated oppofite the village of Shouair, on a fteep
declivity, at the bottom of which a torrent runs in
winter into the Nahr-el-kelb. The convent built amid
rocks and blocks of ftone is far from magnificent,

and confifts of a dormitory with two rows of little cells, above which is a terrace fubftantially vaulted; it maintains forty monks. Its chief merit confifts in an Arabic Printing-Prefs, the only one which has fucceeded in the Turkifh empire. This has been eftablifhed about fifty years, and the reader will perhaps not be offended if I fay fomething of its hiftory.

At the commencement of the prefent century, the Jefuits, profiting by the profpect which the protection of France procured them, manifefted, in their houfe at Aleppo, that zeal for the improvement of knowledge which they have every where fhewn. They had founded a fchool in that city, intended to educate the children of Chriftians in the doctrines of the Catholic religion, and enable them to confute heretics; this latter article is always a principal object with the miffionaries; whence refults a rage for controverfy, which caufes perpetual differences among the partifans of the various fects in the eaft. The Latins of Aleppo, excited by the Jefuits, prefently recommenced, as heretofore, their difputations with the Greeks; but as logic requires a methodical acquaintance with language, and the Chriftians, excluded from the Mahometan-fchools, knew nothing but the vulgar Arabic, they were unable to indulge their paffion for controverfy in writing. To remedy this, the Latins determined to ftudy the Arabic language grammatically. The pride of the Mahometan Doctors at firft refufed to lay open their learning to *Infidels*, but, their avarice overpowered their fcruples; and for a few Purfes, this fo much boafted fcience of grammar, and *the Nahou*, was introduced among the Chriftians. The ftudent who diftinguifhed himfelf moft by his progrefs was named Abd-allah-Zaker, who to his own defire of learning, added an ardent zeal to promulgate his knowledge and his opinions. It is impoffible to determine to what length this fpirit of making profelytes might have been carried at Aleppo, had not an accident not unufual in Turkey, difturbed its progrefs. The Schifmatics, vexed at the attacks of Abd-allah, endeavoured to procure his ruin at Conftantinople. The Patriarch, excited by the priefts, reprefented him to the Vifir as a dangerous man; the Vifir, accuftomed to thefe difputes, feigned to pay no attention to his complaint; but the patriarch, backing his reafons with a few purfes, the Vifir delivered him a *Kat-fherif*, or warrant of the Sultan, which according to cuftom, conveyed an order to cut off Abd-allah's head. Fortunately he received timely warning, and efcaped into Lebanon, where his life was in fafety: but in quitting his country, he by no means abandoned his ideas of reformation, and was more refolutely bent than ever on propagating his opinions. This he was only able to effeft by writings; and manufcripts feemed to him an inadequate method. He was no ftranger to the advantages of the prefs, and had the courage to form the three-fold projeft of writing, founding types, and printing; he fucceeded in this enterprize from the natural goodnefs of his underftanding, and the knowledge he had of the art of engraving, which he had already praftifed in his profeffion as a jeweller. He ftood in need of an affociate, and was lucky enough to find one who entered into his defigns: his brother, who was fuperior at Mar-Hanna, prevailed on him to make that convent his refidence, and from that time, abandoning every other care, he gave himfelf up entirely to the execution of his projeft. His zeal and induftry had fuch fuccefs, that in the year 1733, he publifhed the Pfalms of David in one volume. His charafters were found fo correft and beautiful, that even his enemies purchafed his books; and fince that period there have been ten impreffions of it; new charafters have been founded, but nothing has been executed fuperior to his. They perfeftly imitate hand-writing; they exprefs the full and the fine let-

ters, and have not the meagre and ftraggling appearance of the Arabic charaçters of Europe. He paffed
twenty years in this manner, printing different works,
which, in general, were tranflations of our books of
devotion. Not that he was acquainted with any of
the European languages, but the Jefuits had already
tranflated feveral books, and as their Arabic was extremely bad, he correçted their tranflations, and often
fubftituted his own verfion, which is a model of
purity and elegance. The Arabic he wrote was remarkable for a clear, precife, and harmonious ftile,
of which that language had been thought incapable,
and which proves that, fhould it ever be cultivated
by a learned people, it will become one of the moft
copious and expreffive in the world. After the death
of Abd-allah, which happened about 1755, he was
fucceeded by his pupil; and his fucceffors were the
religious of the houfe itfelf; they have continued to
found letters and to print, but the bufinefs is at prefent on the decline, and feems likely to be foon entirely laid afide. The books have but little fale, except the Pfalter, which is the claffic of the Chriftian
children, and for which there is a continual demand.
The expenfes are confiderable, as the paper comes
from Europe, and the labour is very flow. A little
art would remedy the firft inconvenience, but the
latter is radical. The Arabic charaçters requiring to
be conneçted together, to join them well and place
them in a right line requires an immenfe and minute
attention. Befides this, the combination of the letters varying according as they occur, at the beginning,
in the middle, or at the end of a word, it is neceffary to found a great number of double letters; by
which means the cafes being too multiplied, are not
colleçted under the hand of a compofitor; but he is
obliged to run the whole length of a table eighteen
feet long, and feek for his letters in near nine hundred divifions: hence a lofs of time which will never

allow Arabic Preffes to attain the perfection of ours. As for the inconfiderable fale of the books, this muft be attributed to the bad choice they have made of them; inftead of tranflating works of real utility, calculated to awaken a tafte for the arts indifcrimi-nately among all the Arabs, they have only tranf-lated myftic books peculiar to the Chriftians, which, by their mifanthropic morality, are formed to ex-cite a difguft for all fcience, and even for life itfelf. Of this the reader will judge from the following Catalogue.

CATALOGUE *of the* BOOKS *printed at the Convent of* MAR-HANNA-EL-SHOUAIR, *in the mountains of the Druzes.*

1. THE balance of Time, or the Difference be-tween Time and Eternity, by Father Nieremberg, Jefuit.

2. The Vanity of the World, by Didaco Stella, Jefuit.

3. The Sinner's Guide, by Louis de Grenade Jefuit.

4. The Prieft's Guide.

5. The Chriftian's Guide.

6. The Food of the Soul.

7. The Contemplation of Paffion Week.

8. Chriftian Doctrine.

9. Explication of the Seven Penitential Pfalms.

10. The Pfalms of David, *tranflated from the Greek.*

11. The Prophecies.

12. The Gofpel and Epiftles.

1. Mizan-el-Zaman. 2. Abatil-el-Aalam. 3. Morfhed-el-Ka-ti. 4. Morfhed-el-Kahen. 5. Morfhed-el-Mafihi. 6. Kout-el Nafs. 7. Taammol-el-Afboua. 8. Taalim-el-Mafihi. 9. Taffir-el-Sabat. 10. Mazamir. 11. El Onbouat. 12. El-Endjil oua el Rafayel.

13. Les Heures Chretiennes (hourly prayers ;) to which is added, the Chriſtian Perfeſtion of Rodriguez, and the Regulation of the Monks ; *both printed at Rome.*

IN MANUSCRIPTS THIS CONVENT POSSESSES ;

1. The Imitation of Jeſus Chriſt.
2. The Garden of the Monks, or Life of the Holy Fathers of the Deſert.
3. Moral Theology of Buzembaum.
4. The Sermoms of Segneri.
5. Theology of St. Thomas, in 4 vol. *folio*, the copying of which coſt one thouſand two hundred and fifty livres (52*l.*)
6. Sermons of St. John Chryſoſtom.
7. Principles of Laws, by Claude Virtieu.
8. * Theological Diſputes of the Monk George.
9. Logic, tranſlated from the Italian, by a Maronite.
10. The Light of Hearts, by Paul of Smyrna, a converted Jew.
11. * Queſtions and Enquiries concerning Grammar, and *the Nahou*, by Biſhop Germain, Maronite.
12. * Poems of the ſame, on pious ſubjeſts.
13. * Poems of the Curate Nicholas, brother of Abd-allah-Zakar.
14. * Abridgment of the Arabic Diſtionary, called *the Ocean.*

13. El-Soueyat.

1. Taklid-el-*Masih.* 2. Beſtan el Rohoban. 3. Elm el Nia l'Bouzembaoum. 4. Maouaez Sainari. 5. Lahout Mar Touma. 6. Mawaez Fomm el Dahab. 7. Kawaed el Naouamis l'Kloud Firtiou. 8. Madjadalat el Anba Djordji. 9. El Mantek. 10. Nour el Aebab. 11. El Mataleb wa el Mebâhes. 12. Diwan Djermanos. 13. Diwan Ankoula. 14. Moktaſar el Kamous.

N. B. *All thefe are the productions of Chriftians ; thofe marked with a ftar* were originally written in Arabic : the following are Mahometan works.*

1. The Koran.
2. The *Ocean* of the Arabic Tongue, tranflated by Golius.
3. The thoufand Diftichs of Ebn-el-Malek, on Grammar.
4. Explication of the Thoufand Diftichs.
5. Grammar of Adjeroumia.
6. Rhetoric of Taftazani.
7. Seffions, or Pleafant Stories of Hariri.
8. Poems of Omar-ebn-el-Fardi, of the amorous kind.
9. Science of the Arabic Tongue ; a fmall book in the nature of the *Synonymes Français*, of Abbé Girard.
10. Medicine of Ebn-Sina, (Avicenna.)
11. Simples and Drugs, tranflated from Diofcorides, by Ebn-el-Bitar.
12. Difpute of the Phyficians.
13. Theological Fragments on the different Sects of the World.
14. A little Book of Tales (of little value) from which I have an extract.
15. Hiftory of the Jews, by Jofephus, a very incorrect tranflation.

A fmall book of Aftronomy, on the principles of Ptolemy, and fome others of no value.

1. Koran. 2. El Kamous l'Firowzàbadi. 3. El Alf bait l'Ebnel-malek. 4. Taffir el-alf-bait. 5. El-Adjiroumia. 6. Elm el Bayan l'Taftazàni. 7. Makamat el Hariri. 8. Diwan omar Ebn el fardi. 9. Fakah el Logat. 1c. El tob l'Ebn fina. 11. El Mofràdat. 12. Daouat el Otobba. 13. Abarat el Motakal
lamin. 14. Nadim el wahid. 15. Tarik el Yhoud, l'Youfefous.

This is all the library of the convent of Mar-Hanna from which we may form an idea of the literature of Syria, since, excepting one possessed by Djezzar, there does not exist another. Among the original books, there is not one, which, in fact, merits a translation. Even the *Sessions* of *Hariri*, are only interesting from their style, and, in the whole order, there is but one monk who understands them, nor are the others found much more intelligible by his brethren in general. In the administration of this house, and the manners of the religious who inhabit it, we find some singularities which deserve our notice.

Their order is that of Saint Basil, who is to the orientals what Saint Benedict is to the western Christians, except that they have adopted a few alterations in consequence of their peculiar situation, and the court of Rome has given her sanction to the code they drew up thirty years ago. They may pronounce the vows at the age of sixteen, for it has ever been the aim of all Monastic legislators to captivate the minds of their proselytes at an early age, that they may more implicitely comply with their institutions. These vows are, as every where else, vows of poverty, obedience, devotion to the order, and chastity; and it must be allowed that they are more strictly observed in this country than in Europe. The condition of the oriental Monks is infinitely more hard than that of the European. We may judge of this from the following description of their domestic life. Every day they have seven hours prayers at church, from which no person is exempted. They rise at four in the morning, go to bed at nine in the evening, and make only too meals, viz. at nine and five. They live perpetually on a meagre diet, and hardly allow themselves flesh meat in the most critical disorders. Like the other Greeks, they have three Lents a year, and a multitude of fasts, during which they can neither eat eggs, nor milk, nor butter, nor even cheefe. Almoft the whole year they live on lentils and beans with oil, rice and butter, curds, olives, and a little falt fifh. Their bread is a little clumfy loaf badly levened, which ferves two days, and is frefh made only once a week. With this food they pretend to be lefs fubject to maladies than the peafants; but it muft be remarked that they have all iffues in their arms and many of them are attacked by Hernias, owing, as I imagine, to their immoderate ufe of oil. The lodging of each is a narrow cell and his whole furnature confifts in a mat, a matrafs and a blanket; but no fheets, for of thefe they have no need, as they fleep with their cloathes on. Their cloathing is a coarfe cotton fhirt ftriped with blue, a pair of drawers, a waiftcoat, and a furplice of coarfe brown cloath, fo ftiff and thick, that it will ftand upright without a fold. Contrary to the cuftom of the country they wear their hair eight inches long, and, inftead of a hood, a cylinder of felt, ten inches high, like thofe of the Turkifh cavalry. Every one of them, in fhort, except the Superior, Purveyor, and Vicar, exercifes fome trade either neceffary or ufeful to the houfe; one is a weaver, and weaves ftuffs; another a tailor, and makes cloaths; this is a fhoe-maker, and makes their fhoes; that a mafon, and fuperintends their buildings. Two of them have the management of the kitchen, four work at the Printing-prefs, four are employed in Book-binding, and all affift at the Bake-houfe, on the day of making bread. The expence of maintaining forty or five and forty perfons, of which the convent is compofed, does not exceed the annual fum of twelve purfes, or fix hundred and twenty-five pounds; and from this fum muft be deducted the expences of their hofpitality to all paffengers, which of itfelf forms a confiderable article. It is true, moft of thefe paffengers leave prefents or alms, which make a part of the revenue of the houfe; the other part arifes from the culture of the lands. They farm a confiderable extent of ground, for which they pay four hundred piaftres to two Emirs: thefe lands were cleared out by the firft Monks themfelves; but at prefent they commit the culture of them to peafants, who pay them one half of all the produce. This produce confifts of white and yellow filks, which are fold at Bairout, fome corn and wines,* which, for want of demand, are fent as prefents to their benefactors, or confumed in the houfe. Formerly the religious abftained from drinking wine; but, as is cuftomary in all focieties, they have gradually relaxed from their primative aufterity: they have alfo begun to allow the ufe of tobacco and coffee, notwithftanding the

---

* Thefe wines are of three forts, the red, the white, and the yellow; the white, which are the moft rare, are fo bitter as to be difagreeable. The two others, on the contrary, are too fweet and fugary. This arifes from their being boiled, which makes them refemble the baked wines of Provence. The general cuftom of the country is, to reduce the muft to two thirds of its quantity. It is improper for a common drink at meals, becaufe it ferments in the ftomach. In fome places, however, they do not boil the red, which then acquires a quality almoft equal to that of Bordeaux. The yellow wine is much efteemed among our merchants, under the name of *Golden Wine (Vin d'or)*, which has been given it from its colour. The moft efteemed is produced from the hill fides of the Mouk, or village of Maf beh near Antoura. It is not neceffary to heat it, but it is too fugary. Such are the wines of Lebanon, fo boafted by the Grecian and Roman epicures. The Europeans may try them, and fee how far they agree with the ancients in opinion: but they fhould obferve, that the paffage by fea ferments boiled wines a fecond time, and burfts the cafks. It is probable, that the inhabitants of Lebanon have made no change in their ancient method of making wines, nor in the culture of their vines. They are difpofed on poles of fix or eight feet high. They are not pruned as in France, which certainly muft greatly injure both the quantity and quality of the crop. The vintage begins about the end of September. The convent of Mar-Hanna makes about one hundred and fifty *Rabia*, or earthen jars, containing about one hundred and ten pints each; the price current in the country, is about feven or eight fols, (four pence) the French pint.

remonstrances of the older Monks, who are ever jealous of too much indulging the habits of youth.

The same regulations are observed in all the houses
of the order, which, as I have already said, amount
to twelve. The whole number of these religious is
estimated at one hundred and fifty; to which must
be added, five convents of women which depend on
them. The first superiors who founded them, thought
they had performed a good work; but at present the
order repent it has been done, because nuns in a
Turkish country are very dangerous, as they are connected with the wealthiest merchants of Aleppo,
Damascus, and Cairo, who for a stipulated sum get
rid of their daughters by placing them in these convents. The merchants likewise bestow on them
considerable alms. Several of them give an hundred
pistoles yearly, and even as high as one hundred Louis
d'or, or three thousand livres (one hundred and
twenty-five pounds,) without requiring any other interest than their prayers to God, that he would preserve them from the rapacity of the Pachas. But,
as they imprudently attract their notice, by the extreme
luxury of their dress and furniture, neither their presents, nor the prayers of the religious, can save them
from extortion. Not long since, one of these merchants ventured to build a house at Damascus, which
cost him upwards of one hundred and twenty thousand
livres, (five thousand pounds.) The Pacha observed
it, and presently gave the owner to understand, he
had a curiosity to see his new house, and would pay
him a visit, and take a dish of coffee with him. As
the Pacha, therefore, might have been so delighted
with it, as not to have quitted it again, it became necessary to avoid his politeness, by making him a present
of thirty thousand livres, (seven thousand five hundred pounds.)

Next to Mar-Hanna, the most remarkable convent
is that of *Dair Mokalles*, or St. Saviour. It is situ-

ated three hours journey to the north-east of Saide. The religious had collected there a confiderable number of printed Arabic books, and manufcripts; but Djezzar, having carried the war into thefe diftricts about eight years ago, his foldiers pillaged the houfe, and took away all the books.

As we return to the fea-coaft, we muft firft remark Saide, the degenerate offspring of ancient Sidon.* This town, formerly the refidence of the Pacha, is like all the Turkifh towns, ill built, dirty, and full of modern ruins. Its length along the fea fhore is about fix hundred paces, and its breadth one hundred and fifty. On the fouth fide, on a fmall eminence, is a fort built by Degnizla. From hence we have a view of the fea, the city, and the country: but a few cannon would eafily deftroy this whole work, which is only a large tower of a fingle ftory, already half in ruins. At the other extremity of the town, that is, to the north-weft, is the caftle, which is built in the fea itfelf, eighty paces from the main land, to which it is joined by arches. To the weft of this caftle is a fhoal fifteen feet high above the fea, and about two hundred paces long. The fpace between this fhoal and the caftle forms the road, but veffels are not fafe there in bad weather. The fhoal, which extends along the town, has a bafon enclofed by a decayed pier. This was the ancient port; but it is fo choaked up by fands, that boats alone can enter its mouth, near the caftle. Fakr-el-din, Emir of the Druzes, deftroyed all thefe little ports, from Bairout to Acre, by finking boats and ftones to prevent the Turkifh fhips from entering them. The bafon of Saide, if it were emptied, might contain twenty or twenty-five fmall veffels. On the fide of the fea, the town is abfolutely without any wall; and

* The name of Sidon ftill fubfifts in a fmall village half a league from Saide.

that which enclofes it on the land fide is no better than a prifon wall. The whole artillery does not exceed fix cannon; and thefe are without carriages and gunners. The garrifon fcarcely amounts to one hundred men. The water comes from the river Aoula, through open canals, from which it is fetched by the women. Thefe canals ferve alfo to water the orchards of mulberry and lemon-trees.

Saide is a confiderable trading town, and is the chief emporium of Damafcus, and the interior country. The French, who are the only Europeans to be found there, have a conful, and five or fix commercial houfes. Their exports confift in filks, and particularly in raw and fpun cottons. The manufacture of this cotton is the principal art of the inhabitants, the number of whom may be eftimated at about five thoufand.

Six leagues to the fouth of Saide, following the coaft, we arrive by a very level plain at the village of Sour. In this name we, with difficulty, recognize that of *Tyre, to,* which we receive from the Latins; but if we recollect that the *y* was formerly pronounced *ou;* and obferve, that the Latins have fubftituted the *t* for the *θ* of the Greeks, and that the *θ* had the found of the Englifh *th,* in the word *think,* we fhall be lefs furprifed at the alteration. This has not happened among the orientals, who have always called this place *Tfour* and *Sour.*

The name of Tyre recalls to the memory of the hiftorical reader fo many great events, and fuggefts, fo many reflections, that I think I may be allowed to enter with fome minutenefs into the defcription of a place, which was, in ancient times, the theatre of an immenfe commerce and navigation, the nurfe of arts and fciences, and the city of, perhaps, the moft induftrious and active people the world has yet feen.

Sour is fituated on a peninfula, which projects from the fhore into the fea, in the form of a mallet with an oval head. This head is a folid rock, covered with a brown cultivable earth, which forms a fmall plain of about eight hundred paces long, by four hundred broad. The ifthmus, which joins this plain to the continent, is of pure fea fand. This difference of foil renders the ancient infular ftate of the plain, before Alexander joined it to the fhore by a mole, very vifible. The fea, by covering this mole with fand, has enlarged it by fucceffive accumulations, and formed the prefent ifthmus. The village of Sour is fituated at the junction of this ifthmus with the ancient ifland, of which it does not cover above one third. The point to the north is occupied by a bafon, which was a port evidently formed by art, but is at prefent fo choaked up that children pafs it without being wet above the middle. The opening at the point is defended by two towers, correfponding with each other, between which formerly paffed a chain fifty or fixty feet long, to fhut the harbour. From thefe towers began a line of walls, which, after furrounding the bafon, enclofed the whole ifland; but at prefent we can only follow its traces by the foundations which run along the fhore, except in the vicinity of the port, where the Motoualis made fome repairs twenty years ago, but thefe are again fallen to decay.

Further on in the fea, to the north-weft of the point, at the diftance of about three hundred paces, is a ridge of rocks on a level with the water. The fpace which feparates them from the main land in front, forms a fort of road, where veffels may anchor with more fafety than at Saide; they are not, however, free from danger, for they are expofed to the north-weft winds, and the bottom injures the cables. That part of the ifland which lies between the village and the fea, that is the weftern fide, is open; and

this ground the inhabitants have laid out in gardens;
but such is their sloth, that they contain far more
weeds than useful plants. The south side is sandy,
and more covered with rubbish. The whole village
contains only fifty or sixty poor families, which live
obscurely on the produce of their little grounds, and
a trifling fishery. The houses they occupy are no
longer, as in the time of Strabo, edifices of three or
four stories high, but wretched huts, ready to crum-
ble to pieces. Formerly they were defenceless towards
the land, but the Motoualis, who took possession of
it in 1766, enclosed it with a wall of twenty feet
high, which still subsists. The most remarkable building is a ruin at the south-east corner. This was a
Christian church, built probably by the Crusaders; a
part of the choir only is remaining; close to which,
amid heaps of stones, lie two beautiful columns, with
shafts of red granite, of a kind unknown in Syria.
Djezzar, who has stripped all this country to ornament his mosque at Acre, wished to carry them
away; but his engineers were not able even to move
them.

  Leaving the village on the side of the isthmus, at
a hundred paces from the gate, we come to a ruined
tower, in which is a well, where the women go to
fetch water. This well is fifteen or sixteen feet deep;
but the depth of the water is not more than two or
three feet. Better water is not to be found upon the
coast. From some unknown cause, it becomes troubled in September, and continues some days full of
a reddish clay. This season is observed as a kind of
festival by the inhabitants, who then come in crowds
to the well, and pour into it a bucket of sea water,
which, according to them, has the virtue of restoring
the clearness of the spring. As we proceed along the
isthmus, towards the continent, we perceive, at
equal distances, the ruins of arcades, which lead in
a right line to an eminence, the only one in the plain.

This hill is not factitious, like those of the desert ;
it is a natural rock of about one hundred and fifty feet
in circumference, by forty or fifty high : nothing is to
be discovered there but a house in ruins, and the tomb
of a Shaik or Santon,* remarkable for the white
dome at the top. The distance of this rock from
Sour is about a quarter of an hour's walk. As we
approach it, the arcades I have mentioned become
more numerous, and are not so high ; they terminate
by a continued line, and, at the foot of the rock, form
suddenly a right angle to the south, and proceed ob-
liquely toward the sea : we may follow their direction
for above an hour's walk at a horse's pace, till, at
length, we distinctly perceive, by the channel on the
arches, that this is no other than an aqueduct. This
channel is three feet wide, by two and a half deep ;
and is formed of a cement harder than the stones themselves. At last we arrive at the well where it terminates, or rather from which it begins. This is
what some travellers have called the well of Solomon,
but, among the inhabitants of the country, it is known
only by the name of *Ras-el-aen*, or, Head of the
Spring. They reckon one principal, two lesser and
several small ones ; the whole forming a piece of
masonry which is neither of hewn or rough stone,
but of cement mixed with sea pebbles. To the south,
this stone-work rises about eighteen feet from the
ground, and fifteen to the northward. On this side
is a slope, wide and gradual enough to permit carts to
ascend to the top : when there, we discover what is
very surprising ; for, instead of finding the water low,
or no higher than the ground level, it reaches to the
top, that is the column which fills the well, is fifteen

---

* Among the Mahometans, the word *Shaik* bears the various
significations of *santon, hermit, ideot* and *madam*. They have
the same religious respect for persons disordered in their intel-
lects, which was usual in the time of David.

feet higher than the ground. Besides this, the water is not calm, but bubbles up like a torrent, and rushes through channels formed at the surface of the well. It is so abundant as to drive three mills which are near it, and form a little rivulet before it reaches the sea, which is only four hundred paces distant. The mouth of the principal well is an octagon, each side of which is twenty-three feet three inches, the diameter, therefore, must be sixty-one feet. It has been said that this well has no bottom; but the traveller La Roque asserts, that in his time he found it at six and thirty fathom. It is remarkable, that the motion of the water at the surface, has corroded the interior lining of the well, so that its edge rests almost upon nothing, and forms a half arch suspended over the water; among the channels which branch out from it, is a principal one which joins that of the arches I have mentioned : by means of these arches, the water was formerly conveyed to the rock, and from the rock, by the isthmus, to the tower, whence the water was drawn. In other respects, the country is a plain of about two leagues wide surrounded by a chain of considerably high mountains, which stretch from Kasmia to Cape Blanco. The soil is a black fat earth, on which a small quantity of corn and cotton are successfully cultivated.

Such is the present state of Tyre, which may suggest several observations relative to the situation of that ancient city. We know, that at the time when Nabuchodonosor laid siege to it, Tyre was on the continent ; and appears to have stood near *Palæ-Tyrus*, that is, near the well ; but, in that case, why was this aqueduct constructed at so much expence* from the rock ? Will it be alledged it was built after the Tyrians had removed into the island ? But prior to the time of Salmanasar, that is, one hundred and

* The piles of the arches are nine feet wide.

thirty-fix years before Nabuchodonofor, their annals
mention it as already exifting. " In the time of
" Eululæus, king of Tyre," fays the hiftorian Me-
nander, as cited by Jofephus,* " Salmanafas, king
" of Afyria, having carried the war into Phœnicia,
" feveral towns fubmitted to his arms : the Tyrians
" refifted him ; but being foon abandoned by Sidon,
" Acre, and Palæ-Tyrus, which depended on them,
" they were reduced to their own forces. However,
" they continued to defend themfelves, and Salman-
" afar, recalled to Ninevah, left a part of his army
" near the rivulets and the aqueduct, to cut off their
" fupply of water. Thefe remained there five years,
" during which time the Tyrians obtained water by
" means of the wells they dug."

If Palæ-Tyrus was a dependence of Tyre, Tyre
then muft have been fituated elfewhere. It was not
in the ifland, fince the inhabitants did not remove
thither until after Nabuchodonofor. Its original fituation muft, therefore, have been on the rock. The
name of this city is a proof it ; for *Tfour*, in Phœnician fignifies rock, and ftrong hold. On this rock
the colony of Sidonians eftablifhed themfelves, when
driven from their country, two hundred and forty
years before the building of Solomon's Temple.
They made choice of this fituation, from the double
advantage of a place which might be eafily defended,
and the convenience of the adjacent road, which
would contain and cover a great number of veffels.
The population of this colony augmenting in time,
and by the advantages of commerce, the Tyrians were
in want of more water, and conftructed the aqueduct.
The induftry we find them remarkable for in the
days of Solomon, may perhaps, induce us to attribute this work to that age. It muft, however, be
very ancient, fince the water of the aqueduct has

* *Antiq. Judaic.* lib. 9. c. 14.

had time to form, by filtration, a confiderable incruſtation, which, falling from the ſides of the channel, or the inſide of the vaults, has obſtructed whole arches. In order to ſecure the aqueduct, it was neceſſary that a number of inhabitants ſhould ſettle there, and hence the origin of Palæ-Tyrus. It may be alledged, this is a factitious ſpring, formed by a ſubterraneous canal from the mountains; but if ſo, why was it not conducted directly to the rock? It ſeems much more probable it is natural; and that they availed themſelves of one of thoſe ſubterraneous rivers of which we find many in Syria. The idea of confining this water to force it to riſe is worthy of the Phœnicians.

Things were thus ſituated, when the king of Babylon, conqueror of Jeruſalem, determined to deſtroy the only city which continued to brave his power. The Tyrians reſiſted him for thirteen years, at the end of which, wearied with endleſs efforts, they reſolved to place the ſea between them and their enemy, and paſſed accordingly into the oppoſite iſland, a quarter of a league's diſtance. Till this period the iſland muſt have contained few inhabitants, on account of the want of water.* Neceſſity taught them to remedy this inconvenience by ciſterns, the remains of which are ſtill to be found in the form of vaulted caves, paved and walled with the utmoſt care.† Alexander invaded the eaſt, and, to gratify his barbarous pride, Tyre was deſtroyed, but ſoon rebuilt; her new inhabitants profited by the mole, by which the Macedonians had made themſelves a

---

* Joſephus is miſtaken, when he ſpeaks of Tyre as built in an iſland in the time of Hiram. In his uſual manner he confounds its ancient with its poſterior ſtate. See *Antiq. Judaic.* lib. 8. c. 5.

† A confiderable one has been lately diſcovered without the walls, but nothing was found in it, and the *Motſallam* ordered it to be ſhut up.

paffage to the ifland, and continued the aqueduct to
the tower, where the water is drawn at this day. But
the arches being in many places wafting, and fer-
viceable in none, how is it that the water is conveyed
thither ? This muft be done by fecret conduits contrived in the foundations and which ftill continue to
bring it from the well. A proof that the water of
the tower comes from Ras-el-aen is, that it is troubled in September as at the tower, at which time it
is of the fame colour, and it has at all times the fame
tafte. Thefe conduits muft be very numerous; for
though there are feveral lakes near the Tower, yet
the well does not ceafe to fupply a confiderable quantity of water.

The power of the city of Tyre on the Mediterranean, and in the weft, is well known; of this Carthage, Utica, and Cadiz are celebrated monuments.
We know that fhe extended her navigation even into
the ocean, and carried her commerce beyond England to the north, and the Canaries to the fouth.
Her connections with the eaft, though lefs known,
were not lefs confiderable : the iflands of Tyrus, and
Aradus, (the modern Barhain) in the Perfian Gulph ;
the cities of Faran and *Phænicum Oppidum*, on the
Red Sea, in ruins even in the time of the Greeks,
prove, that the Tyrians had long frequented the coafts
of Arabia and the Indian fea : but there exifts an
hiftorical fragment, which contains defcriptions the
more valuable, as they prefent a picture of diftant
ages, perfectly fimilar to that of modern times. I
fhall cite the words of the writer in all their prophetic
enthufiafm, only correcting thefe expreffions which
have hitherto been mifunderftood.

" Proud city, that art fituate at the entry of the
" fea! Tyre, who haft faid, My borders are in the
" midft of the feas; hearken to the judgments pro-
" nounced againft thee! Thou haft extended thy
" commerce to (diftant) iflands, among the inhabi-

" tants of (unknown) coasts. Thou makest the fir
" trees of Sanir* into ships; the cedars of Lebanon
" are thy masts; the poplars of Bisan thy oars. Thy.
" sailors are seated upon the box-wood of Cyprus,†
" inlaid with ivory. Thy sails and streamers are
" woven with fine flax from Egypt; thy garments
" are dyed with the blue and purple of Hellas (the
" Archipelago.) Sidon and Arvad send thee their
" rowers; Djábal (Djebila) her skilful ship-builders;
" thy mathematicians and thy sages guide thy barks;
" all the ships of the sea are employed in thy com-
" merce. The Persian, the Lydian, and the Egyp-
" tian, receive thy wages; thy walls are hung round
" with their bucklers, and their cuirasses. The sons
" of Arvad line thy parapets; and thy towers, guard-
" ed by the Djimedeans, (a Phœnician people), glit-
" ter with their brilliant quivers. Every country is
" desirous of trading with thee. Tarsus sends to thy
" markets iron, tin, and lead. Yonia‡, the country
" of the Mosques, and of Teblis§, supply thee with
" slaves, and brasen vessels. Armenia sends thee.
" mules, horses, and horsemen. The Arab of De-
" dan (between Aleppo and Damascus), conveys thy
" merchandize. Numerous isles exchange with thee
" ivory and ebony. The Aramean (the Syrian)‖

* Possibly Mount *Sannine.*

† Box of *Katim.* By comparing different passages, we shall
be convinced this word does not mean *Greece,* but the isle of
Cyprus, and perhaps the coast of *Cilicia,* where the box abounds.
It agrees particularly with Cyprus, from its analogy with the
town of *Kitium,* and the people of the *Kitiens,* on whom
Eululeus made war in the time of Salmanasar.

‡ *Youn,* pleasantly travestied into *javan,* though the ancients
never knew our *j.*

§ *Tobel* or *Teblis,* is also written *Teflis,* and lies to the north
of Armenia, on the frontiers of Georgia. These countries are
celebrated among the Greeks for slaves, and for the iron of the
Chalybes.

‖ This name extended to the Cappadocians, and the inhabitants of the Upper Mesopatamia,

" brings thee rubies, purple, embroidered work, fine
" linen, coral, and agate. The children of Ifrael
" and Judah fell thee cheefe, balm, myrrh, raifins,
" and oil, and Damafcus fupplies the wine of Hal-
" boun, (perhaps Halab, where there are ftill vines),
" and fine wool. The Arabs of Oman offer to thy
" merchants polifhed iron, cinnamon, and the aro-
" matic reed ; and the Arabians of Dedan bring thee
" rich carpets. The inhabitants of the Defert, and
" the Shaiks of Kedar, exchange their lambs and
" their goats for thy valuable merchandize. The
" Arabs of Saba and Rama (in the Yemen) enrich
" thee with aromatics, precious ftones, and gold.*
" The inhabitants of Haran, of Kalana, (in Mefo-
" potamia), and of Adana (near to Tarfus), the fac-
" tors of the Arabs of Sheba (near the Dedan), the
" Affyrians, and the Chaldeans, trade alfo with thee,
" and fell thee fhawls, garments artfully embroidered,
" filver, mafts, cordage, and cedars ; yea, the (boalt-
" ed) veffels of Tarfus, are in thy pay. O Tyre !
" elate with the greatnefs of thy glory, and the im-
" menfity of thy riches ; the waves of the fea fhall
" rife up againft thee ; and the tempeft plunge thee
" to the bottom of the waters. Then fhall thy
" wealth be fwallowed up with thee ; and with thee
" in one day fhall perifh thy commerce, thy mer-
" chants and correfpondents, thy failors, pilots, ar-
" tifts, and foldiers, and the numberlefs people who
" dwell within thy walls. Thy rowers fhall defert
" thy veffels. Thy pilots fhall fit upon the fhore,
" looking forrowfully toward the land. The nations
" whom thou enrichedft, the kings whom thou didft
" gratify with the multitude of thy merchandize,
" fore afraid at thy ruin, fhall cry bitterly in defpair ;

---

* Strabo, lib. 16, fays, that the Sabeans furnifhed Syria with
all the gold that country received, before they were fupplanted
by the inhabitants of Gerrha, near the mouth of the Euphrates.

" they fhall cut off their hair; they fhall caft afhes
" on their heads; they fhall roll in the duft, and
" lament over thee, faying, " Who fhall equal Tyre,
" that queen of the fea?"*

The viciffitudes of time, or rather the barbarifm
of the Greeks of the Lower Empire, and the Mahometans, have accomplifhed this prediction. Inftead
of that ancient commerce fo active and fo extenfive,
Sour, reduced to a miferable village, has no other
trade than the exportation of a few facks of corn,
and raw cotton, nor any merchant but a fingle Greek
factor in the fervice of the French of Saide, who
fcarcely makes fufficient profit to maintain his family.
Nine leagues to the fouth of Sour, is the city of Acre,
in Arabic called Akk, known in the times of remote
antiquity under the name of Aco, and afterwards
under that of Ptolemaïs. It is fituated at the north
angle of a bay which extends in a femicircle of three
leagues, as far as the point of Carmel. After the
expulfion of the Crufaders, it remained almoft deferted ; but in our time has again revived by the induftry of Daher ; and the works erected by Djezzar,
within the laft ten years, have rendered it one of the
principal towns upon the coaft.

The mofque of this Pacha is boafted as a mafter-
piece of eaftern tafte. The bazar, or covered market, is not inferior even to thofe of Aleppo, and its
public fountain furpaffes in elegance thofe of Damafcus. This laft is alfo the moft ufeful work ; for,
till then, Acre was only fupplied by a ruinous well ;
the water, however, is ftill, as formerly, of a very
indifferent quality. The Pacha has derived the more
honour from thefe works, as he was himfelf both the
engineer and architect : he formed the plans, drew
the defigns, and fuperintended the execution. The
port of Acre is one of the beft fituated on the coaft,

---

* See Ezekiel, chap. xxvii.

as it is fheltered from the north north-weft winds by the town itfelf; but it is greatly choaked up fince the time of Fakr-el-din. Djezzar has contented himfelf with making a landing-place for boats. The fortifications, though more frequently repaired than any other in all Syria, are of no importance; there are only a few wretched low towers, near the port, on which cannon are mounted, but thefe rufty iron pieces are fo bad, that fome of them burft every time they are fired. Its defence on the land fide, is only a mere garden wall without any ditch.

This country is a naked plain, longer than that of Sour, but not fo wide; it is furrounded by fmall mountains, which make an angle at Cape Blanco, and extend as far as Carmel. The unevennefs of the country caufes the winter rains to fettle in the low grounds, and form lakes which are unwholefome in fummer from their infectious vapours. In other refpects, the foil is fertile, and both corn and cotton are cultivated with the greateft fuccefs. Thefe articles form the bafis of the commerce of Acre, which is becoming more flourifhing every day. Of late, the Pacha, by an abufe common throughout all the Turkifh empire, has monopolized all the trade in his own hands; no cotton can be fold but to him, and from him every purchafe muft be made; in vain have the European merchants claimed the privilege granted them by the Sultan; Djezzar replied, that he was the Sultan in his country, and continued his monopoly. Thefe merchants in general are French, and have fix houfes at Acre, with a conful; an Imperial agent too is lately fettled there, and about a year ago, a Refident for Ruffia.

That part of the bay of Acre in which fhips anchor with the greateft fecurity lies to the north of Mount Carmel, below the village of Haifa, (commonly called Caiffa). The bottom is good holding ground, and does not chafe the cables; but this harbour is open to the north-weft wind, which blows violently along all this coaft. Mount Carmel, which commands it to the fouth, is a flattened cone, and very rocky; it is about two thoufand feet high. We ftill find among the brambles, wild vines and olive-trees, which prove that induftry has formerly been employ-ed even in this ungrateful foil: on the fummit is a chapel dedicated to the prophet Elias, which affords an extenfive profpect over the fea and land. To the fouth, the country prefents a chain of rugged hills, on the tops of which are a great number of oak and fir-trees, the retreat of wild boars and lynxes. As we turn towards the eaft, at fix leagues diftance, we perceive *Nafra*, or Nazareth, fo celebrated in the hiftory of Chriftianity; it is an inconfiderable village, one third of whofe inhabitants are Mahometans, and the remaining two thirds Greek Catholics. The fa-thers of the holy land, who are dependant on the Great Convent of Jerufalem, have an Hofpitium and a church here. They are ufually the farmers of the country. In the time of Daher, they were obliged to make a prefent to every wife he married, and he took great care to marry almoft every week.

About two leagues to the fouth-eaft of Nafra is Mount Tabor, from which we have one of the fineft views in Syria. This mountain is of the figure of a broken cone, eight hundred, or a thoufand yards in height. The fummit is two thirds of a league in cir-cumference. Formerly it had a citadel, of which now only a few ftones remain. From hence we dif-cover, to the fouth, a feries of vallies and mountains, which extend as far as Jerufalem, while, to the eaft, the valley of Jordan, and Lake Tabaria, appear as if under our feet; the lake feems as if enclofed in the crater of a volcano. Beyond this, the eye lofes itfelf, towards the plains of the Hauran; and then turning to the north, returns by the mountains of Hafbeya, and the Kafmia, to repofe on the fertile plains of Galilee, without being able to reach the fea.

The eaftern bank of Lake Tabaria offers nothing remarkable but the town whofe name it bears, and the fountain of warm mineral waters in the neighbourhood. This fountain is fituated in the open country, at the diftance of a quarter of a league from Tabaria. For want of cleaning it is filled with a black mud, which is a genuine Ethiops Martial. Perfons attacked by rheumatic complaints find great relief, and are frequently cured by baths of this mud. The town is little elfe than a heap of ruins, and not inhabited at moft by more than one hundred families. Seven leagues to the north of Tabaria, on the brow of a hill, ftands the town or village of Safad, the feat of Daher's power. Under the government of this Shaik an Arabian college flourifhed there, in which the Motoualis doctors inftructed youth in the fcience of grammar, and the allegorical interpretation of the Koran. The Jews, who believe the Meffiah will eftablifh the feat of his emipire at Safad, had alfo taken an affection to this place, and collected there to the number of fifty or fixty families; but the earthquake of 1759, deftroyed every thing, and Safad, regarded by the Turks with an unfavourable eye, is now only a village almoft deferted. As we afcend from Safad to the north, we follow a chain of lofty mountains, named Djebal-el-Shaik, among which are the fources of the Jordan, and likewife thofe of a number of rivulets which water the plain of Damafcus. The high grounds from whence thefe rivulets flow, form a fmall diftrict called Hafbeya, which is at prefent governed by an Emir, a relation and rival of the Emir Youfef, who farms it of Djezzar for fixty purfes. The country is mountainous, and greatly refembles the Lower Lebanon; the chain of mountains which ftretch along the vale of Bekaa, was called by the ancients Anti-Lebanon, from their being parallel to the Lebanon of the Druzes and

Maronites; and the vale of Bekaa, which feparates them, is properly the ancient Cœle Syria, or *hollow Syria*. This valley, by collecting the water of the mountains, has rendered it conftantly one of the moft fertile diftricts of all Syria, but the mountains concentrating the rays of the fun, produce likewife a heat in fummer not inferior to that of Egypt. The air neverthelefs is not unhealthy, no doubt becaufe perpetually renewed by the north wind, and becaufe the waters never ftagnate. The inhabitants fleep without injury upon their terraces. Before the earthquake of 1759, this whole country was covered with villages and plantations of the Motoualis; but the deftruction occafioned by this terrible calamity, and the fubfequent wars with the Turks, have almoft deftroyed every thing. The only place which merits attention is the city of Balbek.

Balbek, celebrated by the Greeks and Latins, under the name of *Heliopolis*, or the City of the Sun, is fituated at the foot of Anti-Lebanon, precifely on the laft rifing ground where the mountain terminates in the plain. As we arrive from the fouth we difcover the city only at the diftance of a league and a half, behind a hedge of trees, over the verdant tops of which appears a white edging of domes and Minarets. After an hour's journey we reach thefe trees, which are very fine walnuts; and foon after, crofling fome ill cultivated gardens, by winding paths, arrive at the entrance of the city. We there perceive a ruined wall, flanked with fquare towers, which afcends the declivity to the right, and traces the precincts of the ancient city. This wall, which is only ten or twelve feet high, permits us to have a view of thofe void fpaces, and heaps of ruins, which are the invariable appendage of every Turkifh city; but what principally attracts our attention, is a large edifice on the left, which, by its lofty walls, and rich columns, manifeftly appears to be one of thofe temples which antiquity has left for our admiration. Thefe ruins, which are fome of the moft beautiful and beft pre-ferved of any in Afia, merit a particular defcription.

To give a juft idea of them, we muft fuppofe ourfelves defcending from the interior of the town. After having croffed the rubbifh and huts with which it is filled, we arrive at a vacant place which appears to have been a Square ; there, in front, towards the weft, we perceive a grand ruin, which confifts of two pavillions ornamented with pilafters, joined at their bottom angle by a wall one hundred and fixty feet in length. This front commands the open country from a fort of terrace, on the edge of which we diftinguifh, with difficulty, the bafes or twelve columns, which formerly extended from one pavillion to the other, and formed a portico. The principal gate is obftructed by heaps of ftones ; but that obftacle furmounted, we enter an empty fpace, which is an hexagonal court of one hundred and eighty feet diameter. The court is ftrewed with broken columns, mutilated capitals, and the remains of pilafters, entablatures, and cornices ; around it is a row of ruined edifices, which difplay all the ornaments of the richeft archi-tecture. At the end of this court, oppofite the weft, is an outlet, which formerly was a gate, through which we perceive a ftill more extenfive range of ruins, whofe magnificence ftrongly excites curiofity. To have a full profpect of thefe, we muft afcend a flope, up which were the fteps to this gate, and we then arrive at the entrance of a fquare court, much more fpacious than the former.* The eye is firft attracted by the end of this court, where fix enor-mous and majeftic columns, render the fcene afton-ifhingly grand and picturefque. Another object not lefs interefting, is a fecond range of columns to the

* It is three hundred and fifty feet wide, and three hundred and thirty fix in length,

left, which appear to have been part of the Periftyle
of a temple ; but before we pafs thither, we cannot
refufe particular attention to the edifices which enclofe
this court on each fide. They form a fort of gallery
which contains various chambers, feven of which may
be reckoned in each of the principal wings : viz.
two in a femicircle, and five in an oblong fquare,
The bottom of thefe apartments ftill retains pediments
of niches and tabernacles, the fupporters of which
are deftroyed. On the fide of the court they are
open, and prefent only four and fix columns totally
deftroyed. It is not eafy to conceive the ufe of thefe
apartments ; but this does not diminifh our admiration at the beauty of their pilafters and the richnefs
of the frize of the entablature. Neither is it poffible to avoid remarking the fingular effect which
refults from the mixture of the garlands, the large
foliage of the capitals, and the fculpture of wild plants
with which they are every where ornamented. In
traverfing the length of the court, we find in the
middle a little fquare Efplanade, where was a pavillion, of which nothing remains but the foundation.
At length we arrive at the foot of the fix columns ;
and then firft conceive all the boldnefs of their eleva-
tion, and the richnefs of their workmanfhip. Their
fhafts are twenty-one feet eight inches in circumference, and fifty-eight feet high ; fo that the total
height, including the entablature, is from feventy-one
to feventy-two feet. The fight of this fuperb ruin
thus folitary and unaccompanied, at firft ftrikes us
with aftonifhment ; but, on a more attentive examination, we difcover a feries of foundations, which mark
an oblong fquare of two hundred and fixty-eight feet
in length, and one hundred and forty-fix wide ; and,
which, it feems probable, was the Periftyle of a grand
temple, the primary purpofe of this whole ftructure.
It prefented to the great court, that is to the eaft, a
front of ten columns, with nineteen on each fide,

which with the other fix, make in all fifty-four. The
ground on which it stood was an oblong square, on
a level with this court, but narrower than it, so that
there was only a terrace of twenty-feven feet wide
round the colonade; the efplanade this produces,
fronts the open country, toward the weft, by a floping wall of about thirty feet. This defcent as you
approach the city becomes lefs fteep, fo that the foundation of the pavillion is on a level with the termina-
tion of the hill, whence it is evident that the whole
ground of the courts has been artificially raifed. Such
was the former ftate of this edifice, but the fouthward
fide of the grand temple was afterwards blocked up
to build a fmaller one, the Peryftile and walls of
which are ftill remaining. This temple, fituated fome
feet lower than the other, prefents a fide of thirteen
columns, by eight in front, (in all thirty-four), which
are likewife of the Corinthian order; their fhafts are
fifteen feet eight inches in circumference, and forty-
four in height. The building they furround is an
oblong fquare, the front of which turned toward the
eaft, is out of the line of the left wing of the great
court. To reach it you muft crofs trunks of columns,
heaps of ftone, and a ruinous wall by which it is now
hid. After furmounting thefe obftacles, you arrive
at the gate, where you may furvey the enclofure
which was once the habitation of a god; but inftead
of the awful fcene of a proftrate people, and facrifices offering by a multitude of priefts, the fky, which
is open from the falling in of the roof, only lets in
light to fhew a chaos of ruins covered with duft and
weeds. The walls, formerly enriched with all the
ornaments of the Corinthian order, now prefent nothing but pediments of niches, and tabernacles of which
almoft all the fupporters are fallen to the ground.
Between the niches is a range of fluted pilafters, whofe
capitals fupport a broken entablature; but what remains of it difplays a rich frize of foliage refting on

the heads of satyrs, horses, bulls, &c. Over this entablature was the ancient roof, which was fifty-seven
feet wide, and one hundred and ten in length. The
walls which supported it are thirty-one feet high,
and without a window. It is impossible to form any
idea of the ornaments of this roof, except from the
fragments lying on the ground; but it could not
have been richer than the gallery of the Periftyle: the principal remaining parts contain tablets
in the form of lozenges, on which are reprefented
Jupiter feated on his eagle; Leda careffed by the
fwan; Diana with her bow and crefcent, and feveral
bufts which feem to be figures of emperors and em-
preffes. It would lead me too far, to enter more
minutely into the defcription of this aftonifhing edifice. The lovers of the arts will find it defcribed
with the greateft truth and accuracy in a work publifhed at London in 1757, under the title of *Ruins of
Balbek.* This work, compiled by Mr. Robert Wood,
the world owes to the attention and liberality of Mr.
Dawkins, who in 1751 vifited Balbek, and Palmyra.
It is impoffible to add any thing to the fidelity of their
defcription.

Several changes however have taken place fince
their journey: for example, they found nine large
columns ftanding, and, in 1784, I found but fix.
They reckoned nine and twenty at the leffer temple,
but their now remain but twenty; the others have
been overthrown by the earthquake of 1759. It has
likewife fo fhaken the walls of the leffer temple, that
the ftone of the foffit* of the gate has flid between
the two adjoining ones, and defcended eight inches;
by which means the body of the bird fculptured on
that ftone, is fufpended, detached from its wings, and
the two garlands, which hung from its beak and ter-
minated in two Genii. Nature alone has not effected

---

* The *Soffit* is the crofs ftone at the top of a gate.

this devaftation; the Turks have had their fhare in
the deftruction of the columns. Their motive is to
procure the iron cramps, which ferve to join the feveral blocks of which each column is compofed. Thefe
cramps anfwer fo well the end intended, that feveral
of the columns are not even disjointed by their fall;
one, among others, as Mr. Wood obferves, has penetrated a ftone of the temple wall without giving
way; nothing can furpafs the workmanfhip of thefe
columns; they are joined without any cement, yet
there is not room for the blade of a knife between
their interftices. After fo many ages, they in general
ftill retain their original whitenefs. But, what is ftill
more aftonifhing is, the enormous ftones which compofe the floping wall. To the weft, the fecond layer
is formed of ftones which are from twenty-eight to
thirty-five feet long, by about nine in height. Over
this layer, at the north-weft angle, there are three
ftones, which alone occupy a fpace of one hundred
and feventy-five feet and one half; viz. the firft,
fifty-eight feet feven inches; the fecond, fifty-eight
feet eleven, and the third, exactly fifty eight feet,
and each of thefe are twelve feet thick. Thefe ftones
are of a white granite, with large fhining flakes, like
Gypfe; there is a quarry of this kind of ftone under
the whole city, and in the adjacent mountain, which
is open in feveral places, and, among others, on the
right, as we approach the city. There is ftill lying
there a ftone, hewn on three fides, which is fixty-
nine feet two inches long, twelve feet ten inches
broad, and thirteen feet three inches in thicknefs.
By what means could the ancients move thofe enormous maffes? This is doubtlefs a problem in me-
chanics curious to refolve. The inhabitants of Balbek have a very commodious manner of explaining
it, by fuppofing thefe edifices to have been conftructed
by *Djenoun*, or Genii, who obeyed the orders of king
Solomon, adding, that the motive of fuch immenfe

VOL. II.   T

works was to conceal in fubterraneous caverns vaſt treaſures, which ſtill remain there. To difcover thefe, many have defcended into the vaults which range under the whole edifice; but the inutility of their refearches, added to the oppreffions and extortions of the governors, who have made their fuppoſed dif- coveries a pretext, have at length diſheartened them; but they imagine the Europeans will be more fuccefs- ful, nor would it be poffible to perfuade them but -what we are poffeffed of the magic art of deſtroying Taliſmans. It is in vain to oppofe reafon to ignorance and prejudice: and it would be no lefs ridiculous to attempt to prove to them that Solomon never was acquainted with the Corinthian order, which was only in ufe under the Roman emperors. But their tradi- tion on the fubjeĉt of this prince may fuggeſt three important obfervations.

Firſt, that all tradition relative to high antiquity, is as falfe among the orientals as the Europeans. With them, as with us, faĉts which happened a hun- dred years before, when not preferved in writing, are altered, mutilated, or forgotton. To expeĉt infor- mation from them with refpeĉt to events in the time of David or Alexander, would be as abfurd as to make enquiries of the Flemiſh peafants concerning Clovis or Charlemagne.

Secondly, that throughout Syria, the Mahometans, as well as the Jews and Chriſtians, attribute every great work to Solomon: not that the memory of him ſtill remains by tradition in thofe countries, but from certain paffages in the Old Teſtament; which, with the gofpel, is the fource of almoſt all their tradition, as thefe are the only hiſtorical books read or known; but as their expounders are very ignorant, their appli- cations of what they are told, are generally very re- mote from truth: by an error of this kind, they pre- tend that Balbek is *the houfe of the foreſt of Lebanon,* built by Solomon; nor do they approach nearer probability, when they attribute to that king the well of Tyre, and the buildings of Palmyra.

A third remark is, that the belief in hidden treasures has been confirmed by discoveries which have been really made from time to time. It is not ten years since a small coffer was found at *Hebron*, full of gold and silver medals, with an ancient Arabic book on medicine. In the country of the Druzes, an individual discovered, likewise, some time since, a jar with gold coin in the form of a crescent; but as the chiefs and governors claim a right to these discoveries, and ruin those who have made them, under pretext of obliging them to make restoration, those who find any thing endeavour carefully to conceal it; they secretly melt the antique coins, nay, frequently bury them again in the same place where they found them, from the same fears which caused their first concealment, and which prove the same tyranny formerly existed in these countries.

When we consider the extraordinary magnificence of the temple of Balbek, we cannot but be astonished at the silence of the Greek and Roman authors. Mr. Wood, who has carefully examined all the ancient writers, has found no mention of it, except in a fragment of John of Antioch, who attributes the construction of this edifice to Antoninus Pius. The inscriptions which remain corroborate this opinion, which perfectly accounts for the constant use of the Corinthian order, since that order was not in general use before the third age of Rome; but we ought by no means to alledge as an additional proof, the bird sculptured over the gate; for if his crooked beak, large claws, and the caduceus he bears, give him the appearance of an eagle, the tuft of feathers on his head, like that of certain pigeons, proves that he is not the Roman eagle: besides that the same bird is found in the temple of Palmyra, and is therefore evidently an oriental eagle, consecrated to the sun,

who was the divinity adored in both these temples.
His worship existed at Balbek, in the most remote
antiquity. His statue, which resembled that of Osi-
ris, had been transported there from the Heliopolis
of Egypt, and the ceremonies with which he was
worshipped there have been described by Macrobius,
in his curious work entitled Saturnalia*. Mr. Wood
supposes, with reason, that the name of Balbek, which
in Syriac signifies *City of Bal*, or of the Sun, originated in this worship. The Greeks, by naming it
Heliopolis, have, in this instance, only given a literal
translation of the oriental word, a practice to which
they have not always adhered. We are ignorant of
the state of this city in remote antiquity; but it is to
be presumed that its situation, on the road from Tyre
to Palmyra, gave it some part of the commerce of
these opulent capitals. Under the Romans, in the
time of Augustus it is mentioned as a garrison town;
and there is still remaining, on the wall of the south-
ern gate, on the right, as we enter, an inscription
which proves the truth of this, the words KENTURIA
PRIMA, in Greek characters, being very legible. One
hundred and forty years after, Antoninus built there
the present temple, instead of the ancient one, which
was doubtless falling into ruins; but Christianity having gained the ascendency under Constantine, the
modern temple was neglected, and afterwards converted into a church, a wall of which is now remaining, that hid the sanctuary of the idols. It continued
thus until the invasion of the Arabs, when it is probable they envied the Christians so beautiful a building. The church being less frequented fell to decay;
wars succeeded, and it was converted into a place of
defence, battlements were built on the wall which
surrounded it, on the pavillions and at the angles,

---

* He there calls it Heliopolis, a city of the *Assyrians*, the
ancients frequently confounded that nation with the *Syrians*.

which ftill fubfift; and from that time, the temple, expofed to the fate of 'war, fell rapidly to ruin.

The ftate of the city is not lefs deplorable; the wretched government of the Emirs of the houfe of Harfoufhe, had already greatly impaired it, and the earthquake of 1759 completed its deftruction. The wars of the Emir Youfef, and Djezzar, have rendered it ftill more deferted and ruinous; of five thoufand inhabitants, at which number they were eftimated in 1751, not twelve hundred are now remaining and all thefe poor, without induftry or commerce, and cultivating nothing but a little cotton, fome maize, and water-melons. Throughout this part of the country, the foil is poor, and continues to be fo, both as we proceed to the north, or to the fouth-eaft, towards Damafcus.

CHAP. XI.

Of the Pachalics of Damafcus.

THE Pachalics of Damafcus, the fourth and laft of Syria, comprehends nearly the whole eaftern part of that country. It extends to the north from Marra, on the road to Aleppo, as far as Habroun, in the fouth-eaft of Paleftine. It is bounded to the weft by the mountains of the Anfarians, thofe of Anti-Lebanon, and the upper part of the Jordan; then croffing that river in the country of Bifan, it includes Nablous, Jerufalem, and Habroun, and enters the defert to the eaft, into which it advances more or lefs, according as the country is capable of cultivation; but in general it does not extend to any confiderable diftance from the latter mountains, except in the diftrict of Tadmour or Palmyra, towards which it ftretches full five days journey.

In this vaft extent of country, the foil and its productions are very various ; but the plains of the
Hauran, and thofe on the banks of the Orontes, are
the moft fertile : they produce wheat, barley, doura,
fefamum, and cotton. The country of Damafcus,
and the Upper Bekaa, are of a gravelly and poor foil,
better adapted to fruits and tobacco, than any thing
elfe. All the mountains are appropriated to olive,
mulberry, and fruit trees, and in fome places to vines,
from which the Greeks make wine, and the Mahometans dried raifins.

The Pacha enjoys all the privileges of his poft,
which are more confiderable than thofe of any other
Pachalic ; for befides the farm of all the cuftoms
and impofts, and an abfolute authority, he is alfo conductor of the facred caravan of Mecca, under the
highly refpected title of *Emir Hadj*.* The Mahometans confider this office as fo important, and entitled
to fuch reverence, that the perfon of a Pacha who
acquits himfelf well of it, becomes inviolable even
by the Sultan : it is no longer permitted to *fhed his
blood*. But the Divan has invented a method of fa-
tisfying its vengeance on thofe who are protected by
this privilege, without departing from this literal
expreffion of the law, by ordering them to be pounded
in a mortar, or fmothered in a fack, of which there
have been various inftances.

The tribute of the Pacha to the Sultan, is no more
than forty-five purfes (two thoufand three hundred
and forty three pounds ;) but he is charged with
all the expences of the Hadj : thefe are eftimated at
fix thoufand purfes, or three hundred and twelve
thoufand five hundred pounds. They confift of provifions of corn, barley, rice, &c. and in the hire of
camels, which muft be provided for the efcort and a

* The caravan of Mecca bears exclufively the name of *Hadj*,
which fignifies pilgrimage : the others are called fimply *Kafle*.

great number of pilgrims. Befides this, eighteen hundred purfes muft be paid to the Arab tribes, who dwell near the road, to fecure a free paffage. The Pacha reimburfes himfelf by the miri, or duty upon lands, either by collecting it himfelf, or by farming it out, as he does in many places. He does not receive the cuftoms, thefe are collected by a *Deftardar*, or mafter of the regifters, and are appointed for the pay of the Janifaries, and governors of caftles, which are on the route to Mecca. Befides his other emoluments, the Pacha is the heir of all the pilgrims who die on the journey, and this is not the leaft of his perquifites; for it is invariably obferved that thofe are the richeft of the pilgrims. Befides all this, he has the profits he makes by lending money for intereft to merchants and farmers, and taking from them whatever he thinks proper, in the way of *balfe*, or extortion.

His military eftablifhment confifts in fix or feven hundred Janifaries, better conditioned, and more infolent, than in other parts of the country; as many Barbary Arabs, who are naked, and plunderers as they are every where, and in eight or nine hundred Dellibaches, or horfemen. Thefe troops, which in Syria pafs for a confiderable army, are neceffary, not only by way of efcort for the caravan, and to reftrain the Arabs, but likewife to enable him to collect the miri from his own fubjects. Every year, three months prior to the departure of the Hadj, he makes what is called his circuit; that is, he travels through his vaft government, at the head of his foldiers, and raifes contributions on the towns and villages. This is feldom effected without refiftance; the ignorant populace, excited by factious chiefs, or provoked by the injuftice of the Pacha, frequently revolt, and pay the fums levied on them with the mufket; the inhabitants of Nablous, Bethlehem, and Habroun, are famous for this refractorinefs, which has procured them pe-

culiar privileges ; but when opportunity offers, they
are made to pay ten-fold.   The Pachalic of Damafcus,
from its fituation, is more expofed than any other to
the incurfions of the Bedouin Arabs ; yet it is remarked to be the leaft ravaged of any in Syria.   ·
The reafon affigned is, that inftead of frequently
changing the Pachas, as is practifed in the other governments, the Porte ufually beftows this Pachalic
for life : in the prefent century it was held for fifty
years by a rich family of Damafcus, called El-Adm,
a father and three brothers of which fucceeded each
other.   Afad, the laft of them, whom I have before
mentioned in the hiftory of Daher, held it fifteen
years during which time he did an infinite deal of
good.   He had likewife eftablifhed fuch a degree of
difcipline among the foldiers as, to prevent the peafants from being injured by their robberies and extortions.   His paffion, like that of all men in office
throughout Turkey, was to amafs money, but he did
not let it remain idle in his coffers, and, by a moderation unheard of in this country required no more
intereft for it than fix per cent.*   An anecdote is
related of him which will give an idea of his character :   Being one day in want of money, the informers, by whom the Pachas are conftantly furrounded, advifed him to levy a contribution on the
Chriftians, and on the manufacturers of ftuffs.   " How
" much do you think that they may produce ?" faid
Afad. " Fifty or fixty purfes," replied they.   " But,"
anfwered he, " thefe people are by no means rich,
" how will they raife that fum ?"   " My lord they
" will fell their wives jewels ; and, befides, they are
" Chriftian dogs." I'll fhew you," replied the Pacha,
" that I am an abler extortioner than you."   The
fame day he fent an order to the Mufti to wait upon

---

* In Syria and in Egypt, the ordinary intereft is from twelve
to fifteen, nay, frequently from twenty to thirty per cent.

him fecretly, and at night. As foon as the Mufti arrived, Afad told him, " he was informed he had " long led a very irregular life in private; that he, " though the head of the law, had indulged himfelf " in drinking wine and eating pork, contrary to the " precepts of the moft pure book; affuring him, at " the fame time, he was determined to inform againft " him to the Mufti of Stamboul (Conftantinople), " but that he wifhed to give him timely notice, that " he might not reproach him with perfidioufnefs." The Mufti, terrified at this menace, conjured him to defift; and, as fuch offers are an open and allowed traffic among the Turks, promifed him a prefent of a thoufand piaftres. The Pacha rejected the offer; the Mufti doubled and trebled the fum, till at length they ftrike a bargain for fix thoufand piaftres, with the reciprocal engagement to obferve a profound filence. The next day, Afad fends for the Cadi, and addreffes him in the fame manner; tells him he is informed of feveral flagrant abufes in his adminiftra- tion; and that he is no ftranger to a certain affair, which may perhaps coft him his head. The Cadi, confounded, implores his clemency, negociates like the Mufti; accommodates the matter for a like fum, and retires, congratulating himfelf that he has efcaped even at that price. He proceeded in like manner with the Wali, the Nakib, the Aga of the Janifaries, the Mohtefeb, and, after them, with the wealthieft Turkifh and Chriftian merchants. Each of thefe, charged with offences peculiar to their fituations; and, above all, accufed of intrigues, were anxious to purchafe pardon by contributions. When the fum total was collected, the Pacha, being again with his intimates, thus addreffed them, " Have you heard it " reported, in Damafcus, that Afad has been guilty " of extortion?" "No, Seignior." " By what means, " then, have I found the two hundred purfes I now " fhew you?" The informers began to exclaim in great admiration, and enquire what method he had employed. " I have fleeced the rams," replied he, " and not skinned the lambs and the kids."

After fifteen years reign, the people of Damascus were deprived of this man, by intrigues, the history of which is thus related: About the year 1755, one of the black eunuchs of the seraglio, making the pilgrimage of Mecca, took up his quarters with Asad; but not contented with the simple hospitality with which he was entertained, he would not return by Damascus, but took the road to Gaza. Hosein Pacha, who then was governor of that town, took care to give him a sumptuous entertainment. The eunuch on his return to Constantinople, did not forget the treatment he had received from his two hosts; and, to shew at once his gratitude and resentment determined to ruin Asad, and raise Hosein to his dignity. His intrigues were so successful that, after the year 1756, Jerusalem was detached from the government of Damascus, and bestowed upon Hosein, under the title of a Pachalic, and the following year he obtained that of Damascus. Asad, thus deposed retired with his houshold into the desart, to avoid still greater disgrace. The time of the caravan arrived: Hosein conducted it, agreeable to the duty of his station; but, on his return, having quarrelled with the Arabs, concerning some payment they claimed, they attacked him, defeated the escort, and entirely plundered the caravan, in 1757. On the news of this disaster, the whole empire was thrown into as much confusion as could have been occasioned by the loss of the most important battle. The families of twenty thousand pilgrims, who had perished with thirst and hunger, or been slain by the Arabs; the relations of a multitude of women who had been carried into slavery; the merchants interested in the plundered caravan, all demanded vengeance on the cowardice of the Emir Hadj, and the sacrilege of the Bedouins.

The Porte, alarmed, at firſt profcribed the head of Hofein; but he concealed himſelf ſo well, that it was impoſſible to ſurpriſe him; while he, from his retreat, acting in concert with the eunuch his protector, undertook to exculpate himſelf, in which, after three months he ſucceeded, by producing a real or fictitious letter of Aſad, by which it appeared that this Pacha had excited the Arabs to attack the caravan, to revenge himſelf of Hofein. The profcription was now turned againſt Aſad, and nothing but the opportunity wanting to carry it into execution.

The Pachalic, however, remained vacant: Hofein, diſgraced as he was, could not reſume his government. The Porte, deſiring to revenge the late affront, and provide for the ſafety of the pilgrims in future, made choice of a ſingular man, whoſe character and hiſtory deſerve to be noticed. This man, named Abd-allah-el-Satadji, was born near Bagdad, in an obſcure ſtation. Entering very young into the ſervice of the Pacha, he had paſſed the firſt years of his life in camps and war, and been preſent, as a common ſoldier, in all the campaigns of the Turks againſt the famous Shah-Thamas-Kouli-Khan; and the bravery and intelligence he diſplayed, raiſed him, ſtep by ſtep, even to the dignity of Pacha of Bagdad. Advanced to this eminent poſt, he conducted himſelf with ſo much firmneſs and prudence, that he reſtored peace to the country from both foreign and domeſtic wars. The ſimple and military life he continued to lead requiring no great ſupplies of money, he amaſſed none; but the great officers of the Seraglio of Conſtantinople, who derived no profits from his moderation, did not approve of this diſintereſtedneſs, and waited only for a pretext to remove him.

This they ſoon found. Abd-allah had kept back the ſum of one hundred thouſand livres (above four thouſand pounds,) ariſing from the eſtate of a merchant. Scarcely had the Pacha received it, before it was demanded from him. In vain did he reprefent, that he had ufed it to pay fome old arrears of the troops; in vain did he requeſt time: the Viſir only preſſed him the more cloſely; and, on a ſecond reſuſal, diſpatched a black eunuch, ſecretly provided with a kat-ſherif, to take off his head. The eunuch, arriving at Bagdad, feigned himſelf a ſick perſon travelling for his health; and, as ſuch, ſent his reſpeCts to the Pacha; obferving the uſual forms of politeneſs, and requeſting perniſſion to pay him a viſit. Abd-allah, well acquainted with the praCtices of the Divan, was diſtruſtful of ſo much complaiſance, and ſuſpeCted ſome ſecret miſchief. His treaſurer, not leſs verſed in ſuch plots, and greatly attached to his perſon, confirmed him in theſe ſuſpicions; and, in order to diſcover the truth, propoſed to go and ſearch the eunuch's baggage, while he and his retinue ſhould be paying their viſit to the Pacha. Abd-allah approved the expedient, and at the hour appointed, the treaſurer repaired to the tent of the eunuch, and made ſo careful a ſearch, that he found the kat-ſherif concealed in the lapelles of a peliſſe. Immediately he flew to the Pacha, and ſending for him into an adjoining room, told him what he had diſcovered.* Abd-allah, furniſhed with the fatal writing, hid it in his boſom, and returned to the apartment; when reſuming, with an air of the greateſt indifference, his converſation with the eunuch: " The more I think of it," ſaid he, " Seignior Aga, " the more am I aſtoniſhed at your journey into this " country; Bagdad is ſo. far from Stamboul, we can " boaſt ſo little of our air, that I can ſcarcely believe " you have come hither for no other purpoſe but the " re-eſtabliſhment of your health." " It is true,"

* I have theſe faCts from perſon who was intimate with thio treaſurer, and had ſeen Abd-allah at Jeruſalem.

replied the Aga; " I am alfo commiffioned to demand
" of you fomething on account of the four thoufand
" pounds you received." " We will fay nothing
" of that," anfwered the Pacha; " but come" added he with an air of firmnefs, " confefs that you
" have likewife orders to bring with you my head.
" Obferve what I fay, you know my character, and
" you know my word may be depended on: I now
" affure you that, if you make an open declaration
" of the truth you fhall depart without the leaft in-
" jury." The eunuch now began a long defence,
protefting that he came with no fuch black intentions.
" *By my head*," faid Abd-allah, " confefs to me the
" truth :" the eunuch ftill denied. " *By your head;*"
he ftill denied : " Take care, *By the head of the
Sultan;*" he ftill perfifted. " Be it fo," fays Abd-
allah, " the matter is decided : thou haft pronounced
" thy doom ;" and drawing forth the kat-fherif,
" Know you this paper? Thus you govern at Con-
" ftantinople : Yes, you are a troop of villains,
" who fport with the lives of whoever happen to dif-
" pleafe you, and fhed, without remorfe, the blood
" of the fervants of the Sultan. The Vifir muft have
" heads: he fhall have one ; off with the head of
" that dog and fend it to Conftantinople." The
order was executed on the fpot, and the eunuch's
retinue, difmiffed departed with his head.

After this decifive ftroke, Abd-allah might have
availed himfelf of his popularity to revolt; but he
rather chofe to retire among the Curds. Here the
pardon of the Sultan was fent him, and an order,
appointing him Pacha of Damafcus. Wearied of
his exile, and deftitute of money, he accepted the
commiffion, and fet out with one hundred men who
followed his fortune. On his arrival on the frontiers
of his new government, he learnt that Afad was encamped in the neighbourhood : he had heard him
fpoken of as the greateft man in Syria, and was de-

firous of feeing him. He therefore difguifed himfelf,
and, accompanied only by fix horfemen, repaired
to his camp, and defired to fpeak with him. He was
introduced, as is ufual in thefe camps, without much
ceremony; and, after the cuftomary falutations, Afad
enquired of him whither he was going, and whence
he came? Abd-allah replied, he was one of fix or
feven Curd horfemen who were feeking employment,
and hearing Satadji was appointed to the Pachalic of
Damafcus, were going to apply to him; but being
informed on their way that Afad was encamped in
the neighbourhood, they had come to requeft of him
provifions for themfelves and their horfes. With
pleafure, replied Afad; but do you know Satadji?
Yes. What fort of a man is he? Is he fond of money?
No; Satadji cares very little for money or peliffes,
or fhawls or pearls, or women; he is fond of nothing
but well-tempered arms, good horfes, and war. He
does juftice, protects the widow and the orphan,
reads the Koran, and lives on butter and milk. Is
he old? faid Afad. Fatigue has made him appear
older than he is: he is covered with wounds; he has
received a blow with a fabre that has made him lame
of his left leg; and another, which makes him lean
his head on his right fhoulder. In fhort, faid he, haftily rifing, he is in fhape and features, exactly like my
picture. At thefe words Afad turned pale, and gave
himfelf up for loft; but Abd-allah, fitting down again,
faid to him, Brother, fear nothing; I am not fent
by a troop of banditti; I come not to betray thee:
on the contrary, if I can render thee any fervice,
command me, for we are both held in the fame eftimation with our mafters; they have recalled me,
becaufe they wifh to chaftife the Bedouins; when
they have gratified their revenge on them, they will
again lay plots to deprive me of my head. *God is
great; what he has decreed will come to pafs.*

With thefe fentiments, Abd-allah repaired to Damafcus ; where he reftored good order, put an end
to the extortions of the foldiery, and conducted the
caravan, fabre in hand, without paying a piaftre to
the Arabs. During his adminiftration, which lafted
two years, the country enjoyed the moft perfect tranquility. The inhabitants of Damafcus ftill fay, that
under his government they flept in fecurity with open
doors. He himfelf, frequently difguifed as one of
the pooreft of the people, faw every thing with his
own eyes. The acts of juftice he fometimes did, in
confequence of his difcoveries under thefe difguifes,
produced a falutary circumfpection. Some inftances
are ftill told by the people with pleafure. It is faid,
for example, that being on his circuit at Jerufalem,
he had prohibited his foldiers from either taking, or
ordering any thing without paying. One day, when
he was going about in the difguife of a poor man
with a little plate of lentiles in his hand, a foldier, who
had a faggot on his fhoulders, would force him to
carry it. After fome refiftance, he took it on his
back, while the Delibafhe following him, drove him
on with imprecations. Another foldier, knowing the
Pacha, made a fign to his comrade, who inftantly
took to flight, and efcaped through the crofs ftreets.
After proceeding a few paces, Abd-allah no longer
hearing his man, turned round, and vexed at miffing
his aim, threw his burthen on the ground, faying,
the rafcally knavifh dog! he has both robbed me
of my hire and carried off my plate of lentiles. But
the foldier did not long efcape ; for, a few days after,
the Pacha again furprifing him in the act of robbing
a poor woman's garden, and ill treating her, ordered
his head to be ftruck off upon the fpot.

As for himfelf, he was unable to ward off the deftiny he had forefeen. After efcaping feveral times
from hired affaffins, he was poifoned by his nephew.
This he difcovered before he died, and, fending for

his murderer: Wretch that thou art, faid he, the villains have feduced thee, thou haft poifoned me to profit by my fpoils: it is in my power, before I die, to blaft thy hopes, and punifh thy ingratitude; but I know the Turks; they will be my avengers. In fact, Satadji had fcarcely breathed his laft before a Capidji produced an order to ftrangle the nephew: which was executed. The whole hiftory of the Turks proves that they love treafon, but invariably punifh the traitors. Since Abd-allah, the Pachalic of Damafcus has paffed fucceffively into the hands of Selik, Ofman, Mohammed, and Darouifh, the fon of Ofman, who held it in 1784. This man, who has not the talents of his father, refembles him in his tyrannical difpofition, of which the following is a ftriking inftance. In the month of November, 1784, a village of Greek Chriftians, near Damafcus, which had paid the miri, was called upon to pay it a fecond time. The Shaiks, appealing to the regifter, refufed to comply; but a night or two after, a party of foldiers attacked the village, and flew one and thirty perfons. The wretched peafants, in confternation, carried the heads to Damafcus, and demanded juftice of the Pacha. After hearing their complaints, Darouifh told them to leave the heads in the Greek church, while he made the neceffary enquiries. Three days elapfed, and the heads putrifying, the Chriftians wifhed to bury them; but to effect this the Pacha's permiffion was neceffary, for which they were under the neceffity of paying forty purfes, or above two thoufand pounds.

About a year ago, (in 1785), Djezzar, availing himfelf of the credit his money had gained him at the Porte, difpoffeffed Darouifh, and governs at prefent at Damafcus, to which it is faid he is endeavouring to add the Pachalic of Aleppo. But it is not probable the Porte will confent to grant him this, as fuch an increafe of power would render him mafter of all Syria; but befides that the neceffity of obferving the Ruffians, leaves the Divan no leifure to confider thefe affairs, it concerns itfelf but little about the revolt of the governors, fince conftant experience has proved, that, fooner or later, they never fail to fall into the fnares that are laid for them. Nor is Djezzar likely to be an exception to this rule; for though not deftitute of talents, and efpecially cunning*, his abilities are unequal to the tafk of conceiving and accomplifhing a great revolution. The courfe he purfues is that of all his predeceffors: he only concerns himfelf with the welfare of the public, fo far as it coincides with his private intereft. The Mofque he has built at Acre, is a monument of pure vanity, on which he has expended, without any advantage, the fum of three millions of French livres, (one hundred and twenty-five thoufand pounds): his Bazar is undoubtedly of more utility; but before he began to build a market for the fale of corn and vegetables, he fhould have paid fome attention to the ftate of agriculture, by which they are to be produced, and this is in a very languifhing condition indeed, except clofe to the walls of Acre. The principal part of his expences confifts in his gardens, his baths, and his white women: of the latter he poffeffed eighteen in 1784, and the luxury of thefe women is moft enormous. As he is now growing old and has loft the relifh for other pleafures, he regards nothing but amaffing money. His avarice has alienated his foldiers, and his feverity created him enemies even in his own houfe. Two of his pages have already attempted to affaffinate him; he has had the good luck to efcape their piftols, but fortune will not always favour him; he will one day fhare the fate of fo many others, and be taken by furprife, when he will

---

* Baron de Tott has called Djezzar a *lion*: I think he would have defined him better by calling him a *wolf*.

reap no other fruit from his induſtry in heaping up
wealth, than the eagerneſs of the Porte to obtain
poſſeſſion of it, and the hatred of the people he has
oppreſſed. Let us now return to the moſt remarkable places in this Pachalic.

. The firſt that preſents itſelf is the city of Damaſcus,
the capital and reſidence of the Pachas. The Arabs
call it *el-Sham*, agreeable to their cuſtom of beſtow-
ing the name of the country on its capital. The
ancient Oriental name of *Demeſhk* is known only to
geographers. This city is ſituated in a vaſt plain,
open to the ſouth and eaſt, and ſhut in towards the
weſt and north by mountains, which limit the view
at no great diſtance ; but in return, a number of
rivulets ariſe from theſe mountains, which render the
territory of Damaſcus the beſt watered and moſt deli-
cious province of all Syria ; the Arabs ſpeak of it
with enthuſiaſm ; and think they can never ſufficiently extol the freſhneſs and verdure of its orchards,
the abundance and variety of its fruits, its numerous
ſtreams, and the clearneſs of its rills and fountains.
This is alſo the only part of Syria where there are
detatched pleaſure houſes in the open country. The
natives muſt ſet a higher value on theſe advantages,
as they are the more rare in the adjacent provinces.
In other reſpects, the ſoil, which is poor, gravelly,
and of a reddiſh colour, is ill adapted for corn ; but
is on that account more ſuitable to fruits, which are
here excellently flavoured. No city affords ſo many
canals and fountains ; each houſe has one ; and all
theſe waters are furniſhed by three rivulets, or branches
of the ſame river, which after fertilizing the gardens
for a courſe of three leagues, flow into a hollow of
the Deſert to the ſouth-eaſt, where they form a mo-
raſs called *Bæhairat-el-Mardj,* or the Lake of the
Meadow.

With ſuch a ſituation it cannot be diſputed that
Damaſcus is one of the moſt agreeable cities in Tur-

key; but it is still deficient in point of salubrity.
The inhabitants complain with reason, that the white
waters of the Barrada are cold and hard; and it is
observed that the natives are subject to obstructions;
that the whiteness of their skin is rather the paleness
of sickness than the colour of health; and that the
too great use of fruit, particularly of apricots, occasions there, every summer and autumn, intermittent
fevers and dysenteries.

Damascus is much longer than it is broad. M.
Niebuhr, who has given a plan of it, makes it three
thousand two hundred and fifty toises, or something
less than a league and a half in circumference. Comparing these dimensions with those of Aleppo, I sup-
pose that Damascus may contain eighty thousand inhabitants. The greater part of these are Arabs and
Turks; the number of Christians is estimated at
above fifteen thousand, two thirds of whom are Schifmatics. The Turks never speak of the people of
Damascus without observing, that they are the most
mischievous in the whole empire; the Arabs, by a
play on words, have made this proverb: *Shami, shoumi,*
The man of Damascus, wicked: on the contrary,
they say of the people of Aleppo, *Halabi, tchelebi,*
The Aleppo man, a *petit maitre.* From a prejudice
arising from the difference of religions, they also add,
that the Christians there are more vile and knavish
than elsewhere; doubtless, because the Mahometans
are there more fanatic and more infolent. In this
they resemble the inhabitants of Cairo; like them,
they detest the Franks, nor is it possible to appear
at Damascus in an European dress; our merchants
have not been able to form any establishment there;
we only meet with two Capuchin Missionaries, and a
physician who is not permitted to practise.

This hatred the people of Damascus bear the Christians, is maintained and increased by their communication with Mecca. Their city, say they, is a holy

place, since it is one of the gates of the Caaba: for Damascus is the rendezvous for all the pilgrims from the north of Asia, as Cairo is for those from Africa. Their number every year amounts to from twenty to fifty thousand; many of them repair here four months before the time, but the greatest number only at the end of the Ramadan. Damascus then resembles an immense fair; nothing is to be seen but strangers from all parts of Turkey, and even Persia; and every place is full of camels, horses, mules, and merchandize. At length, after some days preparations, all this vast multitude set out confusedly on their march; and, travelling by the confines of the Desert, arrive in forty days at Mecca, for the festival of the Bairam. As this caravan traverses the country of several independent Arab tribes, it is necessary to make treaties with the Bedouins, to allow them certain sums of money for a free passage, and take them for guides. There are frequent disputes on this subject between the Shaiks, of which the Pacha avails himself to make a better bargain; but in general the preference is given to the tribe of Sardia, which encamps to the south of Damascus, along the Hauran; the Pacha sends to the Shaik a mace, a tent, and a pelisse, to signify he takes him as his chief conductor. From this moment it is the Shaik's business to furnish camels at a stated price; these he hires likewise from his tribe and his allies; the Pacha is responsible for no damages, and all losses are on his own account. On an average, ten thousand camels perish yearly; which forms a very advantageous article of commerce for the Arabs.

It must not be imagined that the sole motive of all these expences and fatigues, is devotion. Pecuniary interest has a more considerable share in this expedition. The caravan affords the means of engrossing every lucrative branch of commerce; almost all the pilgrims convert it into a matter of speculation. On leaving their own country, they load themfelves with merchandize, which they fell on the road ; the fpecie arifing from this, added to what they have brought with them, is conveyed to Mecca, where they exchange it for muflins and india goods from Malabar and Bengal, the fhawls of Cafhmire, the aloes of Tonquin, the diamonds of Golconda, the pearls of Barhain, fome pepper, and a great quantity of coffee from the Yemen. Sometimes the Arabs of the Defert deceive the expectation of the merchant, by pillaging the ftragglers, and carrying off detatched parties of the caravan. But in general the pilgrims arrive fafe ; in which cafe their profits are very confiderable. At all events they are recompenfed in the veneration attached to the title of *Hadji*, (Pilgrim ;) and by the pleafure of boafting to their countrymen of the wonders of the Caaba, and Mount Arafat ; of magnifying the prodigious crouds of pilgrims, and the number of victims, on the day of the Bairam ; and recounting the dangers and fatigues they have undergone, the extraordinary figure of the Bedouins, the Defert without water, and the tomb of the prophet at Medina, which, after all, is neither fufpended by a loadftone, nor the principal object of their pilgrimage. Thefe wonderful tales produce their ufual effect, that is, they excite the admiration and enthufiafm of the audience, though, from the confeffion of fincere pilgrims, nothing can be more wretched than this journey. Accordingly, this tranfient admiration has not prevented a proverb, which does little honour to thefe pious travellers. *Diftruft thy neighbour*, fays the Arab, *if he has made a Hadj ; but if he has made two, make hafte to leave thy houfe :* and, in fact, experience has proved that the greater part of the devotees of Mecca are peculiarly infolent and treacherous, as if they wifhed to recompenfe themfelves for having been dupes, by becoming knaves.

By means of this caravan, Damaſcus is become the centre of a very extenſive commerce. By Aleppo the merchants of this city correſpond with Armenia, Anadolia, the Diarbekar, and even with Perſia. They ſend caravans to Cairo, which, following a route frequented in the time of the patriarchs, take their courſe by Djeſr-Yakoub, Tabaria, Nablous and Gaza. In return, they receive the merchandize of Conſtantinople and Europe, by way of Saide and Bairout. The home conſumption is balanced by ſilk and cotton ſtuffs, which are manufactured here in great quantities, and are very well made; by the dried fruits of their own growth, and ſweetmeat cakes of roſes, apricots, and peaches, of which Turkey conſumes to the amount of near a million of livres, (about forty thouſand pounds). The remainder, paid for by the courſe of exchange, occaſions a conſiderable circulation of money in the cuſtom-houſe duties, and the commiſſion of the merchants. This commerce has exiſted in theſe countries from the moſt remote antiquity. It has flowed through different channels, according to the changes of the government, and other circumſtances; but it has every where left very apparent traces of the opulence it produced.

The Pachalic of which I am ſpeaking, affords a monument of this kind too remarkable to be paſſed over in ſilence. I mean the remains of Palmyra, a city celebrated in the third age of Rome, for the part it took in the differences between the Parthians and the Romans, the power and fall of Odenatus and Zenobia, and its deſtruction under Aurelian. From that time hiſtory preſerved the name of this great city, but it was merely the name, for the world had very confuſed ideas of the real grandeur and power it had poſſeſſed. They were ſcarcely even ſuſpected in Europe, until towards the end of the laſt century, when ſome Engliſh merchants of Aleppo, tired with hearing the Bedouins talk of the immenſe ruins to be found

in the Defert, refolved to afcertain the truth of thefe
extraordinary relations. The firft attempt was made
in 1678, but without fuccefs; the adventurers were
robbed of all they had by the Arabs, and obliged to
return without accomplifhing their defign. They
again took courage in 1691, and at length obtained
a fight of the antiquities in queftion. Their narrative,
publifhed in the philofophical tranfactions, met with
many who refufed belief; men could neither conceive
nor perfuade themfelves that in a fpot fo remote from
any habitable place, fuch a magnificent city as their
drawings defcribed could have fubfifted. But fince
Mr. Dawkins publifhed, in 1753, the plans and views
he himfelf had taken on the fpot in 1751, all doubts
are at an end, and it is univerfally acknowledged that
antiquity has left nothing, either in Greece or Italy,
to be compared with the magnificence of the ruins of
Palmyra.

I fhall give a fummary of the relation of Mr.
Wood, the companion and editor of the journey of
Mr. Dawkins.*

" After learning at Damafcus that Tadmour, or
" Palmyra, depended on an Aga who refided at
" Haffia, we repaired in four days, to that village,
" which is fituated in the Defert, on the route from
" Damafcus to Aleppo. The Aga received us with
" that hofpitality which is fo common in thefe coun-
" tries amongft all ranks of people, and, though ex-
" tremely furprized at our curiofity, gave us inftruc-
" tions how to fatisfy it in the beft manner. We
" fet out from Haffia the 11th of March 1751, with
" an efcort of the Aga's beft Arab horfemen, armed
" with guns and long pikes; and travelled in four
" hours to Sudud, through a barren plain, fcarce
" affording a little browfing to antelopes, of which we

* *Ruins of Palmyra,* by Robert Wood, 1 vol, in folio, with
fifty plates, London 1753.

" faw a great number. Sudud is a poor fmall vil-
" lage, inhabited by Maronite Chriftians. Its houfes
" are built of no better materials than mud dried in
" the fun. They cultivate as much good ground
" about the village as is neceffary for their bare
" fubfiftence, and make a good red wine. After
" dinner, we continued our journey, and arrived in
" three hours at Owareen, a Turkifh viliage, where
" we lay.

" Owareen has the fame appearance of poverty as
" Sudud; but we found a few ruins there, which
" fhew it to have been formerly a more confiderable
" place. We remarked a village near this entirely
" abandoned by its inhabitants, which happens often
" in thefe countries; where the lands have no ac-
" quired value from cultivation, and are often defert-
" ed to avoid oppreffion. We fet out from Owareen
" the 12th, and arrived in three hours at Carietein,
" keeping always in the direction of a point and half
" to the fouth of the eaft. This village differs from
" the former, only by being a little larger. It was
" thought proper we fhould ftay here this day, as
" well to collect the reft of our efcort which the
" Aga had ordered to attend us, as to prepare our
" people and cattle for the fatigue of the remaining
" part of our journey; for, though we could not
" perform it in lefs time than twenty-four hours, it
" could not be divided into ftages, as there is no
" water in that part of the Defert.

" We left Carietein the 13th, being in all about
" two hundred perfons, with the fame number of
" beaft of carriage, confifting of an odd mixture of
" affes, mules and camels. Our route was a little
" to the eaft of the north, through a flat fandy plain,
" without either tree or water, the whole about ten
" miles broad, and bounded, to our right and left,
" by a ridge of barren hills, which feemed to join
" about two miles before we arrived at Palmyria.

" The 14th, about noon, we arrived at the end of
" the plain, where the hills feemed to meet. We
" find between thefe hills a vale, through which an
" aquedu&t (now ruined) formerly conveyed water
" to Palmyra. In this vale, to our right and left,
" were feveral fquare towers of a confiderable height,
" which, upon a nearer approach, we found were
" the fepulchres of the ancient Palmyrenes. We
" had fcarce paffed thefe venerable monuments, than
" the hills opening, difcovered to us, all at once,
" the greateft quantity of ruins we had ever feen*,
" and, behind them, towards the Euphrates, a flat
" wafte as far as the eye could reach, without any
" obje&t which fhewed either life or motion. It is
" fcarce poffible to imagine any thing more ftriking
" than this view. So great a number of Corinthian
" pillars, with fo little wall or folid building, afforded
" a moft romantic variety of profpe&t."
Undoubtedly the effe&t of fuch a fight is not to be
communicated. To have a juft conception of the
whole, the dimenfions muft be fupplied by the imagination. In this fpace we fometimes find a palace,
of which nothing remains but the courts and walls;
fometimes a temple whofe periftyle is half thrown
down; and now, a portico, a gallery, or triumphal
arch. Here ftand groups of columns, whofe fymme-
try is deftroyed by the fall of many of them; there
we fee them ranged in rows of fuch length, that fimilar to rows of trees, they deceive the fight, and affume the appearance of continued walls. If from
this ftriking fcene we caft our eyes upon the ground,
another, almoft as varied, prefents itfelf: on all fides
we behold nothing but fubverted fhafts, fome whole,
others fhattered to pieces, or diflocated in their joints;
and on which fide foever we look, the earth is ftrewed
with vaft ftones half buried, with broken entabla-

---

* Though thefe travellers had vifited *Greece* and *Italy*.

tures, damaged capitals, mutilated frizes, disfigured relief, effaced sculptures, violated tombs, and altars defiled by dust.

But I must refer the reader to the plates of Mr. Wood, for a more particular explanation of these various edifices, and to make him sensible of the degree of perfection to which the arts had arrived in those remote ages. Architecture more especially lavished her ornaments and displayed her magnificence in the temple of the sun, the tutelar deity of Palmyra. The square court which enclosed it, was six hundred and seventy-nine feet each way, and a double range of columns was continued all round the inside. In the middle of the vacant space, the temple presents another front of forty-seven feet, by one hundred and twenty-four in depth. Around it runs a peristyle of one hundred and forty columns, and, what is very extraordinary, the gate faces the setting and not the rising sun. The soffit of this gate which is lying on the ground, presents a zodiac, the signs of which are the same as in ours. On another soffit is a bird similar to that of Balbek, sculptured on a ground of stars. It is a remark worthy the observation of historians, that the front of the portico has twelve pillars, like that of Balbek; but what artists will esteem still more curious is, that these two fronts resemble the gallery of the Louvre, built by Perrault, long before the existence of the drawings which made us acquainted with them; the only difference is, that the columns of the Louvre are double, whereas those of Balbek and Palmyra are detached.

Within the court of this same temple, the philosopher may contemplate a scene he will esteem still more interesting. Amid these hallowed ruins of the magnificence of a powerful and polished people, are about thirty mud-walled huts, which contain as many peasant families, who exhibit every external sign of extreme poverty. So wretched are the present inha-

bitants of a place once fo renowned and populous.
Thefe Arabs only cultivate a few olive-trees, and as
much corn as is barely neceffary for their fubfiftence.
All their riches confift in fome goats and fheep they
feed in the Defert. They have no other communication with the reft of the world than by little caravans,
which come to them five or fix times a year from
Homs, of which they are a dependency. Incapable
of defending themfelves from violence, they are compelled to pay frequent contributions to the Bedouins,
who by turns harrafs and protect them. The Englifh
travellers inform us, " Thefe peafants are healthy and
" well fhaped, and the few diftempers they are fubject
" to, prove that the air of Palmyra merits the eulo-
" gium beftowed on it by Longinus, in his epiftle to
" Porphyry. It feldom rains there, except at the
" equinoxes, which are accompanied alfo by thofe
" hurricans of fand, fo dangerous in the Defert.
" The complexion of thefe Arabs is very fwarthy
" from the exceffive heat; but this does not hinder
" the women from having beautiful features. They
" are veiled; but are not fo fcrupulous of fhewing
" their faces as the eaftern women generally are;
" they dye the end of their fingers red, (with henna),
" their lips blue, and their eye-brows and eye-lafhes
" black; and wear very large gold or brafs rings in
" their ears and nofes."

It is impoffible to view fo many monuments of induftry and power, without enquiring what age produced them, and what was the fource of the immenfe
riches they indicate; in a word, without enquiring
into the hiftory of Palmyra, and why it is fo fingu-
larly fituated, in a kind of ifland feparated from the
habitable earth, by an ocean of barren fands. The
travellers I have quoted, have made very judicious
refearches into this queftion, but too long to be in-
ferted here; I muft again refer the reader to that
work, to fee in what manner they diftinguifh two forts

of ruins at Palmyra, one of which muſt be attributed to very remote ages, and are only rude, un-
ſhapen maſſes; while the others, which are the magnificent monuments ſo often mentioned, are the work
of more modern times. He will there ſee, in what
manner they prove from the ſtyle of agriculture, that
theſe latter muſt have been erected in the three centuries preceding Dioclefian, in which the Corinthian
was preferred to every other order. They demon-
ſtrate with great ingenuity, that Palmyra, ſituated
three days journey from the Euphrates, was indebted
for its wealth and ſplendor to the advantage of its
poſition on one of the great roads, by which the valuable commerce that has at all times ſubſiſted between
India and Europe was then carried on; they have
proved, in ſhort, that the Palmyrenes were at the
height of their proſperity; when, become a barrier
between the Romans and the Parthians, they were
politic enough to maintain a neutrality in their diſputes, and to render the luxury of thoſe powerful
empires ſubſervient to their own opulence.

Palmyra was at all times a natural emporium for
the merchandize coming from India by the Perſian
Gulph, which, from thence by way of the Euphrates
or the Deſert, was conveyed into Phœnicia, and Aſia
Minor, to diffuſe its varied luxuries among the nations
with whom they were always in great requeſt. Such
commerce muſt neceſſarily, in the moſt early ages,
have cauſed this ſpot to be inhabited, and rendered
it a place of importance, though at firſt of no great
celebrity. The two ſprings of freſh water* it poſ-
feffes, were, above all, a powerful inducement in
a Deſert every where elſe ſo parched and barren.
Theſe doubtleſs were the two principal motives which

---

* Theſe waters are warm and ſulphureous, but the inhabitants
who, excepting theſe ſprings, have none but what is brackiſh,
find them very good, and they are at leaſt wholeſome.

drew the attention of Solomon, and induced that commercial prince to carry his arms to a place fo remote from the ordinary limits of Judea. " He built " ftrong walls there," fays the Hiftorian Jofephus,[*] " to fecure himfelf in the poffeffion, and named it " Tadmour, which fignifies the place of Palm-trees." Hence it has been inferred that Solomon was its firft founder ; but we fhould, from this paffage, be rather led to conclude that it was already a place of known importance. The Palm-trees he found there are not the trees of uninhabited countries. Prior to the days of Mofes, the journies of Abraham and Jacob, from Mefopotamia into Syria fufficiently prove a communication between thefe countries, which muft foon have made Palmyra flourifh. The cinnamon and pearls mentioned in the time of the Hebrew legiflator, demonftrate a trade with India and the Perfian Gulph, which muft have been carried on by the Euphrates and Palmyra. At this diftance of time, when the greater part of the monuments of thefe early ages have perifhed, we are liable to form very falfe opinions concerning the ftate of thefe countries in thofe remote times, and are the more eafily deceived, as we admit as hiftorical fact antecedent events, of an entirely different character. If we obferve, however, that men in all ages are united by the fame interefts and the fame defires, we cannot help concluding, that a commercial intercourfe muft early have taken place between one nation and another, and that this intercourfe muft have been nearly the fame with that of more modern times. Without therefore going higher than the reign of Solomon, the invafion of Tadmour by that prince, is fufficient alone to throw a great light on the hiftory of that city. The king of Jerufalem would never have carried his attention to fo diftant and detached a fpot, without fome powerful motive

[*] Antiq. Jud. lib. 8. c. 6

of intereſt, and this intereſt could be no other than that of an extenſive commerce, of which this place was already the emporium.   This commerce extended itſelf to India, and the Perſian Gulph was the principal point of union.   Various facts concur in corroborating this laſt aſſertion; nay, neceſſarily force us to acknowledge the Perſian Gulph as the centre of the commerce of that *Ophir*, concerning which ſo many falſe hypotheſis have been framed.   For, was it not in this Gulph that the Tyrians carried on a flouriſhing trade from the moſt remote ages, and are not the iſles of *Tyrus* and *Aradus* ſufficient proofs of the ſettlements they made there?   If Solomon ſought the alliance of the Tyrians, if he ſtood in need of their pilots to guide his veſſels, muſt not the object of their voyage have been thoſe places which they already frequented, and to which they repaired from their port of *Phœnicum oppidum*, on the Red-ſea, and perhaps from *Tor*, in which name we may diſcover traces of that of their own city.   Are not pearls, which were one of the principal articles of the commerce of Solomon, almoſt the excluſive produce of the coaſt of the Gulph, between the iſles of Tyrus and Aradus, (now called Barhain), and Cape Maſandoum?   Have not peacocks, which were ſo much admired by the Jews, been always ſuppoſed natives of that province of Perſia which adjoins to the Gulph?   Did they not procure their monkeys from Yemen, which was in their way, and where they ſtill abound?   Was not Yemen the country of Saba, (or Sheba,) the queen of which brought frankincenſe and gold to the Jewiſh king?   And is not the country of the Sabeans celebrated by Strabo for producing great quantities of gold?   Ophir has been ſought for in India and in Africa; but is it not one of thoſe twelve Arabian diſtricts, or tribes mentioned in the genealogical annals of the Hebrews?   And ought it not therefore to be looked for in the vicinity of the countries they inhabit, fince this genealogical geography always obferves a certain order of fituation, whatever Bochart and Calmet may have faid to the contrary? In fhort, do we not directly perceive the name of Ophir, in that of *Ofar*, a town of the diftrict of Oman, on the pearl coaft? There is no longer any gold in this country; but this is of no confequence fince Strabo pofitively afferts, that in the time of Seleucidæ, the inhabitants of Gerrha, on the road to Babylon, obtained confiderable quantities from it. On weighing all thefe circumftances, it muft be admitted that the Perfian Gulph was the centre of the moft extenfive commerce of the ancient eaftern world, and that it was with a view of communicating with it by a fhorter or more fecure route, that Solomon turned his attention towards the Euphrates; and that, from the convenience of its fituation, Palmyra muft from that period have been a confiderable city. We may even reafonably conjecture, when we reflect on the revolutions of the following ages, that this commerce became a principal caufe of thofe various wars in lower Afia, for which the barren chronicles of thofe early times affign no motives. If after the reign of Solomon the Affyrians of Niniveh turned their ambitious views towards Chaldea, and the lower part of the Euphrates, it was with the intention to approach that great fource of opulence the Perfian Gulph. If Babylon, from being the vaffal of Niniveh, in a fhort time became her rival, and the feat of a new empire, it was becaufe her fituation rendered her the emporium of this lucrative trade; in fhort, if the kings of this great city waged perpetual wars with Jerufalem and Tyre, their object was not only to defpoil thefe cities of their riches but to prevent their invading their trade by the way of the Red-fea. An hiftorian* who has informed us that Nabuchodo-

---

* John of Antioch.

nofor, before he laid fiege to Jerufalem, took poffeffion of Tadmour, clearly indicates that the latter city
acted in concert with the two neighbouring capitals.
Their gradual decline became, under the Perfian empire, and the fucceffors of Alexander, the efficient
caufe of the fudden greatnefs of Palmyra in the time
of the Parthians and Romans ; fhe then enjoyed a long
peace, for many centuries, which allowed her inhabitants to erect thofe monuments of opulence whofe
ruins we ftill admire. They the more readily adopted
this fpecies of luxury, as the nature of the country
permitted no other, and from the natural propenfity
of merchants, in every nation, to difplay their wealth
in magnificent buildings. Odenatus and Zenobia carried this propenfity to its greateft height ; but by
attempting to exceed its natural limits, they at once
deftroyed the equilibrium, and Palmyra, ftripped
by Aurelian of the power fhe had acquired in Syria,
was befieged, taken, and ravaged by the emperor,
and loft in one day her liberty and fecurity, which
were the principal fources of her grandeur. From
that period, the perpetual wars of thefe countries,
the devaftations of conquerors, and the oppreffions
of defpots, by impoverifhing the people, have diminifhed the commerce and deftroyed the fource
which conveyed induftry and opulence into the very
heart of the Deferts : the feeble channels that have
furvived, proceeding from Aleppo and Damafcus,
ferve only at this day to render her defertion more
fenfible and more complete.

Leaving thefe venerable ruins, and returning to the
inhabited world, we firft meet with Homs, the Eme-
fus of the Greeks, fituated on the eaftern bank of
the Orontes : this place, which was formerly a ftrong
and populous city, is, at prefent, only a large ruinous town, containing not more than two thoufand
inhabitants, partly Greeks, and partly Mahometans.
An Aga refides here, who holds, as a fub-renter of

the Pacha of Damafcus, the whole country as far as Palmyra. The Pacha himfelf holds this farm as an appenage deriving immediately from the Sultan. Hama and Merra are held in the fame manner. Thefe three farms pay four hundred purfes, or five hundred thoufand livres (above twenty thoufand pounds); but they produce nearly four times that fum.

Two days journey below Homs, is Hama, celebrated in Syria for its water-works. The wheels are in fact the largeft in this country, being thirty-two feet in diameter. Troughs are faftened to the circumference, and fo difpofed as to fall in the river, and when they reach the vertex of the wheel, difcharge the water into a refervoir, whence it is conveyed by conduits to the public and private baths. The town is fituated in a narrow valley on the banks of the Orontes, contains about four thoufand inhabitants, and poffeffes fome trade from its fituation on the road from Aleppo to Tripoli. The foil, as throughout this whole diftrict, is well adapted to wheat and cotton; but agriculture, expofed to the rapine of the *Motfallam* and the Arabs, is in a very languifhing condition. An Arab Shaik, named Mohammed-el-Korfan, is become fo powerful of late years, as to impofe arbitrary contributions on the country. He is fuppofed to be able to bring into the field thirty thoufand horfemen.

Continuing to defcend the Orontes, by an unfrequented route, we arrive at a marfhy country, where we meet with a place interefting from the change of fortune it has undergone. This place, called Famia, was formerly one of the moft celebrated cities of Syria, under the name of Apamea. "It was there," fays Strabo, "that the Seleucidæ, had eftablifhed the "fchool and nurfery of their cavalry." The foil of the neighbourhood, abounding in pafturage, fed no lefs than thirty thoufand mares, three hundred ftallions, and five hundred elephants; inftead of which the marfhes of *Famia* at prefent fcarcely afford a few

VOL. II.   Z

buffaloes and sheep. To the veteran soldiers of Alexander, who here reposed after their victories, have
succeeded wretched peasants who live in perpetual
dread of the oppressions of the Turks and the inroads
of the Arabs. The same prospect is repeated on
every side throughout these districts. Every town,
every village is built of materials furnished by ruins,
and founded on the rubbish of ancient edifices. We
continually meet with such ruins, both on the desert,
and returning along this road, as far as the mountains of Damascus; and even as we pass to the southward of that city in the immense plains of the Hauran. The pilgrims of Mecca, who traverse the latter
for five or six days journey, assure us they find, at
every step, the vestiges of ancient habitations. They
are, however, less remarkable in these plains, for want
of durable materials. The soil is a pure earth without stones, and almost without pebbles. What is said
of its actual fertility, perfectly corresponds with the
idea given of it in the Hebrew writings. Wherever
wheat is sown, if the rains do not fail, it repays the
cultivator with profusion, and grows to the height of
a man. The pilgrims assert, also, that the inhabitants
are stronger and taller than the rest of the Syrians.
They must differ from them likewise in other respects,
on account of the climate, for this part of the country is so excessively hot and dry, as to resemble Egypt
more than Syria. In the desert, as they have no running waters nor wood, they make their fires with
dung, and build huts with pounded earth and straw.
They are very tawny; they pay a tribute to the Pacha
of Damascus, but the greatest part of their villages
put themselves under the protection of some Arab
tribes; and when the Shaiks are prudent, the country
prospers, and enjoys security. The mountains, however, which border on these plains to the West and
North, are still more secure, on which account a
number of families of the Druzes and Maronites,

wearied with the troubles in Lebanon, have of late years taken refuge there, and built *deo*,* or villages, where they freely profefs their religion, and have priefts and chapels. An intelligent traveller would here, no doubt, be able to make various interefting difcoveries in antiquities and natural hiftory; but no European has been hitherto known to have penetrated thefe recelles.

As we approach the Jordan, the country becomes more hilly and better watered; the valley through which this river flows abounds, in general, in pafturage, efpecially in the upper part of it. As for the river itfelf, it is very far from being of that importance which we are apt to affign to it. The Arabs, who are ignorant of the name of Jordan, call it *el-Sharia.* Its breadth, between the two principal lakes, in few places exceeds fixty or eighty feet; but its depth is about ten or twelve. In winter it overflows its narrow channel, and, fwelled by the rains, forms a fheet of water fometimes a quarter of a league broad. The time of its overflowing is generally in March, when the fnows melt on the mountains of the Shaik; at which time, more than any other, its waters are troubled, and of a yellow hue, and its courfe impetuous. Its banks are covered with a thick foreft of reeds, willows, and various fhrubs, which ferve as an afylum for wild boars, ounces, jackals, hares, and different kinds of birds.

Crofling the Jordan, half way between the two lakes, we enter a hilly country, anciently celebrated under the name of the kingdom of Samaria, but at prefent called the country of *Nablous,* its capital. This town, fituated near to Sichem, and on the ruins of the Neapolis of the Greeks, is the refidence of a Shaik, who farms the tribute, for which he is accountable to the Pacha of Damafcus, when he makes

---

* Hence the Spanish word, *aldea.*

his circuit. The ftate of this country is fimilar to that of the Druzes, with this difference, that its inhabitants are fuch zealous Mahometans as not willingly to fuffer any Chriftians among them. They are difperfed in villages among the mountains; the foil of which is tolerably fertile, and produces a great deal of corn, cotton, olives, and fome filks. Their diftance from Damafcus, and the difficulty of invading their country, by preferving them to a certain degree from the oppreffions of the government, enables them to live in more peace and happinefs, than is to be found elfewhere. They are at prefent even fuppofed the richeft people in Syria; which advantage they owe to their political conduct during the late troubles in Galilee and Paleftine; when the tranquility in which they lived, induced many perfons of property to take refuge there. But, within the laft four or five years, the ambition of certain Shaiks, encouraged by the Turks, has excited a fpirit of faction and difcord, the confequences of which have been almoft as mifchievous as the oppreffions of the Pachas.

Two days journey to the fouth of Nablous, following the courfe of the mountains, which at every ftep became more barren and rocky, we arrive at a town, which, like many others already mentioned, prefents a ftriking example of the viciffitude of human affairs: when we behold its walls levelled, its ditches filled up, and all its buildings embarraffed with ruins, we fcarcely can believe we view that celebrated metropolis, which formerly, withftood the efforts of the moft powerful empires, and, for a time, refifted the arms of Rome herfelf: though, by a whimfical change of fortune, its ruins now receive her homage and reverence; in a word, we with difficulty recognize *Jerufalem*. Still more are we aftonifhed at its ancient greatnefs, when we confider its fituation, amid a rugged foil, deftitute of water, and furrounded by dry channels of torrents, and fteep heights. Remote from every great road, it feems neither to have been calculated for a confiderable mart of commerce, nor the centre of a great confumption. It overcame however every obftacle, and may be adduced as a proof of what popular opinions may effect in the hands of an able Legiflature, or when favoured by happy circumftances. The fame opinions ftill preferve to this city its feeble exiftence. The renown of its miracles perpetuated in the Eaft, invites and retains a certain number of inhabitants within its walls. Mahometans, Chriftians, Jews, without diftinction of fects, all make it a point of honour to fee, or to have feen, what they denominate the *noble* and *holy* city.* To judge from the refpect the inhabitants profefs for the facred places it contains, we fhould be ready to imagine there is not in the world a more devout people; but this has not prevented them from acquiring, and well deferving, the reputation of the vileft people in Syria, without excepting thofe even of Damafcus. Their number is fuppofed to amount to twelve or fourteen thoufand.

Jerufalem has from time to time had Governors of its own, with the title of Pachas; but it is in general, as at this day, a dependency of Damafcus, from which it receives a *Motfallam*, or deputy Governor. This Motfallam farms it and receives the revenues arifing from the Miri, the Cuftoms, and efpecially from the follies of the Chriftian inhabitants. To conceive the nature of this laft article, it muft be underftood that the different communions of fchifmatic, and catholic Greeks, Armenians, Copts, Abyffinians and Franks, mutually envying each other the poffeffion of the holy places, are continually endeavouring to

---

* The Orientals never call Jerufalem by any other name than *El-Kods*, the *Holy*. Sometimes adding the Epithet *El-Sheriff*. the *noble*. This word *El-Kods* feems to me the etymology of all the *Cafius* of antiquity. which like Jerufalem were *high places*, and had *Temples*, or *Holy-places* erected on them.

out-bid one another in the price they offer for them
to the Turkish Governors.   They are constantly
aiming to obtain some privilege for themselves, or
to take it from their rivals: And each sect is perpetually informing against the other for irregularities.
Has a church been clandestinely repaired; or a pro-
cession extended beyond the usual limits: has a pilgrim entered by a different gate from that customary:
all these are subjects of accusation to the government,
which never fails to profit by them, by fines and
extortions.   Hence those hatreds, and that eternal
jangling, which prevail between the different convents;
and the adherents of each communion.   The Turks,
to whom every dispute produces money, are, as we
may imagine, far from wishing to put an end to them.
They all, in whatever station, derive some advantage
from these quarrels: some sell their protection, others
their interest.   Hence a spirit of intrigue and cabal,
which has diffused venality through every class; and
hence perquisites for the Motsallam, which annually
amount to upwards of one hundred thousand piasters.
Every pilgrim pays him an entrance fee of ten piasters,
and another for an escort for the journey to the Jordan, without reckoning the fines imposed in consequence of the imprudencies committed by these
strangers during their stay.   Each convent pays him
so much for the privilege of processions, and so much
for all repairs they undertake, besides presents on the
accession of a new superior, or a new Motsallam;
not to speak of private gratifications to obtain secret
trifles they solicit; all which is carried to a great
length among the Turks, who are as well versed in
the art of squeezing money as the most able law
practitioners in Europe.   Besides all this, the Motsallam collects duties on the exportation of certain
singular commodities from Jerusalem, I mean *beads,
relics, fanctuaries, crosses, passions, agnusdei's, scapula-
ries,* &c. of which near three hundred chests are sent

off annually. The fabrication of these utensils of piety procures subsistence for the greatest part of the Christian and Mahometan families of Jerusalem and its neighbourhood; men, women, and children are employed in carving, and turning wood and coral, and in embroidering in silk, with pearls, and gold and silver thread. The convent of the Holy-land, alone, lays out annually to the amount of fifty thousand piasters in these wares, and those of the Greeks, Armenians, and Copts, taken together, pay a still larger sum. This fort of commerce is the more advantageous to the manufactures as, their goods cost them little beside their labour; and the more lucrative for the sellers as the price is enhanced by superstition. These commodities, exported to Turkey, Italy, Portugal, and more especially to Spain, produce a return of considerable sums, either in the form of alms or payments. To this the convents join another not less important article of traffic, *the visits of the pilgrims.* It is well known that at all times the devout curiosity of visiting the *holy places,* has conducted Christians of every country to Jerusalem. There was even a time when the ministers of religion taught it was indispensibly necessary to salvation, and this pious zeal pervading all Europe, gave rise to the Crusades. Since their unfortunate, issue, the zeal of the Europeans cooling every day, the number of Pilgrims has diminished; and is now reduced to a few Italian, Spanish and German monks, but the case is different with the Orientals. Faithful to the spirit of past times, they continue to consider the journey to Jerusalem as a work of the greatest merit. They are even scandalized at the relaxation of the Franks in this respect, and say, they have all become heretics or infidels. Their priests and monks who find their advantage in this fervor, do not cease to promote it. The Greeks, especially, declare that *the pilgrimage ensures plenary indulgence, not only for the paft, but even for the future ; and that it abfolves not only from murther, inceft, and pederafty ; but even from the neglect of fafting and the non-obfervance of feftivals, which are far more heinous offences.* Such great encouragements are not without their effect ; and every year a crowd of pilgrims of both fexes and all ages, fet out from the Morea, the Archipelago, Conftantinople, Anatolia, Armenia, Egypt and Syria; the number of whom in 1784, amounted to two thoufand. The monks, who find, by their regifters, that formerly ten or twelve thoufand annually made this pilgrimage, never ceafe exclaiming that religion rapidly decays, and that the zeal of the faithful is nearly extinguifhed. It muft be confefled, however, that this zeal is rather expenfive, fince the moft moderate pilgrimage never cofts lefs than four thoufand livres, (one hundred and fixty-fix pounds,) and fome of them, by means of offerings, amount to fifty or fixty thoufand, (twenty five hundred pounds.)

Yafa is the port where the pilgrims difembark. They arrive in November; and repair without delay to Jerufalem, where they remain until after the feftival of Eafter. They are lodged confufedly, by whole families, in the cells of the convents of their refpective communions; the monks take efpecial care to tell them that this lodging is gratuitous ; but it would be neither civil, nor very fafe to depart without making an offering greatly exceeding the ufual price of apartments. Befides this, it is impoffible to difpenfe with paying for maffes, fervices, exorcifms, &c. another confiderable tribute. The pilgrim muft alfo purchafe crucifixes, beads, agnufdei's, &c. On Palm-funday, they go to purify themfelves in the Jordan, an expedition which likewife requires a contribution. One year with another, it produces to the governor fifteen thoufand Turkifh fequins, or four thoufand fix hundred and eighty-feven pounds,* about one half of which,

* At the rate of fix fhillings and three-pence the fequin.

is laid out in the expences of the escort, and the sums demanded by the Arabs. The reader must consult particular relations of this pilgrimage, to form an idea of the tumultuous march of this fanatic multitude into the plain of Jericho; the indecent and superstitious zeal with which they throw themselves, men, women, and children, naked into the Jordan; the fatigue they undergo before they reach the borders of the Dead-sea; the melancholy inspired by the sight of the gloomy rocks of that country, the most savage in nature; their return and visitation of the holy places; and the ceremony *of the new fire, which descends from heaven on the holy Saturday, brought by an angel.* The Orientals still believe in this miracle, though the Franks acknowledge that the priests retire into the Sacricity, and effect what is done by very natural means.

Easter over, each returns to his own country, proud of being able to rival the Mahometan in the title of Pilgrim*; nay, many of them, in order to distinguish themselves as such, imprint on their hands, wrists, or arms, figures of the cross, or spear, with the cypher of Jesus and Mary. This painful, and sometimes dangerous, operation† is performed with needles, and the perforations filled with gunpowder, or gunpowder of antimony, and is never to be effaced. The Mahometans have the same practice, which is also to be found among the Indians, and other savages, as it was likewise among several ancient nations with whom it had a connection with religion, which it still retains wherever it prevails. So much devotion does not however exempt these pilgrims from the proverbial censure thrown upon the

---

* The difference between them is, that those of Mecca are called *Hadjes*, and those of Jerusalem *Mokadst*, a name formed from that of the city, *El-Kods*.

† I have seen a pilgrim who had lost an arm by it, the cubital nerve being wounded in the operation.

Hadjes; fince the Chriftians fay likewife: *beware of the pilgrims of Jerufalem.*

We may well fuppofe that fo great a multitude, refiding at Jerufalem for five or fix months, muft leave behind them confiderable fums; and reckoning only fifteen hundred perfons, at one hundred piftoles each, we fhall find they cannot expend lefs than a million and a half of livres, (fixty two thoufand five hundred pounds). Part of this money is paid to the inhabitants and merchants for neceffaries, and thefe lofe no opportunity of impofing upon ftrangers. Water in 1784, coft twenty fols (ten pence) a fack. Another part goes to the governor and his fubalterns, and the remainder is the profit of the convents. Great complaints are made of the improper ufe the Schifmatics make of this money, and their luxury is fpoken of as a great fcandal, their cells being ornamented with porcelain and tapeftry, nay even with fabres, kandjars and other weapons. The Armenians and the Franks are much more modeft; with the former, who are poor, it is a virtue of neceffity; but with the latter, who are not fo, it is prudence.

The convent of thefe Franks, called *Saint Sauveur*, is the principal religious houfe of all the Miffions of the Holy Land which are in the Turkifh empire. Of thefe they reckon feventeen, compofed of Francifcans of every nation, but who are commonly French, Italian, and Spanifh. The general adminiftration is entrufted to three individuals of thefe nations, but fo that the fuperior muft be always a native fubject of the Pope; the Agent, a fubject of the Catholic king, and the Vicar, a fubject of his moft Chriftian majefty. Each of thefe adminiftrators has a key of the general treafury, that the money may not be touched without common confent. Each of them is affifted by a fecond, called a *Difcreet*: thefe fix and a Portuguefe Difcreet, form together the *Directory*, or fovereign Chapter, which governs the convent and the whole order. The firſt legiſlators had formely fo balanced the powers of theſe adminiſtrators that it was impoſſible for the whole to be governed by the will of one; but as all governments are ſubject to revolutions, ſome circumſtances which happened a few years ſince, have changed the nature of this. The following is a ſhort hiſtory of the tranſaction.

About twenty years ago, in conſequence of ſome irregularities incident to all great adminiſtrations, the convent of the Holy Land incurred a debt of ſix hundred purſes, or thirty-one thouſand two hundred and fifty pounds. This was daily encreaſing, the expenditure continuing to exceed the receipts. It would have been an eaſy matter to liquidate this at one ſtroke, as the treaſury of the holy ſepulchre poſ-ſeſſes, in diamonds and all ſorts of precious ſtones, in chalices, crucifixes, golden ciboires, (boxes contain-ing the Hoſt,) and other preſents of Chriſtian princes, to the amount of upwards of a million of livres; but beſides the averſion which the miniſters of tem-ples have, at all times, to alienate ſacred things, it might be good policy in the preſent caſe, not to ſhew the Turks, nor even the Chriſtians, too great reſour-ces. The ſituation was embarraſſing; and it became ſtill more ſo from the murmurs of the Spaniſh agent, who loudly complained of being alone obliged to ſuſ-tain the burthen of the debt, for, in fact, he it was who furniſhed the moſt conſiderable fund. Under theſe circumſtances, J. Ribadeira, who occupied this poſt died, and chance beſtowed the ſucceſſion on a man, who, ſtill more impatient than himſelf, deter-mined at every hazard to apply a remedy; and he ſet about the execution of his project with the more zeal, as he promiſed himſelf private advantages in the me-ditated reform. He therefore prepared his plan; and addreſſing himſelf directly to the king of Spain, by means of his confeſſor, repreſented to him:

" That the zeal of the Chriſtian princes having
" greatly cooled of late years, their ancient largeſſes
" to the convent of the Holy Land were confiderably
" diminiſhed; that his moſt Faithful Majeſty had re-
" trenched more than one half of the forty thouſand
" dollars he was accuſtomed to beſtow; that his
" moſt Chriſtian Majeſty, thinking the protection he
" granted ſufficient, ſcarcely paid the three thouſand
" livres he had promiſed; that Italy and Germany
" daily became leſs liberal, and that his Catholic
" Majeſty was the only fovereign who continued the
" benefactions of his predeceſſors." He alſo ſtated,
on the other hand, that, " the expences of the eſtab-
" liſhment not having ſuffered a proportionable dimi-
" nution, a deficiency had been incurred, which ren-
" dered it neceſſary to have recourſe to an annual
" loan, that by this means a confiderable debt was
" contracted, which daily encreaſing, menaced the
" inſtitution with final ruin; that among the caufes
" of this debt, the pilgrimage of the monks who
" came to viſit the holy places muſt be particularly
" taken into account, that it was neceſſary to defray
" the expences of their journey, their paſſage by fea,
" their tribute, and board at the convent for two or
" three years, &c. That it fo happened, that the
" greateſt part of theſe monks came from thoſe very
" ſtates which had withdrawn their bounties; that
" is, from Portugal, Germany, and Italy; that it
" feemed unreaſonable for the king of Spain to pay
" for thoſe who were not his ſubjects, and that it
" was a ſtill greater abuſe to fee the adminiſtration
" of theſe funds entruſted to a chapter, almoſt
" wholly compoſed of foreigners. The petitioner,
" infiſting on this laſt article, prayed his Catholic
" Majeſty to interpoſe in the reformation of the
" abufes, and to eſtabliſh new and more equitable
" regulations, the plan of which he ſubmitted,
" &c."

‑Thefe reprefentations produced the defired effect.
The king of Spain firft declared himfelf *Efpecial Protector of the order of the Holy Land, in the Levant ;*
and then named the petitioner, *J. Juan Ribeira,* his
Royal Agent ; he gave him in quality of this office,
a feal, with the arms of Spain, and entrufted him
with the fole management of his *gifts,* without being
accountable to any other than himfelf. From that
moment, J. Juan Ribeira, become a plenipotentiary,
fignified to the confiftory that henceforward he would
have a private treafury, diftinct from the common
ftock ; that the latter could continue, as heretofore,
charged with the general expences, and that in confequence, all the contributions of the different nations
fhould be paid in there ; but as that of Spain bore no
proportion to the others, he fhould apply no more
than what was adequate to their refpective contin-
gents, retaining the furplus for his private treafury ;
that the pilgrimages, henceforth, fhould be at the
expence of the nations from whence they came, except the fubjects of France, the care of whom he
took upon himfelf. By this regulation, the pilgrimages, and the greateft part of the general expences
being limited, the difburfements are more proportionable to the receipts, and they have begun to pay off
the debt ; but the monks do not view with a favourable eye the agent thus become independent ; nor
can they pardon him for concentring in himfelf almoft
as much wealth as is poffeffed by the whole order :
for, in eight years, he has received four *conduits,* or
contributions from Spain, eftimated at eight hundred
thoufand dollars. The money in which thefe contributions are paid, confifting in Spanifh dollars, is
ufually put on board a French fhip which conveys it
to Cyprus, under the care of two monks. From Cyprus, part of thefe dollars are fent to Conftantinople,
where they are fold to advantage, and converted into
Turkifh coin. The other part goes directly by the

way of Yafa to Jerufalem, where the inhabitants expect it with as much anxiety as the Spaniards look
for the galleons. The agents pay a certain fum into
the general treafury, and the remainder is at his difpofal. The ufes he makes of it confifts, firft, in a
penfion of three thoufand livres to the French Vicar
and his *Difcreet*, who by this means, procure him a
majority of fuffrages. Secondly, in prefents to the
governor, the Mufti, the Kadi, the Nakib, other great
officers, whofe credit may be of ufe to him. He has
likewife to fupport the dignity of his office, which is
by no means a trifling expence; for he has his private interpreters, like a conful, his table and his
Janifaries : he alone, of all the Franks, mounts on
horfeback in Jerufalem, and is attended by a body
of cavalry ; in a word, he is, next to the Motfallam,
the firft perfon in the country, and treats with the
powers of it, upon a footing of equality. We may
fuppofe, however, that fo much refpect is not for
nothing. A fingle vifit to Djezzar for the church
of Nazareth, coft thirty thoufand Pataques (above
fix thoufand five hundred and forty-two pounds.)
The Mahometans of Jerufalem who defire his money,
feek his friendfhip. The Chriftians who folicit alms
from him, dread even his indifference. Happy the
family he felects for his favourites, and woe to the man
who has the misfortune to difpleafe him ; for his hatred
can difplay itfelf either by open or indirect means :
a hint to the *Wali* enfures the baftinado, without the
victim knowing whence it proceeds. So much power
made him difdain the cuftomary protection of the
ambaffador of France, and nothing but fuch an affair
as he had lately with the Pacha of Damafcus, could
have reminded him that his protection is more efficacious than twenty thoufand Sequins. His agents,
proud of his protection, abufe their authority, like
all fubalterns. The Spanifh monks of Yafa and Ramla, treat the Chriftians who depend on them with a

rigour which is very far from evangelical. They excommunicate them in the open church, abufing them by name ; they threaten the women who have been indifcreet in talking of them ; and oblige them to do public penitence, with a taper in their hands ; they deliver over the intractable to the Turks, and refufe every fuccour to their families : in fhort, they offend againft the cuftoms' of the country, and all decorum, by vifiting the wives of the Chriftians, who fhould only be feen by their very near relations, and by remaining with them, without witneffes, in their apartments, under pretence of confeffing them. The Turks are not able to conceive fo much liberty without an abufe of it. The Chriftians, who are of the fame opinion, murmer at it, but do no more. Experience has taught them that the indignation of the RR. PP. (reverend fathers) is attended with dreadful confequences. It is whifpered, that, fix or feven years ago, they procured an order from the Captain Pacha, to cut off the head of an inhabitant of Yafa who oppofed them. Fortunately the Aga took upon himfelf to fufpend the execution, and to undeceive the Admiral ; but their animofity has never ceafed to perfecute this man, by every kind of chicanery. Not long ago, they folicited the Englifh ambaffador, under whofe protection he has placed himfelf, to furrender him to a punifhment, which in fact was only an unjuft revenge.

Let us now quit thefe details, which, however, very properly defcribe the prefent fituation of this country. When we leave Jerufalem, we only find three places in this part of the Pachalic which merit attention.

The firft is *Raha*, the ancient Jericho, fituated fix leagues to the north-eaft of Jerufalem, in a plain fix or feven leagues long, by three wide, around which are a number of barren mountains, that render it extremely hot. Here formerly was cultivated the

balm of Mecca.   From the defcription of the Hadjes,
this is a fhrub, fimilar to the pomegranate-tree, with
leaves like thofe of rue : it bears a pulpy nut, in
which is contained a kernal that yields the refinous
juice we call *balm* or *balfam*.   At prefent there is
not a. plant of it remaining at Raha ; but another
fpecies is to be found there, called *Zakkoun*, which
produces a fweet oil, alfo celebrated for healing
wounds.   This Zakkoun refembles a plumb-tree ; it
has thorns four inches long, with leaves like thofe
of the olive-tree, but narrower and greener, and
prickley at the end ; its fruit is a kind of acorn, without calix, under the bark of which is a pulp, and
then a nut, the kernel of which gives an oil that
the Arabs fell very dear : this is the fole commerce
of Raha, which is no more than a ruinous village.

The fecond place deferving notice, is *Bait-el-lahm*,
or Bethlehem, fo celebrated in the hiftory of Chriftianity.   This village, fituated two leagues fouth-
eaft of Jerufalem, is feated on an eminence, in a
country full of hills and vallies, and might be rendered very agreeable.   The foil is the beft in all thefe
diftricts ; fruits, vines, olives, and fefamum fucceed
here extremely well ; but as is the cafe every where
elfe, cultivation is wanting.   They reckon about fix
hundred men in this village capable of bearing arms
upon occafion, and this often occurs, fometimes to
refift the Pacha, fometimes to make war with the
adjoining villages, and fometimes in confequence of
inteftine diffentions.   Of thefe fix hundred men,
about one hundred are Latin Chriftians, who have
a Vicar dependent on the great convent of Jerufalem.
Formerly their whole trade confifted in the manufacture of beads ; but the reverend fathers not being
able to find a fale for all they could furnifh, they
have refumed the cultivation of their lands.   They
make a white wine, which juftifies the former celebrity of the wines of judea, but it has the bad

property of being very heady. The neceſſity of uniting for their common defence prevails over their religious differences, and makes the Chriſtians live here in tolerable harmony with the Mahometans, their fellow citizens. Both are of the party *Yamani*, which, in oppoſition to that called *Kaiſi*, divides all Paleſtine into two factions, perpetually at variance. The courage of theſe peaſants, which has been frequently tried, has rendered them formidable through all that country.

The third and laſt place of note is *Habroun*, or Hebron, ſeven leagues to the ſouth of Bethlehem; the Arabs have no other name for this village than *El-Kalil**, the *well beloved*, which is the epithet they uſually apply to Abraham, whoſe ſepulchral grotto they ſtill ſhew. Habroun is ſeated at the foot of an eminence, on which are ſome wretched ruins, the misſhapen remains of an ancient caſtle. The adjacent country is a ſort of oblong hollow, five or ſix leagues in length, and not diſagreeably varied by rocky hillocks, groves of fir-trees, ſtunted oaks, and a few plantations of vines and olive-trees. Theſe vineyards are not cultivated with a view to make wine, the inhabitants being ſuch zealous Mahometans as not to permit any Chriſtians to live among them : they are only of uſe to procure dried raiſins which are badly prepared, though the grapes are of an excellent kind. The peaſants cultivate cotton, likewiſe, which is ſpun by their wives, and ſold at Jeruſalem and Gaza. They have alſo ſome ſoap manufactories, the Kali for which is ſold them by the Bedouins, and a very ancient glaſs-houſe, the only one in Syria. They make there a great quantity of coloured rings, bracelets for the wriſts and legs, and for the arms above the elbows†, beſides a variety of

---

* The *K* is here uſed for the Spaniſh *Iota*.

† Theſe rings are often more than an inch in diameter; they are paſſed on the arms of children, and it often happens, as I

other trinkets, which are even fent to Conftantinople. In confequence of thefe manufactures, Habroun is the moft powerful village in all this quarter, and is able to arm eight or nine hundred men, who adhere to the faction Kaifi, and are the perpetual enemies of the people of Bethlehem. This difcord, which has prevailed throughout the country, from the earlieft times of the Arabs caufes a perpetual civil war. The peafants are inceffantly making inroads on each other's lands, deftroying their corn, dourra, fefamum, and olive-trees, and carrying off their fheep, goats, and camels. The Turks, who are every where negligent in repreffing fimilar diforders, are the lefs attentive to them here, fince their authority is very precarious ; the Bedouins, whofe camps occupy the level country, are continually at open hoftilities with them, of which the peafants avail themfelves to refift their authority, or do mifchief to each other, according to the blind caprice of their ignorance, or the intereft of the moment. Hence arifes an anarchy, which is ftill more dreadful than the defpotifm which prevails elfewhere, while the mutual devaftations of the contending parties render the appearance of this part of Syria more wretched than that of any other.

Proceeding from Hebron towards the weft we arrive, after five hours journey, at fome eminences, which, on this fide, form the laft branch of the mountains of Judea. There the traveller, wearied with the rugged country he has quitted, views with pleafure the vaft plain which extends beneath his feet, to the fea that lies before him. This is the plain which, under the name of *Falaftin*, or Paleftine, terminates, on this fide, the country of Syria, and forms the laft divifion concerning which it remains for me to fpeak.

have frequently feen, that the arm growing bigger than the ring, a ridge of flefh is formed above and below, fo that the ring is buried in a deep hollow and cannot be got off, and this is confidered as a beauty.

CHAP. XII.

Of Palestine.

PALESTINE, in its present state, comprehends
the whole country included between the Mediterranean to the west, the chain of mountains to the east,
and two lines, one drawn to the south, by Kan
Younes, and the other to the north, between Kaisa-
ria and the rivulet of Yafa. This whole tract is almost entirely a level plain, without either river or
rivulet in summer, but watered by several torrents in
winter. Notwithstanding this dryness the soil is
good, and may even be termed fertile, for when the
winter rains do not fail, every thing springs up in
abundance; and the earth, which is black and fat,
retains moisture sufficient for the growth of grain and
vegetables during the summer. More dourra, sesa-
mum, water-melons, and beans, are sown here than
in any other part of the country. They also raise
cotton, barley, and wheat; but though the latter be
most esteemed, it is less cultivated, for fear of too
much inviting the avarice of the Turkish governors,
and the rapacity of the Arabs. This country is indeed more frequently plundered than any other in
Syria, for being very proper for cavalry, and adjacent
to the Desert, it lies open to the Arabs, who are far
from satisfied with the mountains; they have long
disputed it with every power established in it, and
have succeeded so far as to obtain the concession of
certain places, on paying a tribute, from whence they
infest the roads, so as to render it unsafe to travel
from Gaza to Acre. They might even have obtained
the entire possession of it, had they known how to
avail themselves of their strength; but, divided among
themselves by jarring interests, and family quarrels,

they turn thofe weapons on each other which they fhould employ againft the common enemy, and are at once enfeebled by their difregard of all good order and government, and impoverifhed by their fpirit of rapacity.

Paleftine, as I have faid, is a diftrict independent of every Pachalic. Sometimes it has governors of its own, who refide at Gaza under the title of Pachas; but it is ufually, as at prefent, divided into three appenages, or *Melkana*, viz. Yafa, Loudd, and Gaza. The former belongs to the *Walda*, or Sultana Mother. The Captain Pacha has received the two others as a recompenfe for his fervices, and reward for the head of Daher. He farms them to an Aga, who refides at Ramla, and pays him two hundred and fifteen purfes for them, viz. one hundred and eighty for Gaza and Ramla, and thirty-five for Loudd.

Yafa is held by another Aga, who pays one hundred and twenty purfes to the Sultana. For this he receives the whole miri and poll-tax of the town, and fome adjacent villages; but the chief part of his revenue arifes from the cuftom-houfe, as he receives all the duties on imports and exports. Thefe are pretty confiderable, as it is at Yafa that the rice of Damietta is landed for Jerufalem, and the merchandize of a fmall French factory at Ramla; it is the port likewife for the pilgrims of the Morea and Conftantinople, and the produce of the coaft of Syria, from hence alfo all the fpun cottons of Paleftine, and the commodities exported from this country, along the coaft, are fhipped. The forces this Aga maintains, are only thirty mufketeers, horfe and foot, who fcarcely fuffice as a guard to two wretched gates, and to keep off the Arabs.

As a fea-port, and place of ftrength, Yafa is nothing; but it is capable of becoming one of the moft important on the coaft, on account of two fprings of frefh water which are within its walls, on the fea shore. These springs enabled it to make the obstinate resistance. it did in the late wars. The port, which is formed by a pier, and at present choaked up, might be cleared out, and made to contain twenty vessels of three hundred tons burthen each. Those which come there at present, are obliged to cast anchor at sea, at near a league's distance from the shore: where they are by no means safe, the bottom being a bank of rock and coral, which extends as far as Gaza.

Before the two late sieges, this was one of the most agreeable towns on the coast. Its environs were covered with a forest of orange and lemon trees, citrons, and palms, which here first begin to bear good fruit.* Beyond it the country abounds in olive trees, as large as walnut trees; but the Mamlouks having cut them all down for the pleasure they take in destroying, or to make fires, Yafa has lost its greatest convenience and ornament; fortunately it was impossible to deprive it of the rivulets that water its gardens, and nourish the young suckers, which have already begun to shoot.

Three leagues to the east of Yafa is the village of *Loudd*, the ancient *Lydda*, and *Diospolis*. A place lately ravaged by fire and sword would have precisely the appearence of this village. From the huts of the inhabitants to the Serai, or palace of the Aga, is one continued heap of rubbish and ruins. A weekly market, however, is held at Loudd, to which the peasants of the environs bring their spun cotton for sale. The poor Christians who dwell here, shew, with great veneration, the ruins of the church of St. Peter, and make strangers sit down on a column, which, they say that Saint once rested on. They point out the place where he preached, where he prayed, &c. The whole country is full of such traditions. It is im-

---

* We meet with some after having passed Acre, but their fruit ripens with difficulty.

possible to stir a step without being shewn the traces
of some apostle, some martyr, or some virgin; but
what credit can be due to these traditions, when experience proves that the history of Ali Bey and
Daher is already disputed and uncertain?

One third of a league to the southward of Loudd,
along a road lined with nopals, stands Ramla, the
ancient Arimathea. This town is almost in as ruinous a state as Loudd itself. We meet with nothing
but rubbish within its boundaries; the Aga of Gaza
resides here in a Serai, the floors and walls of which
are tumbling down. " Why," said I, one day to
one of his Sub-Agas, " does he not at least repair
" his own apartment?" " Yes," replied he, " but if
" another should next year obtain his place, who
" would repay him the expence?"

He maintains about one hundred horsemen, and as
many Barbary soldiers, who are lodged in an old
Christian church, the nave of which is used as a stable,
and in an ancient kan, which is disputed with them
by the scorpions. The adjacent country is planted
with lofty olive trees, disposed in quincunces. The
greatest part of them are as large as the walnut trees
of France; but they are daily perishing through age,
the ravages of contending factions, and even from
secret mischief; for, in these countries, when a peasant would revenge himself of his enemy, he comes
by night, and saws or cuts his trees close to the ground,
and the wound, which he takes care to cover, drain-
ing off the sap like an issue, the olive tree languishes
and dies. Amid these plantations, we meet, at every
step, with dry wells, cisterns fallen in, and vast vaulted reservoirs, which prove that, in ancient times, this
town must have been upwards of a league and a half
in circumference. At present it scarcely contains
two hundred families. The little land which is cultivated, by a few of them, belongs to the Mufti, and
two or three persons related to him. The rest con-

tent themſelves with ſpinning cotton, which is chiefly
purchaſed by two French houſes eſtabliſhed there.
They are the laſt in this part of Syria, there being
none either at Jeruſalem or Yafa.   At Ramla there
is alſo a ſoap manufaĉtury, which is almoſt all ſent
into Egypt.   I muſt not forget to mention that the
Aga built here, in 1784, the only wind-mill I have
ſeen in Syria or Egypt, though they are ſaid to have
been originally invented in theſe countries.   It was
completed after the plan, and under the direĉtion of a
Venetian carpenter.

The only remarkable antiquity at Ramla is the
minoret of a ruined moſque on the road to Yafa.   By
an Arabic inſcription it appears to have been built by
Saf-el-din, Sultan of Egypt.   From the ſummit,
which is very lofty, the eye follows the whole chain
of mountains, which begins at Nablous, and ſkirting
the plain, loſes itſelf toward the ſouth.   In this plain,
between Ramla and Gaza, we meet with a number
of villages, badly built, of dried mud, and which,
like their inhabitants, exhibit every mark of poverty
and wretchedneſs.   The houſes, on a nearer view,
are only ſo many huts, ſometimes detached, at others
ranged in the form of cells around a court-yard, in-
cloſed by a mud wall.   The women have there, as
elſewhere, ſeparate apartments.   In winter, they and
their cattle may be ſaid to live together, the part of
the dwelling allotted to themſelves being only raiſed
two feet above that in which they lodge their beaſts.
The peaſants are by this means kept warm, without
burning wood ; and œconomy indiſpenſible in a country abſolutely deſtitute of fuel.   As for the fire neceſſary for culinary purpoſes, they make it of dung
kneaded into cakes, which they dry in the ſun, ex-
poſing them to its rays on the walls of their huts.
In ſummer their lodging is more airy, but all their
furniture conſiſts in a ſingle mat, and a pitcher for
drinking.   The environs of theſe villages are ſown,

at the proper feafon, with grain and water melons;
all the reft is a defart, and abandoned to the Bedouin
Arabs, who feed their flocks on it. At every ftep
we meet with ruins of towers, dungeons, and caftles
with foffes, and fometimes a garrifon, confifting of
the lieutenant of an Aga, and two or three Barbary
foldiers, with nothing but a fhirt and a mufket; but
more frequently they are inhabited by jackals, owls,
and fcorpions.

Among the inhabited places may be diftinguifhed
the village of Mefmia, four leagues from Ramla, on
the road to Gaza, which furnifhes a great deal of
fpun cotton. At the diftance of a fhort league to
the eaft, is a detached eminence, called for that reafon *El-Tell*. It is the capital of the tribe of Wahidia,
one of the Shaiks of which named Bakir, was affaffinated three years ago by the Aga of Gaza, at an entertainment to which he had invited him. On this
hill are found many remains of habitations and caverns,
fuch as are to be met with in the fortifications of the
middle ages. This muft have been at all times a
favourite fituation, from its fteepnefs, and the fpring
which is at the bottom. The channel through which
it flows, is the fame that lofes itfelf near Afkalon
(Afcalon.) To the eaft the foil is rocky, but covered
with fcattered firs, olives, and other trees. Bait-
djibrim, the Betha-Gabris of Antiquity, is an inhabited village not quite three quarters of a league to the
fouthward. Seven hours journey from thence, toward the fouth-weft, is another village of the Bedouins, called the Hefi, which has in its neighbourhood
an artificial fquare hill, above feventy feet high, one
hundred and fifty wide, and two hundred long. The
whole afcent to it has been paved, and on its fummit
we ftill find the remains of a very ftrong citadel.

As we approach the fea, three leagues from Ramla,
on the road to Gaza, is Yabna, the ancient Jamnia.
This village has nothing remarkable, but a fictitious

eminence like that of Hefi, and a rivulet, the only one in thefe diftricts which does not dry up in fummer. Its whole courfe is not more than a league and a half. Before it reaches the fea, it forms a morafs called Roubin, where the country people had begun a plantation of fugar canes, which made the moft promifing appearance; but, after the fecond crop, the Aga demanded a contribution, which compelled them to defert it.

Leaving Yabna, we meet fucceffively with various ruins, the moft confiderable of which are at Ezdoud, the ancient Azotus, famous at prefent for its fcorpions. This town, fo powerful under the Philiftines, affords no proofs of its ancient importance. Three leagues from Ezdoud is the village of El-Majdal, where they fpin the fineft cottons in Paleftine, which, however, are very clumfy. On the right is Azkalan, whofe deferted ruins are every day removing farther from the fea, by which it formerly was wafhed. This whole coaft is daily accumulating fands, infomuch, that moft of the places which it is known anciently were fea ports, are now four or five hundred paces within land; of this Gaza is an example.

Gaza, called by the Arabs *Rezza*, with a ftrong guttural pronunciation of the *r*, is compofed of three villages, one of which, under the name of *the Caftle*, is fituated between the two others, on an inconfiderable eminence. This caftle, which might have been ftrong for the time in which it was built, is now nothing but a heap of rubbifh. The Serai of the Aga, which makes a part of it, is in as ruinous a ftate as that of Ramla; but it has the advantage of a moft extenfive profpect. From its walls, we view at once the fea, from which it is feparated by a fandy beach, a quarter of a league wide, and the country, whofe date trees, and level and naked afpect, as far as the eye can difcern, reminds us of Egypt; and, in fact, in this latitude, the foil and climate both appear to be truly Arabian. The heats, the drought, the winds, and the dews, are the fame as on the banks of the Nile; and the inhabitants have the complection, ftature, manners, and accent of the Egyptians, rather than thofe of the Syrians.

The fituation of Gaza, by fitting it for the medium of communication between thefe two nations, has rendered it at all times a town of fome importance. The ruins of white marble fometimes found there, prove it was formerly the abode of luxury and opulence; nor was it unworthy of this preference. The black foil of the furrounding country is extremely fertile, and the gardens, watered by limpid ftreams, produce, even yet, without art, pomegranates, oranges, exquifite dates, and ranunculus roots, in great requeft, even at Conftantinople. It has, however, fhared in the general deftruction; and, notwithftanding its proud title of the capital of Paleftine, it is no more than a defencelefs village, peopled by at moft only two thoufand inhabitants. The manufacture of cottons is their principal fupport; and, as they have the exclufive fupply of the peafants and Bedouins of the neighbourhood, they may keep going about five hundred looms. There are likewife two or three foap manufactories. The article of afhes, or *kalis*, was formerly a confiderable commerce. The Bedouins, who procured thefe afhes, by fimply burning the plants of the defert, fold them at a reafonable rate; but fince the Aga has monopolized this commodity, the Arabs, compelled to part with it at his price, are no longer anxious to collect it; and the inhabitants, conftrained to purchafe at his pleafure, neglect making foap. Thefe afhes, however, are an object worthy of attention, from the quantity of alkali they contain.

A branch of commerce more advantageous to the people of Gaza, is furnifhed by the caravans which pafs and repafs between Egypt and Syria. The provifions they are obliged to take for their four days

journey in the defert produce a confiderable demand
for their flour, oils, dates, and other neceffaries.
Sometimes they correfpond with Suez, on the arrival
or departure of the Djedda fleet, as they are able to
reach that place in three long days journey. They fit
out, likewife, every year, a great caravan, which goes
to meet the pilgrims of Mecca, and conveys to them
the convoy or *Djerda* of Paleftine, and fupplies of
various kinds, with different refrefhments. They
meet them at Maon, four days journey to the fouth-
fouth-eaft of Gaza, and one day's journey to the
north of Akaba, on the road to Damafcus. They
alfo purchafe the plunder of the Bedouins ; an article
which would be a Peru to them, were thefe accidents
more frequent. It is impoffible to afcertain the profits
they made by the plunder of the great caravan in
1757. Two-thirds of upwards of twenty thoufand
camel loads, of which the Hadj, or caravan of pilgrims, was compofed, were brought to Gaza. The
ignorant and famifhed Bedouins, who know no value
in the fineft ftuffs, but as they ferve to cover them,
fold their cafhmire, fhawls, callicoes, muflins, firfakes,
Perfian ftuffs, coffee, and gums, for a few piaftres.
We may judge from the following ftory, of the ignorance and fimplicity of thefe inhabitants of the deferts.
A Bedouin of Anaza having found, among his booty,
feveral bags of fine pearls took them for doura, and
had them boiled to eat them ; but feeing that they
did not foften, was on the point of throwing them
away, when an inhabitant of Gaza gave him in exchange for them a red bonnet of Faz. A fimilar
incident happened in 1779, at the time of the pillage
of the caravan which M. de St. Germain accompanied ; and but the other day, in 1784, the caravan
of Barbary, confifting of upwards of three thoufand
camels, was likewife pillaged, and the quantity of
coffee difperfed by the Bedouins throughout Paleftine,
was fo great, as to caufe the price of that article to

fall fuddenly to one half of what it was before; and
it would have fallen ftill more, had not the Aga prohibited the fale of it, in order to compel the Bedouins to deliver it all into his hands. A monopoly of
this fort in the affair of 1779, produced him more
than eighty thoufand piaftres. One year with another, adding thefe cafualties to his other extortions,
to the miri, the cuftoms, the twelve hundred camel
loads, which he purloins from the three thoufand he
fhould furnifh for the Mecca convoy, he raifes, one
year with another, a revenue full double the hundred
and eighty purfes he pays for his farm.

Beyond Gaza there are only deferts. It muft not,
however, be underftood, that the country becomes
fuddenly uninhabitable; we ftill continue, for a day's
journey, along the fea coaft, to meet with fome cultivated fpots and villages. Such is Kan-younes, a
fort of caftle, in which the Mamlouks keep a garrifon
of twelve men. Such alfo is El-Arifh, the laft fpot
where water which can be drank, is to be found until
you arrive at Salaiha in Egypt. El-Arifh is three
quarters of a league from the fea, in a fandy country,
as is all that coaft. Returning to the defert, by the
eaft, we meet with other ftrips of cultivable land,
as far as the road to Mecca. Thefe are little vallies,
where a few peafants have been tempted to fettle by
the waters, which collect at the time of the winter
rains, and by fome wells. They cultivate palm-trees
and doura, under the protection, or rather expofed
to the rapine, of the Arabs. Thefe peafants, feparated from the reft of mankind, are half favages, and
more ignorant and wretched than the Bedouins themfelves. Incapable of leaving the foil they cultivate,
they live in perpetual dread of lofing the fruit of
their labours. No fooner have they gathered in their
harveft, than they haften to fecret it in private places,
and retire among the rocks which border on the Dead
Sea. This country has not been vifited by any travel-

ler, but it well merits fuch an attention; for, from the
reports of the Arabs of Bakir, and the inhabitants of
Gaza, who frequently go to Maan, and Karak on the
road of the pilgrims, there are, to the fouth-eaft of
the lake Afphaltites, within three days journey, upwards of thirty ruined towns, abfolutely deferted.
Several of them have large edifices, with columns
which may have belonged to ancient temples, or at
leaft to Greek churches. The Arabs fometimes make
ufe of them to fold their cattle in; but in general
avoid them, on account of the enormous fcorpions
with which they fwarm. We cannot be furprifed at
thefe traces of ancient population, when we recollect that this was the country of the Nabatheans, the
moft powerful of the Arabs; and of the Idumeans,
who, at the time of the deftruction of Jerufalem, were
almoft as numerous as the Jews, as appears from
Jofephus, who informs us, that on the firft rumour of
the march of Titus againft Jerufalem, thirty thoufand
Idumeans inftantly affembled, and threw themfelves
into that city for its defence. It appears that, befides
the advantage of being under a tolerably good government, thefe diftricts enjoyed a confiderable fhare of
the commerce of Arabia and India, which increafed
their induftry and population. We know that, as far
back as, the time of Solomon, the cities of *Atfioum-Ga-
ber* (Efion Geber), and *Ailah* (Eloth) were highly
frequented marts. Thefe towns were fituated on the
adjacent gulf of the Red Sea, where we ftill find the
latter yet retaining its name and perhaps the former
in that of *El-Alkaba*, or the End (of the Sea.)
Thefe two places are in the hands of the Bedouins,
who being deftitute of a navy and commerce, do not
inhabit them. But the pilgrims of Cairo report that
there is at El-Akàba a wretched fort, with a Turkifh
garrifon, and good water; an advantage truly valuable in thefe countries. The Idumeans, from whom
the Jews only took their ports at intervals, muft have

found in them a great fource of wealth and popula⸱
tion. It even appears, that they rivalled the Tyrians,
who alfo poffeffed a town, the name of which is unknown, on the coaft of Hadjaz, in the defert of Tih,
and the city of Faran, and without doubt El-Tor,
which ferved it by way of Port. From this place
the caravans might reach Paleftine and Judea in eight
or ten days. This route which is longer than that
from Suez to Cairo, is infinitely fhorter than that
from Aleppo to Baffora, which requires five and thirty
or forty days, and poffibly in the prefent ftate of things,
would be the beft, if the paffage by Egypt fhould remain entirely fhut up. Nothing more would be
neceffary, than to make an agreement with the Arabs,
treaties with whom are infinitely more fecure than with
the Mamlouks.

The Defert of Tih, which I have juft mentioned,
is that into which Mofes condu&ed the Jews, and
kept them for a whole generation, to initiate them in
the art of war, and transform a multitude of fhepherds into a nation of conquerors. The name *El-
Tih* feems to have a reference to their hiftory, as it
fignifies the Country of Wandering; but we muft
not imagine this to be in confequence of tradition,
fince the prefent inhabitants are foreigners, and men
in all countries find it difficult to recur even to their
grandfathers; it is from reading the Hebrew books
and the Koran, that the name of El-Tih has been
given this tra& by the Arabs; they alfo call it *Barr-
el-tour-Sina*, which fignifies Country of Mount Sinai.

This defert, which is the boundary of Syria to the
fouth, extends itfelf in the form of a peninfula between
the two gulphs of the Red Sea; that of Suez to the
weft, and that of El-Akaba to the eaft. Its breadth
is ordinarily thirty leagues, and its length feventy.
This great fpace is almoft wholly occupied by barren
mountains which join thofe of Syria, on the north,
and, like them, confift of calcareous ftone: but as

we advance to the fouthward they become granitous,
and Sinai and Horeb are only enormous maffes
of that ftone. Hence it was the ancients called this
country *Arabia Petrea*. The foil in general is a dry
gravel, producing nothing but thorny acacias, tam-
arifks, firs, and a few fcattered fhrubs. Springs of
water are very rare, and thofe few are fometimes ful-
phureous, and *Thermal*, as at Hammam-Faraoun, at
others brackifh and difagreeable, as at El-Nabā oppofite Suez ; this faline quality prevails throughout the
country, and there are mines of foffil falt in the northern parts. In fome of the vallies, however, the foil
becoming better, as it is formed of the earth wafhed
from the rocks, is cultivable after the winter rains,
and may almoft be ftiled fertile. Such is the vale of
Djirandel, in which there are even groves of trees.
Such alfo is the vale of Faran, in which the Bedouins
fay there are ruins, which can be no other than thofe
of the ancient city of that name. In former times
every advantage was made of this country that could
be obtained from it,* but at prefent, abandoned to
nature, or rather to barbarifm, it produces nothing
but wild herbs. Yet, with fuch fcanty provifion this
Defert fubfifts three tribes of Bedouins, confifting of
about five or fix thoufand Arabs, difperfed in various
parts. They are called by the general name of *Taw-
ara*, or the Arabs of Tor, the beft known and moft
frequented place in the country. It is fituated on the
eaftern fide of the branch of Suez, in a fandy and
low ground, as is all this coaft. Its whole merit confifts in a pretty good road for fhipping, and water
which may be drank ; the Arabs alfo bring fome thither
from Sinai, which is really good. The fhips of Suez
lay in their provifions here when they fail to Djedda.

---

* M. Niebhur difcovered, on a mountain, fome tombs with
hieroglyphics, which may induce us to believe the Egyptians
had made fettlements in thefe countries.

There is nothing further to notice except that we find here a few palm-trees, the ruins of a wretched fort without a garrifon, a fmall Greek convent, and fome huts of poor Arabs, who live on fifh and ferve as failors for wages. There are alfo to the fouthward, two fmall villages of Greeks, who are equally poor and miferable. As for the fubfiftence of the three tribes, it is derived from their goats, camels, fome acacia gums fold in Egypt, and their robberies on the roads of Suez, Gaza, and Mecca.

Thefe Arabs have no mares, like the other tribes, or at leaft they bring up very few; but they fupply the want of them by a fort of camel, which they call *Hedjina*. This animal is of the fame fhape with the common camel, with this difference, that he is made much more flender, and moves quicker. The ordinary camel only goes a foot pace, and meafures his fteps fo flowly, that he hardly advances thirty-fix hundred yards an hour; the Hedjina, on the contrary, trots at pleafure, and, from the length of his paces, eafily goes two leagues an hour. The great advantage of this animal is to be able to continue this pace thirty or forty hours fucceffively, almoft without reft, and without eating or drinking: he is made ufe of by couriers, and for long journeys which require expedition; if he has once got the ftart by four hours the fwifteft Arabian mare never can overtake him; but one muft be accuftomed to the motion of this animal; his jolts foon flay the fkin, and difable the beft rider, in fpite of the cufhions with which they ftuff the faddle. All that we have heard of the fwiftnefs of the dromedary, may be applied to this animal. He has however only one bunch; nor do I recollect, out of five and twenty or thirty thoufand camels, I may have feen in Syria and Egypt, ever to have obferved a fingle one with two.

But the moft confiderable profits of the Bedouins of Tor arife from the pilgrimage of the Greeks to the convent of Mount Sinai. The fchifmatics have fo much faith in the relics of faint Chatharine, which they fay are depofited there, that they doubt of their falvation if they have not vifited them at leaft once in their lives. They repair thither even as far as from the Morea and Conftantinople. The rendezvous is at Cairo, where the monks of Mount Sinai have corref-pondents, who treat with the Arabs for a convoy. The ordinary price is twenty-eight pataques, (fix pounds two and fix-pence) each paffenger, exclufive of provifions. On their arrival at the convent, the Greeks perform their devotions, vifit the church, kifs the relics and images, mount on their knees more than one hundred fteps off the hill of Mofes, and con-clude by making an offering, the value of which is not fixed, but rarely amounts to lefs than fifty pa-taques*.

Except at the time of thefe vifitations, which only take place once a year, this convent is the moft defert and favage abode in nature. The adjacent country is nothing but a pile of rugged and naked rocks. Mount Sinai, at the foot of which it is feated, is a peak of granite which feems to overwhelm it. The houfe is a fort of fquare prifon, whofe lofty walls have only one window, which, though very high up, ferves likewife by way of door ; for, to enter this convent, you muft get into a bafket, which the monks leave fufpended at the window, and occafionally hoift up with ropes. This precaution arifes from their fear of the Arabs, who might force the convent if the ufual entrance was

---

* To thefe pilgrims we muft attribute the infcriptions and clumfy figures of affes, camels, &c. engraven on thefe rocks, which have from thence acquired the name of *Djebel Mokattab*, or Written Mountain. *Mr. Wortley Montague* who travelled a great deal in thefe countries, and carefully examined thefe in-fcriptions, is of this opinion. *M. Cour de Gebelin*, author of *Le Monde Primitif*, has loft his labour, endeavouring to difco-ver fome myfterious meaning.

by a door: they never open the only one there is, except on a visit from the bishop, at all other times it is kept closely shut. This visitation should take place every two or three years; but, as it necessarily occasions a considerable contribution for the Arabs, the monks evade it as much as possible. They do not, however, so easily escape the daily distribution of a certain quantity of provisions; and the quarrels which arise, on this subject, frequently drawn on them a shower of stones, and even musket-shot from the discontented Bedouins. They never stir into the country, but by dint of labour, have made a garden, on the rocks, with earth they have brought thither, which serves them to walk in. They cultivate excellent fruit there, such as grapes, figs, and especially pears, of which they make presents, and which are highly esteemed at Cairo, where they have no such fruit. Their domestic life is the same with that of the Greeks and Maronites of Lebanon, that is, it is entirely devoted to useful works or to religious duties. But the Monks of Lebanon enjoy the inestimable advantage of liberty and security, which is not possessed by those of Sinai. In other respects, this confined and melancholy state of existence is that of all the monks, in the country of the Turks. Thus live the Greeks of Mar-Simeon to the north of Aleppo, and of Mar-Saba on the Dead-sea; this also is the life of the Copts in the convents of the desert of Saint Macarius, and in that of Saint Anthony. Every where their convents are prisons, with no other light than a window by which they receive their victuals; and every where are they built in dismal places, destitute of whatever can give pleasure, and where nothing is to be found but rocks and stones, without either grass or moss, and yet they are full of monks. There are fifty at Sinai, five and twenty at Mar-Saba, and upwards of three hundred in the two Deserts of Egypt. I one day enquired the reason of this, in a conversation

with one of the fuperiors of Mar-hanna, and afked
him, " What could induce men to engage in a mode
" of life fo miferable ?" " What" faid he, " are not
" you a Chriftian ? Is not this the path which leads
" to heaven ?"——" But," replied I, " we may alfo
" obtain falvation without renouncing the world ;
" (and between ourfelves, father,) I do not perceive
" that the monks, though they are pious, poffefs that
" ancient fervour which throughout life, kept its eyes
" fixed on the hour of death." " It is true," faid
he, " we have no longer the aufterity of the ancient
" Anchorites, and in reality·this is one reafon why our
" convents are fo full. You who come from a coun-
" try where men live in fecurity and abundance, may
" confider our life as an infupportable felf-denial, and
" our retreat from the world as a facrifice. But, in
" the fituation of this country, perhaps, the cafe is
" different. What can we do ? Turn merchants !
" We fhould then be over-whelmed with the cares of
" bufinefs and our families, and, after having work-
" ed hard for thirty years, comes the Aga, the Pacha,
" or the Cadi ; we are brought to trial without even
" the fhadow of a crime ; witneffes are fuborned to
" accufe us ; we are baftinadoed, plundered, and
" turned into the world as naked as the firft day we
" entered it. As for the peafant, his cafe is ftill
" worfe, the Aga oppreffes him, the foldier pillages
" him, and the Arabs rob him. Shall we become
" foldiers ? the profeffion is laborious and dangerous,
" and how it will end not very certain. It may feem
" hard perhaps to fhut ourfelves up in a convent ;
" but, at leaft, we live there in peace, and, though
" in a ftate of habitual abftinence and poverty, we
" perhaps poffefs and enjoy more than we fhould if
" we had continued in the world. Obferve the fitu-
" ation of the peafants, and look at ours. We pof-
" fefs every thing they have, and even what they have
" not ; we are better·clad, and better fed ; we drink

" wine and coffee: and who are our monks but the
" children of peasants? You talk of the Copts of
" Saint Macarius and Saint Anthony! Be assured
" their condition is much better than that of the Be-
" douins and Fellahs who surround them."

I own I was astonished at so much frankness, and
just reasoning; but I felt, more forcibly than ever,
that the human heart is moved by the same springs, in
every situation. The desire of happiness is every
where the motive, whether sought in hope or actual
enjoyment, and there is always the most to gain in
the part which it adopts. The discourse of this monk
may suggest many other reflections, and shew how
far the spirit of retirement from the world is connected with the state of any government; from what
causes and under what circumstances it must originate,
be predominant, decline, &c. But I shall now conclude this geographical view of Syria, and resume, in
a few words, what I have said of its revenues and
forces, to enable the reader to form a compleat idea
of its political state.

CHAP. XIII.

Political state of Syria resumed.

SYRIA may be considered as a country composed
of three long strips of land of different qualities: one
of these, extending along the Mediterranean, is a
warm, humid valley, the healthiness of which is
doubtful, but which is extremely fertile; the other,
which is the frontier of this, is a mountainous and
rude soil, enjoying a more salubrious temperature;
the third, which lies behind the mountains to the east,
combines the dryness of the latter with the warmth
of the former. We have seen by what a happy com-

bination of the properties of climate and foil this province unites in a fmall compafs the advantages and
productions of different zones, infomuch, that nature feems to have defigned it for one of the moft
agreeable habitations of this continent. It may be re-
proached, however, like almoft all hot countries, with
wanting that frefh and animated verdure which almoft
perpetually adorns our fields; we fee there none of
that gay carpeting of grafs and flowers which decorate
the meadows of Normandy and Flanders, nor thofe
clumps of beautiful trees which gave fuch richnefs
and animation to the landfcapes of Burgundy and
Brittany. As in province, the land of Syria has almoft always a dufty afpect, which is only enlivened
here and there by firs, mulberry-trees, and vineyards.
This deficiency is lefs the fault of nature, poffibly,
than that of art; had not thefe countries been ravaged by the hand of man, they might perhaps at
this day have been fhaded with forefts. Thus much
is certain, and it is the advantage of hot over cold
countries, that in the former, wherever there is water, vegetation may be perpetually maintained and
made to produce an uninterrupted fucceffion of fruits
to flowers, and flowers to fruits. In cold, nay even
in temperate climates, on the contrary, nature be-
numbed for feveral months, lofes in a fterile flumber
the third part, or even half the year. The foil
which has produced grain, has not time, before the
decline of the fummer heat, to mature vegetables;
a fecond crop is not to be expected, and the hufbandman fees himfelf condemned to a long and fatal repofe. Syria, as we have feen, is exempt from thefe
inconveniencies; if therefore it fo happens, that its
productions do not correfpond with its natural advantages, this is lefs owing to its phyfical than political
ftate. To fix our ideas on this head, let us refume,
in a few words, what we have already explained in
detail of the revenues, forces, and population of the
province.

From the ftate of the contributions of each pachalic, it appears that the annual fum paid by Syria into
the *Kcfna*, or Treafury of the Sultan, amounts to
two thoufand three hundred and forty-five purfes, viz,

For Aleppo	-	-	800 Purfes
Tripoli	-	-	750
Damafcus	-	-	45
Acre	-	-	750
Paleftine	-	-	—
		Total	2345

Which are equal to 2,931,250 livres, (122,135*l.*
8*s.* 4*d.*)

To this fum muft be added, firft, the cafual inheritance of the fortunes of the Pachas, and of individuals, which may be eftimated at one thoufand purfes,
annually ; fecondly, the poll tax paid by the Chriftians, called *Karadji*, which is almoft every where
diftinct from the other taxes, and is accountable directly to the Kcfna. This capitation does not take
place in the countries which are fub-let, as thofe of
the Maronites and Druzes, but is confined to the
Rayas, or immediate fubjects. The capitation tickets
are from three and five to eleven piafters a head. It
is difficult to eftimate the total produce, but allowing
one hundred and fifty thoufand to pay the tax, at the
mean rate of fix piafters, we have the fum of 2,250,-
000 livres ; and we cannot be far from the truth, if
we compute the total of the Sultan's revenue from
Syria to be 7,500,000 livres, (312,500*l.*).

Let us now eftimate what the country produces to
thofe who farm it, and we fhall have

For	Aleppo	-	-	2,000	Purfes
	Tripoli	-	-	2,000	
	Damafcus	-	-	10,000	
	Acre	-	-	10,000	
	Paleftine	-	-	600	

Total 24,600

Which make 30,750,000 livres, (1,281,250*l.*) This fum muft be confidered as the leaft we can allow for the produce of Syria, the profits of the fub-farms, fuch as the countries of the Druzes, the Maronites, the Anfarians, &c. not being included.

The military eftablifhment is by no means proportionable to what in Europe we fhould expect from fuch a revenue; all the troops of the Pachas united cannot amount to more than 5,700 men, both cavalry and infantry, viz.

			Cavalry.		Natives of Barbary.
For	Aleppo	-	600	-	500
	Tripoli	-	500	-	200
	Acre	-	1,000	-	900
	Damafcus	-	1,000	-	600
	Paleftine	-	300	-	100
	Total		3,400		2,300

The conftant forces of the country then confift in three thoufand four hundred cavalry, and two thoufand three hundred Barbary infantry. It is true, that, in extraordinary cafes, thefe are joined by the Janifaries, and that the Pachas enlift vagabond volunteers from every quarter, which form thofe fudden armies we have feen collected in the wars of Daher and Ali Bey: but the fketch I have given of the military fkill of thefe armies, and the difcipline of fuch troops, may convince us, that Syria is ftill worfe defended

than Egypt. We muſt, however, allow the Turkiſh
ſoldiers two ineſtimiable good qualities ; a frugality
which enables them to ſubſiſt in the moſt exhauſted
country, and a bodil; health capable of enduring the
greateſt fatigues. This is the effect of the hardſhips
to which they are inured, by their manner of living.
Continually on horſeback, and in the field, lying on
the earth, and ſleeping in the open air, they do not experience that contraſt between the luxurious life of
cities, and the fatigue of camps, which is ſo fatal to
the ſoldiers of poliſhed nations.

Syria and Egypt, compared with reſpect to the facility with which they may be attacked or defended,
differ almoſt in every point. Egypt is protected from
a foreign enemy on the land ſide by her deſerts, and
on that of the ſea, by her dangerous coaſt. Syria, on
the contrary, is open on the ſide of the continent by
the Diarbekar, and expoſed alſo on that of the Mediterranean by a coaſt every where acceſſible. It is eaſy
to make a deſcent in Syria, but very difficult to land
in Egypt : Egypt once invaded is conquered ; Syria
may reſiſt ; Egypt when conquered is extremely difficult, to keep, and eaſily loſt ; Syria is ſo eaſily defended, it is impoſſible it ſhould be loſt. Leſs ſkill is
neceſſary to conquer one, than to preſerve the other.
The reaſon is, that Egypt being a country of plains,
war there makes a rapid progreſs ; every moment
brings on a battle, and every battle is deciſive ; Syria,
on the contrary, being a mountainous country, war
there muſt be a war of poſts, and every loſs may be
repaired.

The ſubject of population, which remains to be diſ-
cuſſed, is infinitely more difficult than the two preceding ones. Calculations of this kind can only be made
from analogies always liable to error. The beſt way
will be to compute from two extremes, the populouſ-
neſs of which is pretty well known. The part of the
country which is the beſt peopled, is that of the Maro-

nites and Druzes, and gives nine hundred inhabitants
for each fquare league, which computation will alfo
ferve for the countries of Nablous, Hafbeya, Adjaloun,
the territory of Damafcus, and fome other places.
The other, which is the leaft populous, is that of
Aleppo, which gives from three hundred and eighty
to four hundred inhabitants to each fquare league,
which eftimation will fuit the greater part of Syria.
Calculating from thefe materials by a method too tedious to explain here, it appears to me that the total
population of Syria may be eftimated at 2,305,000
fouls, viz.

For the Pachalic of Aleppo   320,000 ·
    that of Tripoli, not including the
      Kefraouan   -   -   -   200,000
    the Kefraouan   -   -   115,000
    the country of the Druzes   ⸳   120,000
    the Pachalic of Acre   -   ⸳   300,000
    Paleftine   -   -   -   -   50,000
    the Pachalic of Damafcus   -   1,200,000

              Total   2,305,000

    Let us fuppofe it two millions and a half, and fince
Syria contains about five thoufand two hundred and
fifty fquare leagues, at the rate of one hundred and
fifty in length, and thirty-five in breadth, we fhall have
upon an average four hundred and feventy-fix inhabitants for every fquare league. So feeble a population in fo excellent a country may well excite our
aftonifhment, but this will be ftill increafed, if we
compare the prefent number of inhabitants, with that
of ancient times. We are informed by the philofophical geographer, Strabo, that the territories of Yam-
nia and Yoppa in Paleftine, alone, were formerly fo
populous, as to be able to bring forty thoufand armed
men into the fields. At prefent they could fcarcely
furnifh three thoufand. From the accounts we have

of Judea in the time of Titus, and which are to be
efteemed tolerably accurate, that country muft have
contained four millions of inhabitants; but at prefent,
there are not, perhaps, above three thoufand. If we
go ftill farther back into antiquity, we fhall find the
fame populoufnefs among the Philiftines, the Phœnicians, and in the kingdoms of Samaria, and Damafcus. It is true that fome writers, reafoning from
what they fee in Europe, have called in queftion thefe
facts; feveral of which, indeed, appeared to be difput-
able; but the comparifons on which they build, are
not on that account the lefs erroneous; firft, becaufe
the lands of Affia in general are more fertile than
thofe of Europe; fecondly, becaufe a part of thefe
lands are capable of being cultivated, and in fact are
cultivated, without lying fallow or requiring manure;
thirdly, becaufe the Orientals confume one half lefs
for their fubfiftence than the inhabitants of the weftern world, in general; for all which reafons it appears, that a territory of lefs extent may contain double and treble the population. Thefe authors exclaim
againft the armies of two and three hundred thoufand, furnifhed by ftates, which in Europe could not
produce above twenty or thirty thoufand; but it is
not confidered that the conftitutions of ancient nations were wholly different from ours; that thefe nations were purely cultivators; that there was lefs inequality, and lefs idlenefs than among us; that every
cultivator was a foldier; that in war, the army frequently confifted of the whole nation, and, in a word,
that their ftate was that of the prefent Maronites and
Druzes. Not that I wifh to appear an advocate for
thofe rapid populations, which from a fingle man, are
made to pour forth in a few generations, numerous
and powerful nations. In thefe relations there are a
multitude of miftakes in words, and errors of Co-
pyifts; but admitting only what is conformable to
experience and nature, there is nothing to contradict

the great population of high antiquity; without appealing to the pofitive teftimony of hiftory, there are innumerable monuments which depofe in favour of the fact. Such are the prodigious quantity of ruins difperfed over the plains, and even in the mountains, at this day deferted. On the moft remote parts of Carmel are found wild vines and olive-trees, which muft have been conveyed thither by the hand of man; and in the Lebanon of the Druzes and Maronites, the rocks now abandoned to fir-trees and brambles, prefent us in a thoufand places with terraces, which prove they were anciently better cultivated, and confequently much more populous than in our days.

It now only remains for me, to collect the general facts fcattered through this work, and thofe I may have omitted, in order to form a complete defcription of the political, civil, and moral ftate of the inhabitants of Syria.

CHAP. XIV.

Government of the Turks in Syria.

THE reader muft already have been convinced from the various traits that have been laid before him, that the government of the Turks in Syria is a pure military defpotifm; that is, the bulk of the inhabitants are fubject to the caprices of a faction of armed men, who difpofe of every thing according to their intereft and fancy. To form a more perfect conception of the fpirit with which this faction governs, it will be fufficient to confider by what title they claim poffeffion.

When the Ottomans, under Sultan Selim, took Syria, from the Mamlouks, they confidered it only as the fpoil of a vanquifhed enemy; as a poffeffion acquired by the law of arms and war. Now, according to this law, among barbarous nations, the vanquished is wholly at the discretion of the victor, he becomes his slave; his life, his property belongs to his conqueror; he may dispose of all as master, he owes his captive nothing, and accords what he leaves him as a favour. Such was this law among the Greeks and Romans, and among all those societies of robbers whom we have honoured with the name of conquerors. Such, at all times, was that of the Tartars, from whom the Turks derive their origin. On these principles, even their first social state was formed. In the plains of Tartary the hordes, divided by interest, were no other than bands of robbers, armed for attack or defence, and to seize as fair booty, whatever they might covet. Already, all the elements of their present state were formed; continually wandering and encamped, they were at once shepherds and soldiers; each horde was an army; now, in an army, laws are but the orders of the chief, these orders are absolute and suffer no delay, they must proceed from one will, and from a single head: hence, a supreme authority in him who commands; and a passive submission in him who obeys. But as in the transmission of these orders, the instrument becomes an agent in his turn, the consequence is, a spirit at once imperious and servile, which is precisely that exhibited by the Turkish conquerors. Proud, after their victory, of being one of the conquering people, the meanest of the Ottomans treated the most illustrious of the vanquished with the lofty superiority of a master; and this spirit diffusing itself through every rank, we may judge of the distance from whence the Supreme Chief looks down upon the croud of slaves beneath him. The sentiments he conceives of them cannot be better pourtrayed than in the formulary of the titles assumed by the Sultans in their public acts; "I," say they, in their treaties with the kings of France, "I, who am, by the "infinite grace of the great, just, and omnipotent Crea-

" tor, and by the innumerable miracles of the Chief of
" Prophets, Emperor of Powerful Emperors, the Re-
" fuge of Sovereigns, the Diftributor of Crowns to the
" Kings of the Earth, Servant of the two thrice facred
" cities, (Mecca & Medina) Governor of the Holy City
" of Jerufalem, Mafter of Europe, Afia, and Africa,
" conquered by our victorious Sword, and our terrific
" Lance, Lord of the Two Seas, (the White and
" Black Seas) of Damafcus the Odour of Paradife,
" of Bagdad the feat of the Caliphs, of the Fortreffes
" of Belgrade, Agria, and a multitude of Countries,
" Iflands, Straights, Nations, Generations, and of
" fo many victorious armies, which repofe beneath
" the fhade of our Sublime Porte; I, in fhort, who
" am *the Shadow of God* on Earth, &c."

From fuch exalted grandeur, how muft the Sultan
look down on the reft of mankind? In what light
muft he view that earth which he poffeffes, and dif-
tributes, but as a domain of which he is abfolute mafter? What muft the people he has fubdued appear,
but flaves devoted to his fervice? And what the foldiers he commands, but fervants by whofe means he
retains thefe flaves in obedience? Such is the real
character of the Turkifh government. This empire
may be compared to a plantation in one of our Sugar
Iflands, where a multitude of flaves labour to fupply
the luxury of one Great Proprietor, under the infpection of a few fervants who take good care of themfelves. There is no difference, except that the domi-
nions of the Sultan being too vaft for a fingle adminiftration, he is obliged to divide it into fmaller plantations, and feparate governments, adminiftered in the
fame mode as the united empire. Such are the provinces under the government of the Pachas. Thefe
provinces again being too extenfive, the Pachas have
had recourfe to further fubdivifion, and hence that
feries of fubalterns, which, ftep by ftep, defcends to
the loweft employments. In this gradation of autho-

rity, the object in view being invariably the same, the means employed never change their nature. Thus, power being absolute and arbitrary in the monarch, is transmitted absolute and arbitrary to all his sub-delegates. Each of these is the exact image of his next superior. It is still the Sultan who dictates and commands, under the varied names of *Pacha, Motsallam, Kaiem-Makam,* and *Aga,* nor is there one in this descending scale, even to the *Delibashe,* who does not represent him. It is curious to hear with what insolence the lowest of these soldiers, giving his orders in a village, pronounces: *It is the will of the Sultan; it is the Sultan's pleasure.* The reason of this insolence is easily explained: for the bearer of the orders of the Sultan becomes, for that moment, himself the Sultan. It is not difficult to conceive what must be the consequence of such an administration, since all experience invariably proves, that moderation is the most difficult of virtues; and since even those men who preach it most fervently, frequently neglect to practise it; how numerous must be the abuses of unlimited power in the great, who are strangers both to forbearance and to pity, in upstarts proud of authority and eager to profit by it, and in subalterns continually aiming at a greater power. Let us judge therefore, how far certain speculative writers are justified in insinuating, that despotism in Turkey is not so great an evil as we imagine, since, from its residing in the person of the sovereign, it can only affect the great by whom he is immediately surrounded. It is certain, to use the expression of the Turks, *that the sabre of the Sultan does not descend upon the dust;* but this sabre he entrusts to the hands of his Vizir, who delivers it to the Pacha, from whom it passes to the Motsallam, to the Aga, and even to the lowest Delibashe; so that it is, in fact, within the reach of the vilest retainer to office, and its destructive edge descends even to the meanest heads. This erroneous reasoning arises from the state of the people

at Conſtantinople, to whom the Sultan is more attentive than to thoſe of the provinces; but this attention,
which his own perſonal ſafety renders neceſſary there,
is paid to no other part of the empire; and, even
there, it may be ſaid to be attended with diſagreeable
effects; for, if Conſtantinople is in want of proviſions,
ten provinces are famiſhed for a ſupply. Yet, which
is of moſt importance to the empire, the capital or the
provinces? In caſe of war, by which muſt ſoldiers be
furniſhed, and by which fed? To the provinces therefore muſt we look to diſcover the real effects of deſpotiſm, and, in Turkey, as every where elſe, we muſt
be convinced that arbitrary power in the ſovereign is
fatal to the ſtate, as from the ſovereign it muſt neceſſarily devolve upon his ſubalterns, and become more
abuſed the lower it deſcends; ſince it is a maxim veri-
fied by conſtant experience, that the ſlave, become
maſter, is the moſt rigorous of tyrants. Let us now
examine the abuſes of this adminiſtration, as far as it
reſpects Syria.

In each government, the Pacha, being the image of
the Sultan, is, like him, an abſolute deſpot. All power is united in his perſon; he is chief both of the military and the finances, of the police and criminal juſtice.
He has the power of life and death; he has the power
of making peace and war; in a word, he can do every
thing. The main object of ſo much authority is to
collect the tribute, that is, to tranſmit the revenue to
the great proprietor who has conquered, and who poſ-
ſeſſes the country by the right of his *terrific lance*.
This duty fulfilled, no other is required from him;
the means employed by the agent to accompliſh it is a
matter of no concern; thoſe means are at his diſcre-
tion; and ſuch is the nature of his ſituation, that he
cannot be delicate in his choice of them; for, in the
firſt place, he can neither advance, nor even maintain
himſelf, but in proportion as he can procure money.
Secondly, The place he holds depends on the favour

of the Vifir, or fome other great officer ; and this can only be obtained and fecured by bidding higher than his competitors. He muft therefore raife money to pay the tribute, and alfo to indemnify himfelf for all he has paid, fupport his dignity, and make a provifion in cafe of accidents. Accordingly, the firft care of a Pacha, on entering on his government, is to devife methods to procure money, and the quickeft are invariably the beft. The eftablifhed mode of collecting the miri and the cuftoms, is to appoint one or more principal farmers, for the current year, who, in order to facilitate the collection, divide it into leffer farms, which are again fubdivided, even to the fmalleft villages. The Pacha lets thefe employments to the beft bidder, wifhing to draw as much money from them as poffible. The farmers, who, on their fide, have no object in taking them but gain, ftrain every nerve to augment their receipt. Hence an avidity in thefe delegates always bordering on difhonefty ; hence thofe extortions to which they are the more eafily inclined as they are fure of being fupported by authority ; and hence, in the very heart of the people, a faction of men interefted in multiplying impofitions. The Pacha may applaud himfelf for penetrating into the moft hidden fources of private profits, by the clear fighted rapacity of his fubalterns ; but what is the confequence? The people, denied the enjoyment of the fruit of their labour, reftrain their induftry to the fupply of their neceffary wants. The hufbandman only fows to preferve himfelf from ftarving ; the artift labours only to bring up his family ; if he has any furplus, he carefully conceals it. Thus the arbitrary power of the Sultan, tranfmitted to the Pacha, and to all his fubdelegates, by giving a free courfe to extortion becomes the main fpring of a tyranny which circulates through every clafs, whilft its effects, by a reciprocal re-action, are every where fatal to agriculture, the arts, commerce, population; in a word, every thing which conftitutes the power of the ftate, or, which is the fame thing, the power of the Sultan himfelf.

This power is not subject to less abuses in the army. Perpetually urged by the want of money, on which his safety and tranquility depend, the Pacha has retrenched, as far as possible, the usual military establishment. He diminishes the number of his troops, lessens their pay, winks at their disorders; and discipline is no more. Were a foreign war now to happen, were the Russians to appear again in Syria, as in the year 1772, who would defend that province for the Sultan?

It sometimes happens, that the Pachas, who are Sultans in their provinces, have personal hatreds against each other. To gratify these, they avail themselves of their power, and wage secret or open war, the ruinous consequences of which are sure to be felt by the subjects of the Sultan.

It also happens, that these Pachas are tempted to appropriate to themselves the power of which they are the depositaries. The Porte, foreseeing this, endeavours to provide against their defection, by various means. The employments are divided, and particular officers maintained in the castles of the capitals, as at Aleppo, Damascus, and Tripoli; but should a foreign enemy appear, what benefit would result from this division? Every three months Capidjis are sent who keep the Pachas in alarm, on account of the secret orders of which they are the bearers; but not unfrequently the Pachas, as cunning as themselves, get rid of these troublesome spies. The Porte, in short, often changes the residence of the Pachas, that they may not have time to form connections in the country; but as all the consequences of a bad form of government have a mischievous tendency, the Pachas, uncertain of to-morrow, treat their provinces as mere transient possessions, and take care to make no improvement for the benefit of their successors: on the contrary, they hasten to exhaust them of the produce, and to reap in one day, if possible, the fruit of many

years. It is true, thefe irregularities, every now and
then, are punifhed by the cord, one of the practices
of the Porte, which beft difplays the fpirit of its government. When a Pacha has laid wafte a province;
when, in confequence of repeated acts of tyranny, the
clamours of the people have reached Conftantinople,
woe be unto him if he be without a protector, or
fparing of his money! At the end of the year, a
Capidji arrives, producing the firman of prorogation:
fometimes bringing with him a fecond or third tail,
or fome other frefh mark of favour; but, whilft the
Pacha is celebrating a feftival on the occafion, an order appears for his depofition, then another for his
exile, and frequently a kat-fherif for his head. The
oftenfible reafon is always for having oppreffed the
fubjects of the Sultan: but the Porte, by taking poffeffion of the wealth of the extortioner, and reftoring
nothing to the people, leaves fufficient room to think
that the government is far from difapproving a fyftem
of robbery and plunder which it finds fo profitable.
Every day, therefore affords, frefh examples of oppreffive and rebellious Pachas; and if none of them have
hitherto fucceeded in forming a ftable and independent
government; it is lefs owing to the wife meafures of
the Divan, and the vigilence of the Capidjis, than
their own ignorance in the art of governing. In Afia,
thofe moral means are never employed, which, in the
hands of able legiflators, have frequently raifed powerful ftates on foundations at firft extremely feeble.
The Pachas regard nothing but money; nor has repeated experience been able to make them fenfible
that this, fo far from being the pledge of their fecurity,
becomes the certain caufe of their deftruction. They
are wholly devoted to amaffing wealth, as if friends
were to be purchafed. Afa, Pacha of Damafcus, left
eight millions of livres (about three hundred and thirty
thoufand pounds) and was betrayed by his Mamlouk,
and fmothered in the bath. We have feen what was

the fate of Ibrahim Sabbar with his twenty millions.
Djezzar is following the fame courfe, and will end
in the fame way. Not one of them has ever thought
of infpiring and promoting that difinterefted love of
the public welfare, which in Greece and Italy, nay,
even in Holland and Switzerland, has enabled the
lower claffes of people to enter into a fuccefsful conteft
with the greateft empires. The Emirs and Pachas all
immitate the Sultan : all regard the country they govern as their private property, and their fubjects as
their domeftics ; while they, in their turn, fee in
their fuperiors only imperious mafters ; and fince
they are all alike, of what importance is it which they
ferve ? Hence, in thefe ftates, the cuftom of employ-
ing foreign in preference to national troops. The
chiefs are diftruftful of the people, confcious that they
do not merit their attachment ; their aim is not to govern, but to tyrannize over the country, and by a juft
retaliation, their country fees their ruin with indifference. The mercenaries, too, whom they keep in
pay, faithful to their views of intereft, fell them to
the enemy, to profit by their fpoils. Daher had
maintained for ten years the wretch who murdered
him. It is a truth worthy of remark, that the greater part of the African and Afiatic ftates, efpecially
fince the days of Mahomet, have been governed on
thefe principles, and that no part of the world has exhibited fo many commotions in its provinces, or revolutions in its empires. Ought we not then to conclude, that arbitrary power in the fovereign is no lefs
fatal to the military ftrength, than the finances of a
nation. But let us proceed to enquire what are its
effects on the civil government of Syria.

The Pacha, as being the image of the Sultan, is
the head of all the police of government ; under
which title muft be comprehended criminal juftice.
He poffeffes the moft abfolute power of life and death,
and this he exercifes without formality, and without

appeal. Wherever he meets with an offence, he orders the criminal to be feized, and the executioner,
by whom he is accompanied, ftrangles him, or takes
off his head upon the fpot ; nay, fometimes he himfelf does not difdain this office. Three days before
my arrival at Sour, Djezzar had ripped up a Mafon
with an axe. The Pacha frequently ftrolls about difguifed, and woe to the man whom he furprizes in a
fault ! But, as he cannot be prefent every where, he
commits this duty to a deputy, called the *Wali*, whofe
office refembles that of the *Officiers de Guet* in France.
Like them he patroles night and day ; keeps a watch-
ful eye on the feditious; apprehends robbers; and,
like the Pacha, judges and condemns without appeal.
The criminal bends his neck ; the executioner ftrikes ;
the head falls, and the body is carried off in a leathern
fack. This officer has a multitude of fpies, who are
almoft all of them thieves, and by their means knows
every thing that paffes. It is not, therefore, aftonifhing, that cities like Cairo, Aleppo, and Damafcus,
fhould be fafer than Genoa, Rome, or Naples; but
how dearly is this fafety purchafed ? and how many
innocent lives are facrificed to the partiality and injuftice of the Wali and his agents !

The Wali prefides likewife over the police of the
markets ; that is, he infpects their weights and meafures ; and, on this head, his feverity is extreme :
for the fmalleft deficiency in the weight of bread,
meat, *debs*, or confectionary, he inflicts five hundred
ftrokes of the baftinado, and, fometimes, even death.
Examples of this are frequent in the great cities, yet
is there no country wherein falfe weights are more
common ; all the dealer has to do is to keep a fharp
look-out for the paffing of the Wali, and Mohtefeb,
or infpector of the market. As foon as they appear
on horfe-back, the deficient weights are put out of
the way, and others produced. The dealers alfo bargain with the fervants who precede thefe two officers ;
and for a certain fum can enfure impunity.

The office of the Wali by no means extends to thofe various objects of utility which are under the regulation of our police. No attention is paid either to the cleanlinefs or the falubrity of the cities. They are never paved, fwept, or watered, either in Syria or in Egypt. The ftreets are narrow and winding, and almoft always encumbered with rubbifh. Travellers are, above all, fhocked at the fight of a multitude of hideous dogs, which have no owners. They form a fort of independent body, fubfifting on public alms. They are quartered by families and diftricts, and fhould one of them happen to pafs his limits, a combat enfues, which is extremely troublefome to paffengers. The Turks, who fhed the blood of man fo readily, do not kill thefe dogs, though they avoid touching them as unclean. They pretend they enfure the fafety of the cities by night; but this is more owing to the Wali, and the gates with which every ftreet is fecured. It is alledged, likewife, that they devour the carrion; but in this they are affifted by a great number of jackalls, which are concealed by hundreds in the gardens, and among the ruins and tombs. We muft not expect either walks or plantations in the Turkifh cities. In fuch a country, life, doubtlefs, will appear neither fecure nor agreeable; but this alfo is the confequence of the arbitrary power of the Sultan.

CHAP. XV.

Of the Adminiftration of Juftice.

THE adminiftration of juftice in civil fuits, is the only fpecies of authority which the Sultans have withheld from the executive power of the Pachas; whether, from a fenfe of the enormous abufes which might

refult from it, or from knowing that it required more
time and information than fall to the fhare of thefe
their deputies.   Other officers are appointed for this
purpofe, who, by a wife regulation, are independent
of the Pachas ; but as their jurifdiction is founded on
the fame principles with the reft of the government,
it is attended with the fame inconveniencies.

All the magiftrates of the empire, called *Cadis*, or
judges, depend on one principal chief, who refides at
Conftantinople.   The title of his dignity is *Cadi-el-
afkar*[*], or judge of the army ; which title alone indicates, as I have already obferved, that the power is
entirely military, and refides wholly in the army and
its general.   This grand Cadi names the judges of
the capital cities, fuch as Aleppo, Damafcus, Jerufalem &c.   Thefe judges again name others in the
places within their dependency.   But what is the qua-
lification required ? Always money. All thefe employments, like thofe of the government, are fold to the
beft bidder, and, farmed in the fame way from year
to year.   What is the confequence ? That the farmers
endeavour to recover the money advanced ; to obtain
intereft, and alfo a profit.   What therefore can we
expect from fuch difpofitions in men who hold the
balance of juftice in their hand, and decide on the
property of their fellow citizens ?

The tribunal whence thefe Cadis iffue their deci-
fions, is called the *Mahkama*, or place of Judgment.
Sometimes it is at their own houfes ; but never is it at
a place which correfponds with the idea annexed to fo
facred an employment.   In an empty mean apartment,
the Cadi is feated on a mat, or wretched carpet.
On each fide of him are his clerks, and fome domeftics.   The door is open to every body; the parties
appear ; and there, without interpreters, advocates,
or attornies, each pleads his own caufe.   Squatted
on the ground, thay ftate the facts, difcufs, reply,

_____

[*] Commonly called *Cadi Lefkier.*

conteſt, and argue again in their turns. Sometimes the debates are violent; but the cries of the clerks, and the ſtaff of the Cadi, ſoon reſtore order and ſilence. Gravely ſmoaking his pipe, and twiſting the end of his beard round his finger, this judge liſtens, interrogates, and concludes by pronouncing a ſentence without appeal, which at moſt allows but two months delay. The parties are never well ſatisfied; they retire, however, with reſpect; and pay a fee, eſtimated at one tenth of the litigated property, without murmuring at the deciſion, as it is invariably dictated by the *infallible Koran.*

It muſt be owned this ſimplicity of juſtice, which does not conſume the property, either in preliminary, acceſſary or ſubſequent expences; and this proximity of the ſovereign tribunal, which does not compel the pleader's abſence from his place of reſidence, are two ineſtimable advantages; but it cannot be denied that they are counterbalanced by too many abuſes. In vain have ſome writers, to render more conſpicuous the vices of our legal cuſtoms, boaſted the adminiſtration of juſtice among the Turks. Theſe commendations, founded on a ſuperficial knowledge of the theory of Mahometan juriſprudence, are not juſtified, when we conſider what is actually practiſed. Daily experience proves, that their is no country wherein juſtice is more corrupted than in Egypt, Syria, and, no doubt, all the reſt of the Turkiſh empire*. Venality is no where more open, nor more impudent. The parties may bargain for their cauſe with the Cadi, as they would for any common commodity. Inſtances of great ſagacity and equity, no doubt, are to be found; but they are rare, which is the very reaſon why they are ſo celebrated. Corruption is habitual and general; and how is it poſſible to be otherwiſe,

* See, on this ſubject, the obſervations of Sir James Porter, the Engliſh miniſter at Conſtantinople.

where integrity may be ruinous, and injuſtice lucrative; where each Cadi, deciding without appeal, fears
neither a reviſion of his ſentence, nor puniſhment for
his partiality ; and where, in ſhort, the want of clear
and preciſe laws ; affords a thouſand ways of avoid-
ing the ſhame of an evident injuſtice, by opening the
crooked paths of commentaries and interpretations ?

Such is the ſtate of juriſprudence among the Turks,
that their exiſts no public and acknowledged code,
where individuals may inſtruct themſelves in their re-
ſpective rights.   The judgments given, are in general,
founded on unwritten *cuſtoms*, or on the frequently
contradictory *deciſions* of the Doctors.   The collections of the deciſions are the only books wherein the
judges can acquire any notions of their duty ; and in
them they find only particular caſes more calculated
to confound than enlighten their ideas.   The Roman
law in many particulars has ſerved as a baſis for the
determinations of the Mahometan Doctors ; but the
great and inexhauſtible ſource to which they recur, is
the *moſt pure book*, the *depoſitory of all knowledge* the
code of all legiſlation, the *Koran of the Prophet*.

CHAP. XVI.

Of the influence of religion.

IF the object of religion among the Turks were ſuch
as it ought to be among all nations ; did it teach the
great moderation, in the exerciſe of their power, and
the vulgar, toleration amid the diverſity of opinions,
it would ſtill be a matter of doubt whether it could
ſufficiently correct the vices of which we have been
ſpeaking ; ſince the experience of all men proves that
morality only influences conduct, ſo far as it is ſecond-

ed by the civil laws. But nothing can be worfe calculated to remedy the abufes of government than
the fpirit of *Iflamifm :* we may on the contrary, pronounce it to be their original fource. To convince
himfelf of this, the reader has only to examine their
reverend book. In vain do the Mahometans boaft that
the Koran contains the feeds and even the perfection
of all political and legiflative knowledge, and jurifprudence : nothing but the prejudice of education, or
the intereft of fome fecret partiality can dictate, or
admit fuch a judgment. Whoever reads the Koran,
muft be obliged to confefs, that it conveys no notion,
either of the relative duties of mankind in fociety, of
the formation of the body politic, or of the principles
of the art of governing ; nothing, in a word, which
conftitutes a legiflative code. The only laws we find
there may be reduced to four or five ordinances relative to polygamy, divorces, flavery, and the fucceffion
of near relations ; and even thefe form no code of
jurifprudence, but are fo contradictory, that they cannot
be reconciled by the altercations of the doctors. The
reft is merely a chaos of unmeaning phrafes ; an
emphatical declamation on the attributes of God,
from which nothing is to be learnt ; a collection of
puerile tales, and ridiculous fables ; and, on the whole,
fo flat and faftidious a compofition, that no man can
read it to the end, notwithftanding the elegance of
M. Savary's tranflation. But fhould any general
tendencey or femblance of meaning be vifible through
the abfurdities of this delirious effufion, it is the in-
culcation of a fierce and obftinate fanaticifm. We
are wearied with the perpetual recurrence of the words
*impious, incredulous, enemies of God and the Prophet ;
rebels againft God and the Prophet ; devotion towards
God and the Prophet.* Heaven is open to whomfoever
combats in their caufe ; *Houris* ftretch out their arms
to martyrs ; the imagination takes fire, and the profe-
lyte exclaimes, " Oh Mahomet : thou art the meffen-

" ger of God; thy word is his; he is infallible; thou
" canſt neither err nor deceive me: go on, I follow
" thee." Such is the ſpirit of the Koran, and it is
viſible in the very firſt line.   " There is no doubt in
" this book; it guides without error thoſe who believe
" without doubting, who believe in what they do not
" ſee." What is the tendency of this, but to eſtabliſh
the moſt abſolute deſpotiſm in him who commands,
and the blindeſt devotion in him who obeys? and ſuch
was the object of Mahomet.   He did not wiſh to enlighten men, but to rule over them; he ſought not
diſciples, but ſubjects; and obedience, not reaſoning is
required from ſubjects.   It was to lead them the more
eaſily that he aſcribed all to God.   By making himſelf his miniſter, he removed every ſuſpicion of perſonal intereſt; and avoided alarming that diſtruſtful
vanity which is common to all men; he feigned to
obey that he might exalt obedience; he made himſelf
but the firſt of ſervants, with a certainty that every
man would ſtrive to be the ſecond, and command the
reſt.   He allured by promiſes, and terrified by menaces; and, as every novelty is ſure to meet opponents,
by holding out the terrors of his anathemas, he left
them the hope of pardon.   Hence, in ſome paſſages
we find an appearance of toleration; but this toleration
is ſo rigid, that ſooner or later, it muſt lead to abſolute ſubmiſſion; ſo that in fact the fundamental ſpirit
of the Koran continually recurs, and the moſt arbitrary power is delegated to the meſſenger of God,
and by a natural conſequence to his ſucceſſors.   But
by what kind of precepts is the uſe of this power
manifeſted?   " There is only one God, and Maho-
" met is his prophet.   Pray five times a day turning
" towards Mecca.   Eat not in the day time during
" the whole month of the Ramadan.   Make the
" pilgrimage of the Caaba, and give alms, to the
" widow and orphan."   Here is the profound ſource
from whence muſt ſpring all the ſciences, and every

branch of political and moral knowledge. The So-
lons, the Numas, the Lycurgufes ; all the Legiflators
of antiquity have in vain exhaufted their genius to
explain the relations of mankind in fociety, to declare
the duties and rights of every clafs, and every individual : Mahomet more able or more profound than
they, refolves all into five phrafes. It certainly may
be fafely afferted, of all the men who have ever dared
to give laws to nations, none was more ignorant
than Mahomet ; of all the abfurd compofitions ever
produced, none is more truly wretched than his book.
Of this, the tranfactions of the laft twelve hundred
years in Afia, are a proof ; for where I inclined to
pafs from a particular fubject to general confiderations,
it would be eafy to demonftrate, that the convulfions
of the governments, and the ignorance of the people,
in that quarter of the globe, originate more or lefs
immediately in the Koran, and its morality ; but I
muft confine myfelf to the country we are now con-
fidering, and returning to Syria, explain to the reader, the ftate of its inhabitants, relative to religion.
    The people of Syria in general, as I have already
faid, are Mahometans or Chriftians : this difference
of worfhip is productive of the moft difagreeable
effects in their civil ftate.   Treating each other mutually as rebels, infidels, and impious, the followers of
Jefus Chrift and Mahomet, are actuated by a reciprocal averfion which keeps alive a fort of perpetual war.
We may readily conceive the exceffes to which the
prejudices of education may carry the vulgar, at all
times violent ; and the government fo far from inter-
pofing as a mediator in the diffenfions, foments them
by its partiality.   Faithful to the fpirit of the Koran,
it treats the Chriftians with a feverity, which difplays
itfelf in varied forms.   Mention has been fometimes
made of the toleration of the Turks ; the following
is the price at which it is purchafed :

All kind of public worſhip is prohibited the Chriſtians, except in the Kefraouan, where the government has not been able to prevent it. They cannot
build any new churches ; and if the old ones fall to
decay, they are not allowed to repair them, unleſs
by a permiſſion which coſts them very dear. A Chriſtian cannot ſtrike a Mahometan without riſk of his
life, but if a Mahometan kill a Chriſtian, he eſcapes
for a ſtipulated price. Chriſtians muſt not mount on
horſeback in the towns ; they are prohibited the uſe
of yellow ſlippers, white ſhalls, and every ſort of
green colour. Red for the feet, and blue for the
dreſs, are the colours aſſigned them. The Porte has
juſt renewed its ordinances to re-eſtabliſh the ancient
form of their turbans ; they muſt be of a courſe blue
muſlin, with a ſingle white border. When they travel, they are perpetually ſtopped at different places
to pay *Rafars**, or tolls, from which the Mahometans
are exempt : in judicial proceedings, the oath of two
Chriſtians is only reckoned for one ; and ſuch is the
partiality of the Cadis, that it is almoſt impoſſible
for a Chriſtian to gain a ſuit ; in ſhort, they alone are
ſubject to the Capitation, called *Karadji*, the ticket
of which bears theſe remarkable words : *Djazz-
elras* that is (redemption) *from cutting off the head ;*
a clear proof of the title by which they are tole-
rated and governed.

Theſe diſtinctions, ſo proper to ferment hatred and
diviſions, are diſſeminated among the people, and
manifeſt themſelves in all the intercourſe of life. The
meaneſt Mahometan will neither accept from a Chriſtian, nor return the ſalute of *Salam-alai-k* †, health
to thee, on account of the affinity between the word
Salam and *Eſlam*, (Iſlamiſm), the proper name of

---

* The R here is a guttural *r*.

† Or, *Salam-alai-Kom*, health to you. Hence the word
Salamalk.

their religion, and *Moſlem*, (Muſſulman) the name
of the perſon who profeſſes it : the uſual ſalutation is
only good morning, or good evening, and it is well
too if it be not accompanied with a *Djaour*, *Kafer*,
Kelb, i. e. impious, infidel, dog, expreſſions to which
the Chriſtians are familiarized. The Mahometans
even affect to mortify them, by practiſing before them
the ceremonies of their worſhip. At noon, at three
o'clock, and at ſun-ſet, as ſoon as the criers from
the tops of the minarets announce the time of prayer,
they appear at the doors of their houſes, where, after making their ablution, they, gravely ſpread a mat
or carpet, and turning themſelves towards Mecca,
croſs their arms upon their breaſts, ſtretch them towards their knees, and begin nine proſtrations, down
to the ground, reciting the preface to the Koran. In
converſation, they frequently make a break by their
profeſſion of faith, " There is but one God, and
" Mahomet is his prophet." They talk perpetually
of their religion, and conſider themſelves as the only
faithful to God. To confute them, the Chriſtians,
in their turn, affect great devotion ; and hence that
oſtentation of piety which forms one of the principal
characteriſtics of the Orientals ; but the heart makes
no ſacrifice, and the Chriſtians retain a deep remembrance of all theſe inſults, and only wait a favourable opportunity to ſeek their revenge. The effects of
this were viſible in the time of Daher, when, proud
of the protection of his miniſter, in many places
they aſſumed a ſuperiority over the Mahometans.
The exceſſes they committed on that occaſion ſhould
ſerve as a leſſon to any European power, which may
hereafter obtain poſſeſſion of countries inhabited by
Greeks and Mahometans.

CHAP. XVII.

Of property, ranks, and conditions.

THE Sultans having arrogated to themselves, by
right of conqueft, the property of all the lands of
Syria, the inhabitants can no longer pretend to any
real, or even perfonal property; they have nothing
but a temporary poffeffion.   When a father dies, the
inheritance reverts to the Sultan, or his delegate,
and the children can only redeem the fucceffion by a
confiderable fum of money.   Hence arifes an indifference to landed eftates, which proves fatal to agriculture.   In the towns, the poffeffion of houfes is in
fome meafure lefs uncertain and lefs ruinous; but
every where the preference is given to property in money, as more eafy to hide from the rapine of the
Defpot.   In the tributary countries, fuch as thofe of
the Druzes, the Maronites, Hefbeya, &c. there
exifts a real property founded on cuftoms, which
their petty princes dare net violate; on which account the inhabitants are fo attached to their eftates,
that it is very rare to hear of an alienation of lands
among them.   There is neverthelefs one method,
even under the Turkifh adminiftration, of fecuring a
perpetual *ufus-fructus*, which is by making what is
called a *Wakf*, that is an endowment or donation of
an eftate to a Mofque.   The proprietor than becomes
the irremoveable guardian of his property, on condition of a fine, and under the protection of the profeffors of the law; but this act has this inconvenience,
that, inftead of protecting, the men of the law frequently devour the property: and, in that cafe, to whom
are they to look for redrefs, fince the embezzlers of
the property are at the fame time the diftributers of
juftice?   For this reafon, thefe lawyers are almoft the

only landholders, nor do we fee, under the Turkifh government, that multitude of fmall proprietors, who conftitute the ftrength and riches of the tributary countries.

What I have faid of conditions in Egypt will apply equally to Syria : 'they may be reduced to four or five ; the cultivators or peafants, artifans, merchants, military men, and thofe who fill the different departments of the law and juridical offices. Thefe various claffes again may be comprehended under two others : the people, which includes the peafants, artifans and merchants ; and the government, compofed of the military, and legal and judicial officers. According to the principles of their religion, the power fhould refide in the latter order ; but fince the difpoffeffion of the Caliphs by their lieutenants, a diftinction has taken place between the fpiritual and temporal power, which has left but an illufory authoriry to the interpreters of the law : fuch is that of the Grand Mufti*, who reprefents the Caliph, among the Turks. The real power is in the hands of the Sultan, who reprefents the lieutenant or general of the army. That favourable prejudice, however, which the people entertain for dethroned powers, ftill preferves to the profeffors of the law, a credit of which they almoft always avail themfelves, to' form a *party of oppofition ;* the Sultan is awed by it at Conftantinople, nor do the Pachas venture' too openly to thwart it in their provinces. In each city this party is headed by the Mufti, who derives his authority from that of Conftantinople, his employment is hereditary and not venal, which fingle circumftance has preferved more energy in this body than in all the others. From the priviliges they enjoy, the families which compofe it bear a confiderable refemblance to

* This term fignifies *decider* of the cafes which concern religion.

our nobility, although its true type be the army. They resemble also our magistracy, our clergy, and even our citizens, as they are the only persons in that country who live on their rents. From them to the peasantry, the artisans, and traders, the descent is sudden, yet, as the condition of these three classes form the true standard of the police and power of an empire, I shall select the particulars best calculated to enable the reader to form just ideas.

***

CHAP. XVIII.

State of the Peasants and of Agriculture.

IN Syria, and even throughout the Turkish empire, the peasants, like the other inhabitants, are deemed *slaves* of the Sultan; but this term only conveys the meaning of our word *subjects*. Though master of their lives and properties, the Sultan does not sell men; he does not limit them to a certain spot. If he bestows an appanage on some grandee, it is not said, as in Russia and poland, that he gives five hundred or a thousand peasants; in a word, the peasants are oppressed by the tyranny of the government, but not degraded by the servitude of feodality.

When Sultan Selim had conquered Syria, in order to render the collection of the revenue more easy, he established a single territorial tribute called the *miri*. It should seem, that this Sultan, notwithstanding the ferocity of his character, understood the importance of favouring the husbandman, for the miri, compared with the extent of the lands, is an infinitely moderate impost; and it was the more so at the time in which it was fixed, as Syria was then better peopled than at present, and perhaps also possessed a greater trade,

as it lay on the moſt frequented route to India, little
uſe having been yet made of the paſſage by the Cape of
Good Hope.   That this tax might be collected regu-
larly, Selim, gave orders to prepare a *deſtar*, or regiſ-
ter, in which the contingent of each village ſhould be
ſet down.   In ſhort, he eſtabliſhed the miri, at an invariable rate, and ordered it ſhould neither be augmented
nor diminiſhed.   Moderate as it was in its original
eſtabliſhment, it could never be oppreſſive to the people ; but by abuſes inherent in the conſtitution of the
Turkiſh government, the Pachas and their agents have
found the ſecret of rendering it ruinous.   Not daring
to violate the law eſtabliſhed by the Sultan reſpecting
the immutability of the impoſt, they have introduced a
multitude of changes, which, without the name, produce all the effects of an augmentation.   Thus, having
the greateſt part of the land at their diſpoſal, they clog
their conceſſions with burthenſome conditions ; they
exact the half, nay even two thirds, of the crop ; they
monopolize the ſeed and the cattle, ſo that the cultivators are under the neceſſity of purchaſing from them at
their own price.   The harveſt over, they caval about
loſſes, and pretended robberies, and as they have the
power in their hands, they carry off what they think
proper.   If the ſeaſon fails, they ſtill exact the ſame
ſum, and to pay themſelves, expoſe every thing the
poor peaſant poſſeſſes to ſale.   Happily, his perſon at
leaſt remains free, for the Turks are ignorant of the re-
finement of impriſoning for debt the man who has no
longer any property.   To theſe conſtant oppreſſions
are added a thouſand accidental extorſions.   Sometimes the whole village is laid under contribution for
ſome real or imaginary offence ; and ſometimes a ſervice of a new kind is introduced.   A preſent is exacted
on the acceſſion of each governor ; a contribution of
grafs is demanded for his horſes, and barley and ſtraw
for his cavaliers : they muſt provide, likewiſe, for all

the foldiers who pafs, or who carry orders, and the governors take care to multiply thefe commiffions which are a faving to them, but inevitable ruin to the peafants. The villages tremble at every *Lawend* who appears ; he is a real robber under the name of a foldier ; he enters as a conqueror, and commands as a mafter : *Dogs, Rabble ; bread, coffee, tobacco ; I muft have barley, I muft have meat.* If he cafts his eyes on any poultry, he kills them ; and when he takes his departure, adding infult to tyranny, he demands what is called *kera-el-dars*, the hire of his grinders. In vain do the peafants exclaim againft this injuftice ; the fabre impofes filence. Juftice is remote and difficult of accefs ; nay, complaints are even dangerous. What is the confequence of all thefe depredations ? The poorer clafs of inhabitants ruined, and unable any longer to pay the miri, become a burthen to the village, or fly into the cities : but the miri is unalterable and the fum to be levied muft be found fomewhere, their portion falls on the remaining inhabitants, whofe burthen, though at firft light, now becomes infupportable. If they are vifited by a two years drought and famine, the whole village is ruined and abandoned ; but the tax it fhould have paid is levied on the neighbouring lands. They proceed in the fame manner with the *Karadji* of the Chriftians. Its amount having been eftimated at the time they were firft numbered, it muft always produce the fame, though thofe who pay fhould be lefs numerous. Hence it happens that this capitation is fometimes carried from three, five, and eleven piaftres, at which it was firft fixed, to thirty-five and forty ; which abfolutely impoverifhes thofe on whom it is raifed, and obliges them to leave the country. Thefe burthens are more efpecially oppreffive in the countries beftowed as an appanage, and in thofe which are expofed to the Arabs. In the former the Titulary, greedy to augment his revenue, delegates full power to his Leffee to augment the taxes, and he is well feconded by the avidity of the fubalterns. Thefe men, refining on the arts of wringing money from the people, have contrived to impofe duties on every commodity brought to market, on entries, the conveyance of goods, and even the burthen of an afs. It is remarked that thefe exactions have made a rapid progrefs, efpecially in the laft forty years, from which time they date the decline of agriculture, the depopulation of the country, and the diminution in the quantity of fpecie carried to Conftantinople. With refpect to the Bedouins, if they are at war they pillage as enemies ; and if at peace, devour every thing they can find as guefts ; hence the proverb, *Avoid the Bedouin whether friend or enemy.* The leaft wretched of the peafants, are thofe of the countries which raife themfelves a certain ftipulated fum, as is done by the Druzes, the Kefraouan, Nablous &c. yet even there they are liable to be oppreffed and impoverifhed by various abufes. But nothing is more deftructive to Syria, than the fhameful and exceffive ufury cuftomary in that country. When the peafants are in want of money to purchafe grain, cattle, &c. they can find none but by mortgaging the whole or part of the future crop greatly under its value. The danger of letting money appear, clofes the hands of all by whom it is poffeffed ; and if it is parted with it muft be from the hope of a rapid and exorbitant gain ; the moft moderate intereft is twelve per cent. the ufual rate is twenty, and it frequently rifes as high even as thirty.

From all thefe caufes we may eafily conceive how miferable muft be the condition of the peafants. They are every where reduced to a little flat cake of barley or dourra, to onions, lentils, and water. They are fo little acquainted with dainties, that they efteem ftrong oil, and rancid fat as delicacies. Not to lofe any part of their corn, they leave in it all forts of wild grain, even tares*, which occafions vertigoes, and dimnefs of

* In Arabic *Ziwan.*

fight for feveral hours, as I have myfelf experienced.
In the mountains of Lebanon and Nablous, in time of
dearth, they gather the acorns from the oaks, which
they eat, after boiling or roafting them on the afhes.
The truth of this has been authenticated to me among
the Druzes, by perfons who have themfelves made ufe
of them. We muft therefore no longer accufe the po-
ets of hyperbole ; but it will only be the more difficult
to believe that the golden age was the age of abundance.

By a natural confequence of this mifery, the art of
cultivation is in the moft deplorable ftate ; the hufbandman is deftitute of inftruments, or has very bad
ones ; his plough is frequently no more than the branch
of a tree, cut below a bifurcation, and ufed without
wheels. The ground is tilled by affes, and cows, rarely
by oxen ; they would befpeak too much riches ; beef
is therefore very fcarce in Syria and Egypt, where,
befides, it is always lean and bad, like all the meat of
hot countries. In the diftricts expofed to the Arabs,
as in Paleftine, the countryman muft fow with his
mufket in his hand. Scarcely does the corn turn yellow, before it is reaped, and concealed in *Matmoures*,
or fubterraneous caverns. As little as poffible is employed for feed corn, becaufe they fow no more than is
barely neceffary for fubfiftence ; in a word, their whole
induftry is limited to a fupply of their immediate
wants ; and to procure a little bread, a few onions, a
wretched blue fhirt, and a bit of woolen, much labour
is not neceffary. The peafant lives therefore in dif-
trefs ; but at leaft he does not enrich his tyrants, and
the avarice of defpotifm is its own punifhment.

C H A P. XIX.

Of the Artifans, Traders, and Commerce.

THE clafs of men who give value to commodities, by manufacturing them, or bringing them into circulation, is not fo ill treated in Syria, as that which produces them ; the reafon of which is, that the property of the artifans and traders confifting in perfonal effects, is more concealed from the fcrutinizing eye of government than that of the peafants ; befides which, the artifts and merchants, collected in the towns, efcape more eafily, in the crowd, from the rapacity of their rulers. This is one of the principal caufes of the populoufnefs of the towns in Syria, and even throughout Turkey. While in other countries, the cities are in fome meafure the overflow of the country, there they are the effect of its defertion. The peafants, expelled from their villages, fly thither for refuge, and find in them tranquillity and even a degree of eafe and plenty. The Pachas are more particularly attentive to this laft article, as on it depends their perfonal fafety ; for befides the immediate effects of a fedition, which might be fatal to them, the Porte would not pardon them for endangering the fafety of the empire, for want of fupplying the people with bread. They take care therefore to keep provifions cheap in all the confiderable towns, and efpecially in that which they refide : if there be a dearth, it is always leaft felt there. In cafe of a failure in the harveft, they prohibit the exportation of grain, and oblige every perfon who poffeffes any, to fell it at the price they fix under pain of death ; and if there be none in the province, they fend for it to other countries, as was the cafe at Damafcus in November 1784. The Pacha placed guards on all the roads, permitted the Arabs to pillage every carriage going out of the country, and sent orders into the Hauran, to empty all the *Matmoures*, so that while the peasants where dying with hunger in the villages, the people of Damascus paid for their bread but two paras, or two sols and a half, (one penny farthing), the French pound, and thought it dear even at that price ; but as in the political machine no part is independent of the rest, it was not possible to give such a mortal wound to agriculture, without its being felt by the arts and commerce. The reader will judge from a few details, whether the government be not as negligent in this as in every other particular.

Commerce in Syria, considered as to the manner in which it is carried on, is still in that state of infancy which characterizes barbarous ages and uncivilized countries. Along the whole coast there is not a harbour capable of admitting a vessel of four hundred tons, nor are the roads secured by forts. The Maltese corsairs formerly availed themselves of this want of vigilence, to make prizes close in with the shore ; but as the inhabitants made the European merchants responsible for such accidents, France has obtained from the Order of Malta a prohibition of their corsairs from their appearing within fight of land ; so that the natives may peaceably carry on their coasting trade, which is tolerably brisk, from Latakia to Yafa. In the interior parts of the country, there are neither great roads nor canals, nor even bridges over the greatest part of the rivers and torents, however necessary they may be in winter. Between town and town, there are neither posts nor public conveyance. The only conveyance of this kind is the *Tartar* courier, who comes from Constantinople to Damascus, by way of Aleppo. This courier has no relays but in large towns, at very great distances ; but in case of need he may dismount the very first horseman he meets. He leads with him, according to the custom of the Tartars, a second horse in hand, and has frequently a companion for fear of accidents.

The communication between one town and another is maintained by carriers, who have no fixed time of departure. This arifes from the abfolute neceffity of forming troops, or caravans; nobody travels alone, from the infecurity of the roads. One muft wait for feveral travellers who are going to the fame place, or take advantage of the paffage of fome great man, who affumes the office of protector, but is more frequently the oppreffor of the caravan. Thefe precautions are, above all, neceffary in the countries expofed to the Arabs, fuch as Paleftine, and the whole frontier of the defert, and even on the road from Aleppo to Skandaroon, on account of the Curd robbers. In the mountains, and on the coaft, between Latakia and Carmel, we may travel with more fafety; but the roads in the mountains are extremely bad, as the inhabitants are fo far from levelling them, they endeavour to render them more rugged, in order as they fay, to cure the Turks of their defire to introduce their cavalry.

It is remarkable, that we never fee either a waggon or a cart in all Syria; which arifes, no doubt, from the apprehenfion of having them feized by the minions of government, and fuffering a great lofs at one ftroke. Every thing is conveyed on the backs of mules, affes, or camels: all which animals are excellent here. The two former are employed in the mountains, and nothing can equal their addrefs in climbing and fliding over the flopes of the craggy rocks. The camel is more made ufe of in the plains, becaufe he confumes lefs, and carries more. His ufual burthen is about feven hundred and fifty pounds. His food is every thing you chufe to give him; ftraw, brambles, pounded dates; beans, barley, &c. With a fingle pound of food, and as much water in a day, he will travel for weeks together. In the whole way from Cairo to Suez, which is a journey of forty or forty-fix hours, including the time of repofe, they neither eat nor drink; but thefe faftings, repeated, exhauft them as well as other animals. Their breath then becomes fœtid. Their ordinary pace is very flow, not exceeding thirty-four or thirty-fix hundred yards an hour. It is needlefs to prefs them, they go no quicker; but by allowing them to reft, they will travel from fifteen to eighteen hours a day.

There are no inns any where; but the cities, and commonly the villages, have a large building called a *Kan, or Kervan-ferai*, which ferves as an afylum for all travellers. Thefe houfes of reception are always built without the precincts of the towns, and confift of four wings round a fquare court, which ferves by way of inclofure for the beafts of burden. The lodgings are cells, where you find nothing but bare walls, duft, and fometimes fcorpions. The keeper of this Kan gives the traveller the key and a mat; and he provides himfelf the reft. He muft, therefore, carry with him his bed, his kitchen utenfils, and even his provifions; for frequently not even bread is to be found in the villages. On this account the Orientals contrive their equipage in the moft fimple and portable form. The baggage of a man who wifhes to be completely provided, confifts in a carpet, a matrefs, a blanket, two faucepans with lids, contained within each other; two difhes, two plates, and a coffee-pot, all of copper, well-tinned; a fmall wooden box for falt and pepper; fix coffee cups, without handles, in a leathern box; a round leathern table, which he fufpends from the faddle of his horfe; fmall leathern pouches, or bags for oil, melted butter, water and brandy, (if the traveller be a Chriftian) a pipe, a tinder-box, a cup of cocoa-nut, fome rice, dried raifins dates, Cyprus cheefe, and above all, coffee-berries, with a roafter, and wooden mortar to pound them. I am thus particular to prove, that the Orientals are more advanced than we, in the art of difpenfing with many things; an art which is not without its merit.

Our European merchants are not contented with such simple accommodations. Their journeys, therefore, are very expensive, and consequently not frequent; but even the richest natives of the country make no difficulty in passing part of their lives in the manner I have described, on the roads of Bagdad, Baffora, Cairo, and even of Constantinople. Travelling is their education, their science; and to say of any man he is a merchant, is to pronounce him a traveller. They find in it the advantage of purchasing their goods at the first hand, procuring them at a cheaper rate, enfuring their safety by escorting them themselves; preventing many accidents, and obtaining some abatement of the numerous tolls. They learn, in short, to understand weights and measures, the extreme diversity of which renders their's a very complicated profession. Each town has its particular weight, which under the same denomination, differs from that of another. The *Rotle* of Aleppo weighs about six pounds, Paris weight; that of Damascus five and one quarter; that of Saide less than five; that of Ramla near seven. The *Derhem* alone, that is the drachm, which is the first element of these weights, is the same every where. The long measures vary less: only two are known, the Egyptian cubit *(Draa Masri)*, and the cubit of Constantinople *(Draa Stambouli.)*

Coin is still more fixed; and you may travel over the whole empire from Kotchim to Afouan, without experiencing any change in its denomination or its value. The most simple of these coins is the *Para*, called also a *Medin*, a *Fadda*, a *Kata*, or a *Mesria*. It is of the size of an English silver three-pence, and is only worth five liards (a little above a halfpenny). After the para, follow successively pieces of five, ten, and twenty paras; then the *Zolata*, or *Iflote*, which is worth thirty; the *Piastre*, called *Kersh-afadi*, or Pi-

aftre of the Lion, worth forty paras, or fifty French
fols (two fhillings and a penny); and, is moft generally ufed in commerce; and, laftly, the *Abou-Kelb*,
or Piaftre of the Dog, which is worth fixty paras.
All thefe coins are filver, but with fuch a mixture of
copper alloy, that the abou-kelb is as large as a crown
of fix livres, though its value be only four livres five
fols (three and fixpence halfpenny). They bear no
image, becaufe of the prohibition of the Prophet, but
only the cypher of the Sultan on one fide, and on
the other thefe words: *Sultan of the two Continents,*
Kahan*, (i. e.* Lord) *of the two Seas, the Sultan, Son*
of the Sultan N. ftruck at Stamboul (Conftantinople),
or at *Mafr* (Cairo); which are the only two cities
where there is a mint.

The gold coins are the fequin, called *Dahab*, or
piece of gold; and alfo *Zahr-Mahaboub*, or Well-be-
loved Flower. It is worth three piafters of forty
paras, or feven livres ten fols (fix fhillings and three
pence); the half fequin is only worth fixty paras.
There is likewife a fequin, called *Fondoucli*, which is
worth one hundred and feventy paras: but it is very
rare. Befides thefe coins, which are thofe of the
whole Turkifh empire, fome of the European fpecie
has as much currency; fuch are the filver dahlers of
Germany, and the gold fequins of Venice. The dollars are worth in Syria from ninety to ninety-two
paras, and the fequins from two hundred and five, to
two hundred and eight. Thefe two coins are worth
from eight to ten paras more in Egypt. The Venetian fequins are in great requeft from the finenefs of
their ftandard, and the practice they have of employ-
ing them for womens trinkets. The fafhion of thefe
trinkets does not require much art; the piece of gold
is fimply pierced, in order to fufpend it by a chain
likewife of gold, which flows upon the breaft. The

---

* *Kahan* is a Tartarian word.

more fequins there are attached to this chain, and the greater the number of thefe chains, the more is a woman thought to be ornamented. This is the favourite luxury, and the emulation of all ranks. Even the female peafants, for want of gold, wear piafters or fmaller pieces; but the women of a certain rank difdain filver; they will except of nothing but fequins of Venice, or large Spanifh pieces, and crufadoes. Some of them wear two or three hundred, as well lying flat, as ftrung one on another, and hung near the forehead, at the edge of the head-drefs. It is a real load: but they do not think they can pay too dearly for the fatisfaction of exhibiting this treafure at the public bath, before a crowd of rivals, to awaken whofe jealoufy conftitutes their chief pleafure. The effect of this luxury on commerce, is the withdrawing confiderable fums from circulation, which remain dead; befides, that when any of thefe pieces return into common ufe, having loft their weight by being pierced, it becomes neceffary to weigh them. The practice of weighing money is general in Syria, Egypt, and all Turkey. No piece, however defaced, is refufed there; the merchant draws out his fcales and weighs it, as in the days of Abraham, when he purchafed his fepulchre. In confiderable payments, an agent of exchange is fent for, who counts paras by thoufands, rejects a great many pieces of falfe money, and weighs all the fequins, either feparately or together.

Almoft the whole commerce of Syria is in the hands of the Franks, Greeks, and Armenians: formerly it was engroffed by the Jews. The Mahometans take little part in it; not that they are prevented from engaging in it by the prejudices of their religion, or by indolence, as fome political writers have imagined; but from the obftacles thrown in their way by their own government. The Porte, conftant to its ufual fyftem, inftead of giving a decided preference to the Turkifh subjects, finds it more lucrative to sell their rights and industry to foreigners. Some of the European states have, by treaties, obtained a diminution of custom-house duties to three *per. cent.* while the merchandise of the subjects of the Sultan pays strictly ten, or when favoured, seven *per. cent.* Besides this, the duties once paid in any port, the Frank is not liable to pay a second time in another. But the case is different with the Ottoman subject. The Franks, too, having found it convenient to employ Latin Christians as agents, have procured them a participation of their privileges, and they are no longer subject to the power of the Pachas, or amenable to Turkish justice. They cannot be plundered ; and whoever has a commercial process with them, must plead before the European consul. With such disadvantages, is it surprising that the Mahometans should relinquish commerce to their rivals ? These agents of the Franks are known in the Levant under the name of *Baratary Drogmans ;* that is, privileged Interpreters*. The *barat* or *privilege*, is a patent, of which the Sultan makes a present to the ambassadors residing at the Porte. Formerly these ambassadors, in their turn, made presents of them to particular persons in each factory ; but within the last twenty years they have been made to understand, it is more lucrative to sell them. The present price is from five to six thousand livres (two hundred or two hundred and fifty pounds). Each Ambassador has fifty, which are renewed on the death of the possessor, and form a pretty considerable perquisite.

France has the greatest trade to Syria of any European nation. Her imports consist in five principle articles ; 1st. The cloths of Languedoc. 2dly, Cochineal from Cadiz. 3dly, Indigos. 4thly, Sugars. And,

---

* An interpreter in Arabic is called *Terdjeman*, of which our old writers have made *Trachement*. In Egypt it is pronounced *Tergoman* ; of which the Venetians have made *Dragomano*, and the French converted into *Drogman*.

5thly, Weft-India coffee, which is in great requeſt with the Turks, and which they mix with that of Arabia, more eſteemed indeed, but too high priced. To theſe muſt be added hardware, caſt iron, ſheet lead, tin, Lyons laces, ſoap, &c.

The returns conſiſt almoſt wholly in cotton, either ſpun or raw, or manufactured into coarſe ſtuffs ; in ſome ſilks of Tripoli, the others being prohibited ; in gall nuts, in copper and wool, which come from countries out of Syria. The factories, or as we call them, *Echelles**, of the French, are ſeven in number, i. e. Aleppo, Skandaroon, Latakia, Tripoli, Saide, Acre, and Ramla. The ſum of their imports amounts to 6,000,000 of livres (250,000*l.*) viz.

For Aleppo and Skandaroon,   3,000,000
    Saide and Acre,   -   -   2,000,000
    Tripoli and Catagie,   -   -   400,000
    Ramla,   -   -   -   -   600,000

                Total,   6,000,000

All this commerce paſſes through the ſingle channel of Marſeilles, which poſſeſſes the excluſive privilege of ſending ſhips to, and receiving them from, the Levant, notwithſtanding the remonſtrances of the Province of Languedoc, which furniſhes the principal commodities. Strangers, that is, the natives of Turkey, are prohibited from carrying on their commerce, except through the medium of the Marſeilles factors, eſtabliſhed in their country. This prohibition was aboliſhed in 1777, for ſeveral reaſons ſet forth in the ordinance; but the merchants of Marſeilles made ſuch repreſentations, that, ſince the month of April, 1785,

---

* This whimſical name of *Echelles* (in Engliſh *ladders*) was adopted by the inhabitants of Provence, from the Italian *ſcala*, a corruption of the Arabic word *kalla*, which ſignifies a place proper to receive veſſels, a road, a harbour. At preſent the natives ſay, as the Italians, *ſcala, rada.*

matters have again been placed upon their former footing. It is for France to determine how far this trade is to her intereſt. Conſidered relative to the Turkiſh empire, it may be ſaid, that the commerce of the Turks with Europe and India, is more detrimental than advantageous. For the articles exported being all raw unwrought materials, the empire deprives itſelf of all the advantages to be derived from the labour of its own ſubjects. On the other hand, the commodities imported from Europe and India, being articles of pure luxury, only ſerve to increaſe the diſſipation of the rich, and the ſervants of government, whilſt, perhaps, they aggravate the wretched condition of the people, and the claſs of cultivators. Under a government which pays no reſpect to property, the deſire of multiplying enjoyments, cannot but irritate cupidity, and increaſe oppreſſion. In order to procure more clothes, furs, laces, ſugars, ſhawls, and India goods; there muſt be more money, cotton, and ſilks, and more extortions. A momentary advantage may have accrued to the ſtates which furniſh theſe objects of luxury; but are not the advantages of the preſent moment borrowed from the wealth of future times? And can we hope long to carry on an advantageous commerce with the country which is precipitately haſtening to ruin?

CHAP. XX.

Of the Arts, Sciences, and Ignorance of the People.

THE arts and trades in Syria afford room for many conſiderations. Firſt, The different kinds of them are infinitely leſs numerous than with us; we can ſcarcely reckon twenty, even including the moſt neceſſary. In

the firſt place, the religion of Mahomet having pro-
ſcribed every ſort of image and figure, there exiſts
neither painting, nor ſculpture, nor engraving, nor
any of thoſe numerous profeſſions which depend on
them. The Chriſtians alone purchaſe, for the uſe of
their churches, ſome pictures of the Greeks at Conſtantinople, who in point of taſte, are real Turks. In
the ſecond place, a multitude of our trades are rendered unneceſſary, from the ſmall quantity of furniture uſed by the Orientals. The whole inventory of
a wealthy famility conſiſts in a carpet for the feet, in
mats, cuſhions, matraſſes, ſome ſmall cotton cloths,
copper and wooden platters for the table, a few ſtew-
ing pans, a mortar, a portable mill, a little porcelain,
and ſome plates of copper tinned. All our apparatus
of tapeſtry, wooden bedſteads, chairs, ſtools, glaſſes,
deſks, bureaus, cloſets ; our buffets with their plate,
and table ſervices ; in a word, all our cabinet and
upholſtery work, are luxuries totally unknown to them,
ſo that nothing is ſo ſimple as a Turkiſh removal. Pococke is of opinion that theſe cuſtoms originate in the
wandering life formerly led by the anceſtors of theſe
nations ; but they have had ſufficient time to forget
this ſince they have become ſettled ; and we ſhould
rather ſearch for the cauſe of it in the nature of their government, which reduces every thing to what is ſtrict-
ly neceſſary. Their clothing is not more complicated,
though much more expenſive. They are ſtrangers
to the hats, perukes, hair-dreſſing, buttons, buckles,
ſtocks, laced ruffles, and all that ſuperfluity with
which we are ſurrounded. Cotton or ſilk ſhirts,
which even the Pachas, do not count by dozens, and
which have neither ruffles nor wriſtbands, nor plaited
collars ; an enormous pair of breeches, which ſerve
alſo by way of ſtockings ; a handkerchief on the head ;
another round the waiſt, with the three large folds of
cloth and callico I have mentioned in deſcribing the
dreſs of the Mamlouks, compoſe the whole wardrobe

of the Orientals. Their only articles of luxury are goldfmith's work, which is confined to women's trinkets, faucers for coffee wrought like lace, the ornaments of their harnefs, their pipes, and the filk ftuffs of Aleppo and Damafcus. In paffing through the ftreets of the towns, you meet with nothing but a number of beaters of cotton on tenters, retailers of ftuffs and mercery, barbers to fhave the head, tinners, lockfmiths, fadlers, and efpecially fellers of little loaves, hardware, grain, dates, and fweet-meats, but very few butchers, and thefe ill fupplied. There are alfo in the great towns a few wretched gun-fmiths, who can only repair fire-arms, for not one of them can caft a piftol barrel; as for gun-powder, the frequent occafion they have to make ufe of it, has excited the induftry of the peafants in general to make it, but there is no public manufactory.

In the villages, the inhabitants, limited to mere neceffaries, have no arts but thofe without which they cannot fubfift; every one endeavours to fupply his own wants, that he may not be obliged to fhare what he has with others. Each family manufactures the coarfe cottons with which they are cloathed. Every houfe has its portable mill, with which the women grind the barley or the Dourra for their fuftenance. The flour from thefe mills is coarfe, and the little round loaves made of it, ill leavened and badly baked ; but they preferve life, and that is all which is required. I have already obferved how fimple and cheap their inftruments of hufbandry are. In the mountains they do not prune the vines, and they no where ingraft trees ; every thing, in fhort, reminds us of the fimplicity of ancient times, which, poffibly, as at this day, was only the ignorance of poverty. When we enquire the reafon of their want of induftry, the anfwer is uniformly the fame : " It is good enough ; " That is fufficient : What end would it anfwer to do " more ?" They are in the right, fince they would not be permitted to reap the benefit of their labours.

Secondly; The ftate of the arts in thefe countries,
and the manner in which they are exercifed, are interefting, as they preferve, almoft in every refpeft,
the difcoveries and methods of ancient times. For
example, the ftuffs manufaftured at Aleppo are not of
Arabian invention; this art is borrowed from the
Greeks, who themfelves, doubtlefs, imitated the ancient Orientals. The dyes they ufe are, probably, as
old as the time of the Tyrians, and they carry them at
this day to a perfeftion not unworthy of that people;
but the workmen, jealous of their art, make an impenetrable myftery of the the procefs. The manner in
which the ancients fecured the harnefs of their horfes
againft the ftrokes of the fabre, was undoubtedly the
fame which is now made ufe of at Aleppo and Damafcus, for the head ftalls of their bridles*. The fmall
filver plates with which the leather is lined, hold together without nails, and are fo jointed, that without de-
priving the leather of its pliancy, there remains no in-
terftice for the edge of the weapon.

The cement they make ufe of, is no doubt that of
the Greeks and Romans. To make it properly, they
take care only to ufe the lime when boiling : they mix
with it one third of fand, and another of afhes and
pounded brick-duft. With this compofition they form
wells, cifterns, and vaults, which the water cannot
pafs through. I have feen a fingular fpecies of the
latter in Paleftine that deferves to be defcribed. The
vault is built with cylinders of brick, eight or ten inches long. Thefe cylinders are hollow, and may be
about two inches diameter within. They are in a

* On this fubjeft, I fhall obferve, that the Mamlouks of
Cairo exhibit every year at the proceffions of the Caravan, coats
of mail, helmets, and vizors, braffets, and all the armour of the
time of the Croifades. There is alfo a colleftion of old arms in
the mofque of the Dervifes, a league above Cairo, on the banks
of the Nile.

flight degree tapering, the wideft end is clofed, the other open. To form the roof, they are ranged by the fide of each other, with the clofe end expofed to the weather : they are faftened with plaifter of Jerufalem or Nablous, and four workmen can complete the roof of a chamber in a day. The firft rains ufually penetrate it ; but a coat of oil is then laid over it, which effectually keeps the water out. The cracks withinfide are clofed by a layer of plaifter, and the whole forms a durable and very light roof. With thefe cylinders they build the walls at the edges of the terraces on the houfe tops, throughout Syria, to pre‐vent the women, who wafh and dry their linen there, from being feen. The ufe of them has been lately in‐troduced at Paris ; but the invention is of great anti‐quity in the eaft.

We may affirm the fame of the manner of working the iron mines in Lebanon, on account of its great fimplicity. It is the method now employed in the Pyrenees, and known under the name of the *Catalonian Forge.* The furnace confifts in a fort of chimney form‐ed in the fide of a fteep declivity. The funnel is filled with wood ; which is fet fire to. The bellows is applied to the inferior mouth, and the iron ore poured in from above ; the metal falls to the bottom, and is taken out by the fame mouth at which the fire is lighted. Even their ingenious wooden fliding locks may be traced back to the time of Solomon, who mentions them in his fong.

To their mufic we muft not afcribe fo high an an‐tiquity. It does not appear to have an earlier origin than the age of the Califs, under whom the Arabs applied themfelves to it with more ardour, as all the learned men of that day added the title of Mufician, to that of Phyfician, Geometrician, and Aftronomer ; yet, as its principles were borrowed from the Greeks, it might afford matter of curious obfervation to adepts in that fcience. Such perfons are very rarely to be met with in the eaſt. Cairo is perhaps the only place in Egypt or in Syria, where there are a few Shaiks who underſtand the principles of the art. They have collections of airs which are not noted in our manner, but written in characters, all the names of which are Perſian. They have no muſic but vocal; for they neither know nor eſteem inſtrumental, and they are in the right; for ſuch inſtruments as they have, not excepting their flutes, are deteſtable. They are ſtrangers likewiſe to any other accompaniment than the uniſon, and the continued baſe of the Monochord. They are fond of ſinging with a forced voice in the high tones, and one muſt have lungs like theirs to ſupport the effort for a quarter of an hour. Their airs, in point of character and execution, reſemble nothing we have heard in Europe, except the Seguidillas of the Spaniards. They have diviſions more laboured even than thoſe of the Italians, and cadences and inflexions of tones impoſſible to be imitated by European throats. Their performance is accompanied with ſighs and geſtures, which paint the paſſions in a more lively manner than we ſhould venture to allow. They may be ſaid to excel moſt in the melancholy ſtrain. To behold an Arab with his head inclined, his hand applied to his ear, his eyebrows knit, his eyes languiſhing; to hear his plaintive tones, his lengthened notes, his ſighs and ſobs, it is almoſt impoſſible to refrain from tears, which, as their expreſſion is, are far from bitter: and indeed they muſt certainly find a pleaſure in ſhedding them, ſince among all their ſongs, they conſtantly prefer that which excites them moſt, as among all accompliſhments ſinging is that they moſt admire.

Dancing, which with us holds an equal rank with muſic, is far from being held in the ſame eſtimation by the Arabs. This art, among them, is branded with all kind of ſhame; a man cannot practiſe it with-

out difhonour,* and the exercife of it is only permitted
to women.   This judgment will appear to us fevere,
but before we condemn it, it muft be confidered, that
in the eaftern world, dancing is not an imitation of war,
as among the Greeks, nor a combination of graceful
attitudes and movements, as with us ; but a licentious
imitation of the utmoft wantonnefs of love.   This is
the fpecies of dance which, brought from Carthage
to Rome, announced the decline of her republican
manners, and which, fince arrived in Spain by the
Arabs, ftill fubfifts there under the title of the *Fan-
dango*.   Notwithftanding the freedom of our manners, it would be difficult, without wounding the ear,
accurately to defcribe it ; it will be fufficient to fay
that the female dancer, with her arms extended, and
an empaffioned air, finging and accompanying her
fong with caftanets, which fhe holds between her
fingers, executes without changing her place, all thofe
motions of the body which paffion itfelf carefully conceals under the veil of night.   Such is their licentiouf-
nefs, that none but proftitutes venture to dance in
public.   Thofe who make a profeffion of it are called
Rawazi, and thofe who excel, affume the name of
Alma, or proficients in the art.   The moft celebrated
are thofe of Cairo.   A late traveller, (M. Savary,)
has drawn a flattering picture of them ; but I confefs
the originals did not produce the fame enthufiafm in
me.   With their yellow linnen, their tawny fkins,
their naked pendent breafts, their blackened eye-
lafhes, their blue lips, and their hands ftained with
henna, thefe Alma only reminded me of the *Bacchantes* of the *Porcherons†* ; and if we reflect that, even

---

* The facred dance of the Dervifes, the motions of which
are fuppofed to imitate the revolutions of the ftars, muft be
excepted.

† Wine-houfes without Paris, and free from the city duties ;
the refort of the populace—the idea might, perhaps, be better
conveyed by the term *Bacchantes of Billingfgate*.

among the moſt poliſhed nations, this claſs of women
retain not a little vulgarity, it is not credible, that
among a people, where the moſt ſimple arts are ſtill
in a ſtate of barbariſm, they can ſhew much refine-
ment and delicacy in one which requires the moſt.

The intimate connection between the arts and ſciences, leaves no room to doubt that the latter are ſtill
more neglected, or to confeſs the truth, totally unknown. The barbariſm of Syria, as well as that of
Egypt, is complete ; and, from the ſimilarity which
is uſually found in the different provinces of the ſame
empire, we may form the like judgment of all the countries under the dominion of the Turks. In vain have
ſome perſons denied this aſſertion ; in vain do they
talk of *colleges, places of education, and books* : theſe
words in Turkey convey not the ſame ideas as with
us. The age of the Califs is paſt among the Arabs,
and yet to begin among the Turks. Theſe two nations have at preſent neither geometricians, aſtronomers, muſicians, nor phyſicians. Scarcely can we
meet with one of the latter who knows how to bleed
with a fleam ; when they have ordered a cautery, applied fire, or preſcribed ſome common recipe, their
knowledge is exhauſted : and conſequently the valet
de chambre of an European is conſulted as an Eſcula-
pius ; where indeed ſhould phyſicians be formed,
ſince there are no eſtabliſhments of the kind, and
anatomy is directly repugnant to the prejudices of
their religion ? Aſtronomy might gain more admirers,
but by aſtronomy they underſtand only the art of diſ-
covering the decrees of fate by the motions of the
ſtars, and not the profound ſcience of calculating
their revolutions. The monks of Mar-Hanna, who
are poſſeſſed of books, and maintained a correſpon-
dence with Rome, are not leſs ignorant than the reſt.
Never, before my arrival among them, had they
heard that the earth turned round the ſun, and this
opinion was very near giving great offence to the bro-

therhood; for the zealots, finding that it contradicted the Holy Bible, were inclined to treat me as a he-
retic: fortunately the Vicar General had good fenfe
enough to doubt, and to fay : " Without blindly cre-
" diting the Franks, we muft not too haftily deny all
" they affert ; for every thing they bring us, the pro-
" duce of their arts, is fo infinitely fuperior to our
" own, that they may poffibly difcover things which
" are beyond our ideas." I efcaped by not taking the
blame of this novel hypothefis on myfelf, but reftoring the difcovery to our modern philofophers, who
are efteemed by the monks at this day, as Vifionaries.

A great difference than fhould be made between the
prefent Arabs, and thofe of the times of El-Mamoun,
and Aroun-el-Rafchid, and it muft be admitted that,
even of them, we have formed very extravagant ideas.
Their empire was too often deftroyed to fuffer them to
make any great progrefs in the fciences. What we
fee happen in our days in fome of the European ftates
proves that they require ages to become eftablifhed in
any country. And from what we know of the Arabian writers, do we not conftantly find them either the
tranflators or echoes of the Greeks ? The only fcience
which is peculiar to them, and the only one they continue to cultivate, is that of their own language ; but,
by the ftudy of language, we muft not underftand
that philofophical fpirit of refearch, which, in words,
inveftigates the hiftory of ideas, in order to perfect
the art by which they are communicated. Among the
Mahometans, the ftudy of the Arabic is only cultivated on account of its connection with religion; and
this is in fact very confined, for the Koran is " the immediate word of God :" but, as this word only retains
the identity of its nature, fo far as it correfponds with
the meaning of God and his prophet, it is a matter of
the greateft moment to learn, not only the exact fignification of the words employed, but, likewife, the
accents, inflexions, fighs and paufes, in fhort, all the

moſt minute niceties of profody and reading; and it
is impoſſible to form an idea how complicated all this
is without having heard their declaration in the Moſques.   As for the principles of the language, thofe of
the grammar alone take feveral years to acquire.
Next is taught the *Nahou*, a part of grammar which
may be defined, the fcience of terminations foreign to
the vulgar Arabic, which are fuperadded to words,
and vary according to the numbers, cafes, genders
and perfons.   When this is attained, the ſtudent is
reckoned among the learned.   Eloquence is next to
be ſtudied, and that requires whole years; for the
maſters, myſterious like the Brachmans, difcover the
fecrets of their art only by degrees.   At length, they
proceed to the ſtudy of the law and the *Fakah*, or
Science, *per excellentiam*, by which they mean theology.   Now, if we confider that the perpetual object of thefe ſtudies is always the Koran, and that it
is neceſſary thoroughly to be acquainted with all the
myſtical and allegorical fignifications afcribed to it,
and to read all the commentaries and paraphrafes upon it, of which there are two hundred volumes on
the firſt verfe; if we reflect that it is requifite to difpute on thoufands of ridiculous cafes of confcience;
fuch as, if it be allowed to mix mortar with impure
water, whether a man who has an iſſue be not in the
cafe of a defiled woman; as alfo to be able to difcufs
· the various queſtions, whether the foul of the prophet
was not created before that of Adam; whether he
did not counfel God in the creation; and what was
the counfel he gave: it cannot but be allowed, that
one may pafs one's whole life-time in learning a great
deal, and knowing nothing.

As for the inſtruction beſtowed on the vulgar, as
the profeſſors of the law do not perform the function
of our vicars and prieſts, as they neither preach, nor
catechize, nor confefs, it may be pronounced that
they receive none: all the education of children con-

fifts in attending private mafters, who reach them to read the Koran, if they are Mahometans, or the Pfalms, if Chriftians, and a little writing, and reckoning from memory : this continues till they arrive almoft at manhood, when each of them chufes fome profeffion, in order to marry and gain a livelihood. The contagion of ignorance infects even the children of the Franks, and it is a maxim at Marfeilles, that a *Levantin* muft be a diffipated youth, idle, and without emulation, and whofe whole knowledge will be confined to being able to fpeak feveral languages, though this rule, like all others, has its exceptions.

In examining the caufes of the general ignorance of the Orientals, I fhall not fay with a late traveller, that it arifes from the difficulties of the language, and of reading and writing ; undoubtedly the difficulty of the dialects, the perplexity of the characters, and the defects of their alphabet, multiply the oftacles to inftruction. But habit furmounts them, and the Arabs attain as perfect a facility in writing and reading, as the Europeans themfelves. The real caufe is the few means of inftruction they poffefs, among which muft be firft reckoned the fcarcity of books. With us nothing is fo common as this valuable affiftance : nothing fo general among all ranks as the practice of reading. In the Eaft, on the contrary, nothing is fo rare. There are but two libraries throughout Syria, that of Mar-hanna, of which I have fpoken, and that of Djezzar at Acre. The reader has feen how infignificant the former is, both with refpect to the number and the choice of its books. I fhall not fpeak of the latter as an eye witnefs ; but two perfons who have feen it, have affured me, that it did not contain more than three hundred volumes ; yet thefe are the fpoils of all Syria, and among others, of the Convent of St. Sauveur, near Saide, and of the Shaik Kairi, Mufti of Ramla. At Aleppo, the houfe of Bitar is the only one which poffefes any books, and thofe are aftro-

nomical, which nobody underftands. At Damafcus
the lawyers hold even their own fcience in no eftimation. Cairo alone is rich in books. There is a collection of very ancient ones at the Mofque of El-
azhar, and a confiderable number is in daily circulation; but Chriftians are forbid to touch them.
Twelve years ago, however, the monks of Mar-hanna
defirous of procuring fome, fent one of their number
thither to purchafe them. By a fortunate accident he
got acquainted with an Effendi, with whom he became
a favourite, and who wifhing to obtain from him fome
leffons in Aftrology, in which he thought him an
adept, procured him fome books. In the fpace of fix
months this monk affured me, that upwards of two
hundred paffed through his hands; and on my enquiring on what fubjects, he replied, treatifes on grammar, the Nahou, eloquence, and the interpretation of
the Koran; but very few hiftories, or even tales. He
had never feen two copies of the Arabian Nights En-
tertainments. From this ftate of facts, we are certainly authorized to confirm, not only that there is a
fcarcity of good books in the eaft, but that books of
any kind are very rare. The reafon of this is evident.
In thefe countries every book is a manufcript; the
writing of which is neceffarily flow, difficult, and expenfive. The labour of many months produces but
one copy. That muft be without erafure, and is liable to be deftroyed by a thoufand accidents. It is impoffible therefore for books to multiply, and confequently for knowledge to be propagated. If we compare this ftate of things with what paffes among ourfelves, we cannot but be deeply impreffed with the advantages of printing. We fhall even be convinced,
on reflection, that this art alone is poffibly the main
fpring of thofe great revolutions, which, within the
laft three centuries, have taken place in the moral fyftem of Europe. The prefs, by rendering books com-

mon, has diffufed a more equal fhare of knowledge
through every clafs; and by rapidly communicating
ideas and difcoveries, has produced a more fpeedy improvement and more univerfal acquaintance with the
arts and fciences: by its means, all thofe who occupy
themfelves in literary purfuits, are become a body
perpetually affembled, who purfue without intermif-
fion the fame labours. By printing, every writer is
become a public orator, who addreffes himfelf not
only to his city, but to his nation, and to all Europe.
If in this new fpecies of popular affembly he has loft
the advantage of declamation and gefture to excite the
paffions, he is amply indemnified by that of having a
more felect audience, and being able to reafon with
more temperance; and if the impreffion he makes be
lefs lively, it is certainly more durable. Since the difcovery of the art of printing, therefore, fingle men
have been feen to produce by the mere effects of their
writings, moral revolutions in whole nations, and
have obtained an influence over the minds of men,
which has even awed and controuled the authority of
the reigning powers.

Another very remarkable effect of the prefs, is that
which it has had on hiftory. By giving a general and
rapid publicity to facts, it has rendered their certainty
more eafy to be afcertained; whereas, when books
were written by hand, the collection made by one
man, producing only one copy, could be feen and
criticized by only a very fmall number of readers;
and thefe readers are the more to be fufpected, as they
muft depend on the choice of the author. If he
fhould permit copies to be taken, they multiply and
fpread very flowly. In the mean time witneffes drop
off, proofs which might once have been produced
lofe their force, contradictions ftart up, and a wide
field is open to error, paffion, and mifreprefentation.
This is the caufe of all thefe monftrous relations with
which the hiftories of antiquity, as well as thofe of

Modern Afia abound. If among thofe hiftories we
find fome which bear ftriking marks of probability,
they are thofe whofe writers were either eye-witneffes
of the facts they relate, or public men who wrote to an
enlightened people, able to contradict them whenever
they departed from truth. Such was Cæfar, the principal actor in the events related in his own memoirs ;
fuch was Xenophon, the general of the ten thoufand,
whofe able retreat he has fo well defcribed ; fuch was
Polybius, the friend and companion of Scipio, the
conqueror of Carthage; fuch alfo were Salluft and
Tacitus, who had been confuls ; Thucidides, the com-
mander of an army, and Herodotus, fenator, and de-
liverer of Halicarnaffus. When hiftory on the contrary is only a collection of ancient events, delivered
down by tradition ; when thefe facts are merely collected by individuals, it is neither of the fame fpecies,
nor does it bear the fame character. How great is the
difference between the preceding writers and Livy,
Quintus Curtius, and Diodorus Siculus! Fortunately,
however, for them, the countries in which they wrote
were civilized, and public information might ferve to
guide them refpecting recent facts. But when nations
were in a ftate of anarchy, or groaning under fuch a
defpotifm as prevails at this day in the eaft, writers,
abforbed in that ignorance and credulity which ever
accompany fuch a ftate, might boldly commit their
errors and prejudices to hiftory ; and we may remark,
that it is in the productions of fuch ages and nations
that we meet with all the monfters of fiction, while
in polifhed periods, and in the hands of original writers, the annals of hiftory only prefent us with a narrative of facts fimilar to thofe which are daily paffing
before our eyes.

This influence of the prefs is fo efficacious, that the
eftablifhment of Mar-Hanna alone, imperfect as it is,
has already produced a fenfible difference among the
Chriftians. The art of reading and writing, and even

a fort of information, are more common among them
at prefent, than they were thirty years ago.   Unfortunately their outfet has been of that kind, which long
retarded the progrefs of improvement, and excited
innumerable diforders in Europe.   For bibles and religious books being the firft which proceeded from the
prefs, the general attention was turned towards theological difcuffions, whence refulted a fermentation
which was the fource of the Schifms of England and
Germany, and the unhappy political troubles of France.
If inftead of tranflating their Buzembaum, and the
Mifanthropical reveries of Nieremberg and Didaco
Stella, the Jefuits had printed and difperfed books of
practical morality and public utility, adapted to the
ftate of the Kefraouan and the Druzes, their labours
might have produced in thofe countries, and even
through all Syria, political confequences which might
eventually have changed its whole fyftem.   At prefent,
all hope of fuch improvement is over, or at leaft
greatly retarded ; the firft fervor has been fpent on
ufelefs objects.   Befides, the monks are poor, and if
Djezzar takes it into his head he will deftroy their
prefs.   To this he will probably be induced by the
fanaticifm of the profeffors of the law, who, without
very well knowing what they have to dread from the
prefs, have, notwithftanding, conceived an averfion
to it ; as if folly poffeffed the natural inftinct of divin-
ing what may prove its deftruction.

The fcarcity of books, and the want of the means
of information are then, as I have juft faid, the caufes
of the ignorance of the Orientals ; but thefe muft,
after all be regarded merely as acceffaries : the radical
fource is ftill in the government, which not only does
not encourage the propagation of knowledge, but ex-
erts every effort to ftifle it in the birth.   Under the
adminiftration of the Turks, there is no profpect of
obtaining rank or fortune through the channel of the
arts and fciences, or polite literature.   The talents of

the moſt diſtinguiſhed geometricians, aſtronomers, or engineers of Europe, would not preſerve their poſſeſ-for from languiſhing in obſcurity, or groaning beneath the perſecution of tyranny. If ſcience, therefore, which itſelf is acquired with ſo much difficulty and labour, can only make us regret its inutility, and even expoſe us to danger; it is better never to poſſeſs it. For this reaſon, the orientals are ignorant, and muſt neceſſarily be ſo, from the ſame principle which makes them poor, as they may apply with juſtice to ſcience, what they ſay of the arts: "What good purpoſe will it anſwer " to do more?"

CHAP. XXI.

Of the manners and character of the Inhabitants of Syria.

OF all the ſubjects of obſervation any country affords, the moral character of its inhabitants is un-queſtionably the moſt important; but it muſt likewiſe be acknowledged, it is at the ſame time moſt difficult: for it is not ſufficient to make a barren enquiry into facts; the eſſential object is to inveſtigate their various cauſes and relations; to diſcover the open or ſecret, the remote or immediate ſprings, which produce in men thoſe habits of action we call manners, and that uniform diſpoſition of mind we name character. Now, to ſucceed in ſuch an enquiry, it is neceſſary to com-municate with the men we wiſh to know; we muſt place ourſelves in their ſituations, in order to feel by what agents they are influenced, and the conſequences which reſult; we muſt live in their country, learn their language, and adopt their cuſtoms; conditions ſeldom complied with by travellers; and which even when they are, ftill leave to be furmounted numerous difficulties, which arife from the nature of the thing itfelf; for we have not only to combat the prejudices we may meet in our way, but to overcome our own against which we can never be fufficiently on our guard; habits are powerful, facts liable to be miftaken, and error eafy. The obferver, then, fhould be circumfpect though not timid, and the reader, obliged to fee with the eyes of others, fhould watch attentively both the reafoning of his guide, and the deductions he may be inclined to draw himfelf.

When an European arrives in Syria, or indeed in any part of the eaftern world, what appears moft extraordinary to him, in the exterior of the inhabitants, is the almoft total oppofition of their manners to our own: it feems as if fome premeditated defign had determined to produce an infinity of the moft ftriking contrafts between the people of Afia and thofe of Europe. We wear fhort and clofe dreffes; theirs are long and ample. We fuffer our hair to grow, and fhave the beard; they let the beard grow, and fhave the head. With us, to uncover the head is a mark of refpect; with them a naked head is a fign of folly. We falute in an inclined pofture; they upright. We pafs our lives erect; they are almoft continually feated. They fit and eat upon the ground; we upon raifed feats. With refpect to language, likewife, their manner of writing is directly contrary to ours, and the greateft part of our mafculine nouns are feminine with them. To the bulk of travellers thefe contrafts only appear whimfical; but it may be interefting to philofophers, to enquire into the caufes of fo great a diverfity of habits, in men who have the fame wants, and in nations which appear to have one common origin.

Another diftinguifhing characterestic, no lefs remarkable is that religious exterior obfervable in the countenances, converfation, and geftures of the inhabitants of Turkey. In the ftreets every one appears with his ſtring of beads. We hear nothing but emphatical exclamations of *Ya allah!* O God! *Allah akbar!* God moſt great! *Allah taala,* God moſt high! Every inſtant the ear is ſtruck with a profound ſigh, or noiſy eruɛtation which follows the pronouncing of ſome of the ninety-nine epithets of God; ſuch as *Ya rani!* Source of riches! *Ya ſobhan!* O moſt to be praiſed! *Ya maſtour!* O impenetrable! If a man ſells bread in the ſtreets, he does not cry bread, but exclaims *Allah Kerim,* God is liberal. If he ſells water he cries, *Allah djawad,* God is generous; and ſo of other articles. The uſual form of ſalutation is, *God preſerve thee;* and of thanks, *God proteɛt thee:* in a word, God is in every thing, and every where. Theſe men then are very devout, ſays the reader? Yes, but without being the better in conſequence of this devotion, for I have already obſerved, their zeal is no other than a ſpirit of jealouſy, and contradiɛtion ariſing from the diverſity of religions; ſince in the Chriſtian a profeſſion of his faith is a bravado, an aɛt of independence; and in the Mahometan, an aɛt of ſuperiority and power. This devoutneſs, therefore, merely the offspring of pride and profound ignorance, is no better than a fanatic ſuperſtition, and the ſource of innumerable diſorders.

There is ſtill another charaɛtereſtic in the exterior of the Orientals, which attraɛts the attention of an obſerver: I mean their grave and phlegmatic air in every thing they do, or ſay. Inſtead of that open and cheerful countenance, which we either naturally poſſeſs or aſſume, their behaviour is ſerious, auſtere, and melancholy; they rarely laugh, and the gaiety of the French appears to them a fit of delerium. When they ſpeak it is with deliberation, without geſtures, and without paſſion; they liſten without interrupting you; they are ſilent for whole days together, and by no means pique themſelves on ſupporting converſation. If they walk, it is always leiſurely, and on buſineſs;

they have no idea of our troublefome activity, and
our *walks* backward and forward for amufement.
Continually feated, they pafs whole days mufing, with
their legs croffed, their pipes in their mouths and
almoft without changing their attitude. It fhould
feem as if motion were a punifhment to them, and
that like the Indians, they regard inaction as effential
to happinefs.

This obfervation, which may be extended to the
greater part of their habits and cuftoms, has in our
time, given occafion to a great fummary fyftem of
the caufes of the peculiar character of the Orientals,
and feveral other nations. A celebrated writer, re-
flecting on what the Greeks and Romans have faid
of Afiatic effeminacy, and the accounts given by
travellers of the indolence of the Indians, is of opinion,
that this indolence forms the diftinguifhing character
of the inhabitants of thofe countries; purfuing his
enquiries into the common caufe of this general fact,
and finding, that all thefe nations inhabit what are
called *hot countries*, he has attributed the caufe of
their indolence to heat; and affuming the fact as a
principle, has laid it down as an axiom, that the inhabitants of hot countries muft neceffarily be indolent,
inert of body, and from analogy, likewife inert of
mind and character. He goes even ftill farther; remarking, that unlimited monarchy is the moft habitual
ftate of government among thefe nations; and con-
fidering defpotifm as the effect of the fupinenefs of a
people, he concludes, that defpotifm is as much the
natural government of thefe countries, and as neceffary as the climate under which they live. It fhould
feem as if the feverity, or, more properly fpeaking,
the barbarity of the inference fhould have put men
upon their guard againft fuch erroneous principles :
yet this fyftem has been received with great applaufe
in France, nay, even throughout Europe; and the
opinion of the author of the *Spirit of Laws*, is become

among the moſt numerous claſs of reaſoners, an authority from which it is preſumptuous to differ. This is not the place to write a formal treatiſe completely to overthrow this error : beſides that ſuch a refutation already exiſts in the work of a philoſopher, whoſe name is at leaſt equal to that of Monteſquieu. But in order to raiſe ſome doubts at leaſt in the minds of thoſe who, without giving themſelves time to reflect, have adopted this opinion, 1 ſhall offer a few objections which the ſubject naturally ſuggeſts.

The doctrine of the general indolence of the Oriental and ſouthern nations, is founded on that opinion of Aſiatic effeminacy originally traſmitted to us by the Greeks and Romans ; but what are the facts on which that was built ? Were they fixed and determinate, or did this opinion rely on vague and general ideas like the ſyſtems of the moderns ? Had the ancients a more accurate knowledge of thoſe countries in their time, than we have obtained in ours ; and are we juſtified in founding on their report an hypotheſis difficult to eſtabliſh from our own more minute examination ? But, admitting the facts as we receive them from hiſtory, were the Aſſyrians, whoſe ambition and wars during five hundred years, threw Aſia into confuſion ; the Medes, who ſhook off their yoke, and diſpoſſeſſed them ; the Perſians who, under Cyrus, within the ſpace of thirty years, extended their conqueſts from the Indus to the Mediterranean : were theſe inert and indolent people ? May we not oppoſe to this ſyſtem the Phœnicians, who, for ſo many centuries, were in poſſeſſion of the commerce of the whole ancient world ; the Palmyrenians, of whoſe induſtry we poſſeſs ſuch ſtupendous monuments ; the Carduchi of Xenophon, who braved the power of the *Great King* in the very heart of his empire ; the Parthians, thoſe unconquerable rivals of Rome ; and even the Jews, who, limited to a little ſtate, never ceaſed to ſtruggle, for a thouſand years, againſt the moſt powerful em-

pires? If the men of thefe nations were inert, what is
activity? If they were active, where then is the influence of climate? Why in the fame countries,
where fo much energy was difplayed in former times,
do we at prefent find fuch profound indolence? Why
are the modern Greeks fo debafed amid the very ruins
of Sparta and Athens, and in the fields of Marathon
and Themopylæ? Will it be alledged, that the climate
has changed? Where are the proofs? Suppofing this
true, it muft have changed by irregular fits; the climate of Perfia muft have altered greatly from Cyrus
to Xerxes; that of Athens from Ariftides to Deme-
trius Phalereus; and that of Rome from Scipio to
Sylla, and from Sylla to Tiberius. The climate of
the Portugueze muft have changed fince the days of
Albuquerque; and that of the Turks fince Soliman.
If indolence be peculiar to the fouthern countries,
whence is it that we he have feen Carthage in Africa,
Rome in Italy, and the Buccaneers at St. Domingo?
Why do we meet with the Malays in India, and the
Bedouins in Arabia? Why, too, at the fame period,
and under the fame fky, do we find a Sybaris near
Crotona, a Capua in the vicinity of Rome, and a Sardes
contiguous to Miletus? Whence is it, that we fee, under our own eyes, and in Europe itfelf, northern
governments as languid as thofe of the fouth? Why,
in our own empire, are the fouthern more active
than the northern provinces? If the fame effects are
obfervable under directly contrary circumftances,
and different effects under the fame circumftances,
what becomes of thefe pretended principles? What is
this influence of climate? and what is to be underftood
by activity? Is it only to be accorded to warlike nations?
and was Sparta, when not engaged in war to be efteemed inert? What do we mean by hot countries? Where
are we to draw the line of cold and temperate? Let
the Partifans of Montefquieu afcertain this, that we
may henceforward be enabled to determine the quan-

tity of energy in a nation by the temperature, and at what degree of the thermometer we are to fix its aptitude to flavery or freedom!

But a phyfical obfervation has been called in to corroborate this pofition; and we are told that heat abates our ftrength; we are more indolent in fummer than in winter: the inhabitants of hot countries, therefore, muft be indolent. Let us fuppofe this true. Whence is it then, that, under the fame influence of climate, the tyrant poffeffes more energy to opprefs, than the people to defend themfelves? But, is it not evident that we reafon like the inhabitants of a country where cold is more prevalent than heat? Were a fimilar thefis to be maintained in Egypt and Africa, it would there be faid, the cold prevents motion, and obftructs the circulation. The truth is, that our fenfations are relative to our habits, and that bodies affume a temperament analogous to the climate in which they live; fo that they are only affected by the extremes of the ordinary medium. We hate fweating; the Egyptian loves it, and dreads nothing fo much as a failure of perfpiration. Thus, whether we refer to hiftorical, or natural facts, the fyftem of Montefquieu, fo fpecious at firft fight, turns out, when examined, to be a mere paradox, which has owed its fuccefs only to the impreffion made by the novelty of the fubject, at the time the Spirit of Laws appeared, and the indirect flattery it offered to thofe nations by which it was fo favourably received.

To give precifion to our ideas, refpecting the queftion of activity, a fhorter and more certain method than thefe far-fetched and equivocal reafonings would have been, to have ftudied nature herfelf, and to have examined the origin and motives of activity in man. If we purfue this mode of inveftigation, we fhall perceive that all action, whether of body or mind, has its fource in our neceffities; and augments as they increafe. We may follow its gradations from the rudeft

beginnings, to the ftate of the moft mature improvement. In man yet favage, hunger and thirft awaken
the firft exertions of the foul and body. Thefe are
the wants which prompt him to run, fearch, watch,
and employ cunning or violence, as he finds them
neceffary: all his activity depends on the means of
providing for his fubfiftence. Is that eafily obtained,
has he fruit, game and fifh, within his reach, he is
lefs active, fince by putting forth his hand, he can
fatisfy himfelf: and being fatisfied, nothing invites
him to ftir, till the experience of various employments has awakened in him defires which become new
wants, and new motives of activity. On the other
hand, are the means of fupplying his neceffities difficult to be obtained; is game hard to be found, and
poffeffed of agility to avoid him; are the fifh wily,
and do the fruits foon decay; man is forced to be
more active; he muft exercife his body and mind, to
maintain life; he muft become fwift like the beafts,
wily like the fifh, and provident to preferve his fruits;
he muft endeavour the improvement of his mental
faculties. He, therefore, beftirs himfelf, he thinks,
he meditates; he conceives the idea of bending the
branch of a tree to form a bow, and pointing a reed
to make an arrow, he faftens a handle to a fharp ftone,
and procures him a hatchet; he then labours to make
nets, to fell trees, to hollow out their trunks, and
build canoes. Already has he provided for his moft
urgent neceffities; already the experience of a multitude of fenfations has made him acquainted with enjoyments and fufferings; and his activity is redoubled
to remove the one, and multiply the others. He has
felt the pleafure of being fhaded from the heat of the
fun; he builds himfelf a cabin: he has experienced
that a fkin fecures him from the cold; he makes himfelf clothing: he has tafted brandy and fmoaked tobacco; he likes them, and wifhes to have more; but
to procure them he muft bring beaver fkins, elephants

teeth, gold duſt, &c. He redoubles his activity, and
carries his induſtry ſo far as to ſell even his fellow
creature. In ſuch a progreſs, as in the primary cauſe,
it muſt be acknowledged, that activity has little or no
connection with heat; only the inhabitants of the
north being reputed to ſtand more in need of nouriſh-
ment than thoſe of the ſouth, it may be alledged,
that they muſt conſequently be poſſeſſed of more activity; but this difference in neceſſary wants, has very
narrow limits. Beſides, it is well aſcertained, that
an Eſquimaux or a Samoyede, requires really a greater
quantity of aliment, than a Bedouin or an Ichthyo-
phagus of Perſia? Are the ſavages of Brazil and
Guinea leſs voracious than thoſe of Canada and Cali-
fornia?. Let my opponents beware : the facility of obtaining a great quantity of food, is perhaps the primary cauſe of voracioufneſs; and this facility, eſpecially in a ſavage ſtate, depends leſs on climate than
on the nature of the ſoil, and its richneſs or poverty
in paſturage, in foreſts, and in lakes, and conſequently
in game, fiſh, and fruits; circumſtances which are
found indifferently under every parallel.

From theſe reflections it appears, that the nature of
the ſoil has a real influence on activity. We muſt
perceive, that in the ſocial as in the ſavage ſtate, a
country, in which the means of ſubſiſtence are ſome-
what difficult to be procured, will have more active,
and more induſtrious inhabitants; while in an other
where nature has laviſhed every thing, the people will
be indolent and inactive. And this is perfectly conformable to hiſtorical facts, for we always find the
conquering nations poor, and iſſuing from lands either
barren or difficult of cultivation, while the coquered
people are inhabitants of fertile and opulent countries.
It is even worthy of obſervation, that theſe needy
conquerors, eſtabliſhed among rich nations, ſhortly
loſe their energy, and become effeminate. Such was
the caſe with the Perſians, who, under Cyrus, deſcended

from the Elymaïs, into the fertile fields watered by the
Euphrates ; fuch was the Macedonians under Alexander, when tranfplanted from Mount Rhodope to
the plains of Afia ; fuch the Tartars of Djenkis-kan,
when fettled in China and Bengal ; and fuch the Arabs
fo victorious under Mahomet, after the conqueft of
Spain and Egypt.   Hence we may affirm, that it is
not as inhabitants of hot, but as inhabitants of rich,
countries that nations are inclined to indolence ; and
this maxim is exactly conformable with what we obferve in fociety in general, fince we fee there is always
leaft activity among the more opulent claffes ; but as
this fatiety and poverty do not exift for all the individuals of a nation, we muft recur to reafons more general, and more efficacious, than the nature of the
foil ; I mean the focial inftitutions called *Government*
and *Religion*.   Thefe are the true fources and regu-
lators of the activity or indolence of individuals, and
nations.   Thefe are the efficient caufes, which as they
extend or limit the natural or fuperfluous wants, limit
or extend the activity of all men.   A proof that their
influence operates in fpite of the difference of climate
and foil, is, that Tyre, Carthage, and Alexandria,
formerly poffeffed the fame induftry as London, Paris,
and Amfterdam ; that the Buccanneers, and the
Malayans have difplayed equal turbulence and courage with the Normans ; and that the Ruffians and
Polanders have the apathy and indifference of the
Hindoos, and the negroes.   But as their nature
varies and changes with the paffions of men, their
influence changes and varies in very fhort intervals
of time.   Hence it is, that the Romans, commanded
by Scipio, refembled fo little thofe governed by Tybe-
rius ; and that the Greeks of the age of Ariftides and
Themiftocles, were fo unlike thofe of the time of
Conftantine.   Let us examine what paffes within ourfelves.   Do we not experience, that our activity has
lefs dependence on phyfical caufes, than the actual

circumſtances of the ſociety of which we are members?
Are our deſires excited by neceſſary or ſupurfluous
wants, both our bodies and minds are animated with
new life; paſſion inſpires us with an activity ardent as
our deſires, and perſevering as our hopes. Are theſe
hopes diſappointed, deſire decays, activity languiſhes,
and diſcouragement induces apathy and indolence.
This explains why our activity varies with our conditions, our ſituations and the different periods of our
life. Why does the man, who was active in his youth,
become indolent in his old age? Why is there more
activity in capital and commercial cities, than in towns
without commerce, and in the country? To awaken
activity there muſt be objects of deſire; and to maintain it, the hope of arriving at enjoyment. If theſe
two eſſentials are wanting, there is an end to individual and national activity. And ſuch is the condition
of the Orientals in general, and particularly of thoſe
of whom we are treating. What ſhould induce them
to move, if no motion procures them the hope of
an enjoyment equivalent to the trouble they muſt take?
How can they be otherwiſe than indolent in their
moſt ſimple habits, if their ſocial inſtitutions render it
a ſort of neceſſity?

The moſt intelligent obſerver of antiquity, after
having made the ſame remark on the Aſiatics of his
time, has aſſigned the ſame reaſon. " As to the
" effeminacy and indolence of the Aſiatics, (ſays he
" in a paſſage which well deſerves to be cited,)* if
" they are leſs warlike, and more gentle in their
" manners than the Europeans, no doubt the nature
" of their climate, more temperate than ours, con-
" tributes greatly to this difference. But we muſt
" not forget the form of their governments, which are
" all deſpotic, and ſubject to the arbitrary will of their
" kings. Men who are not permitted the enjoyment

---

* *Hippocrates de acre, locis et aquis.*

" of their natural rights, but whofe paffions are per-
" petually under the guidance of their mafters, will
" never be found courageous in battle. To them the
" rifks and advantages of war are by no means equal.
" Obliged to forfake their friends, their country, their
" families; to fupport cruel fatigues and even death
" itfelf, what is the recompence of fo many facrifices?
" Danger and death. Their mafters alone enjoy the
" booty and the fpoils they have purchafed with their
" blood. But let them combat in their own caufe,
" and reap the reward of their victory, or feel the
" fhame of their defeat, they will no longer be defi-
" cient in courage; and the truth of this is fufficiently
" proved by both the Greeks and Barbarians, who,
" in thofe countries, live under their own laws, and
" are free; for they are more courageous than any
" other race of men."

This is precifely the definition of the Orientals of
our days; and what the Grecian philofopher has faid
of fome particular tribes, who refifted the power of
the Great king and his Satraps, correfponds exactly
with what we have feen of the Druzes, the Maronites,
the Curds, the Arabs, Shaik Daher, and the Bedouins. It muft be admitted, the moral character of nations, like that of individuals, chiefly depends on the
focial ftate in which they live; fince it is true, that
our actions are governed by our civil and religious
laws, and fince our habits are no more than a repeti-
tion of thofe actions, and our character only the difpofition to act in fuch a manner, under fuch circumftances, it evidently follows, that every thing depends on government and religion. In all the obfervations I have made, I have never failed to remark
the influence of thefe two caufes operating more or
lefs immediately. This will become ftill clearer, when
we confidered more circumftantially.

I have faid that the Orientals, in general, have a
grave and phlegmatic exterior, a ftayed and almoft

liftlefs deportment, and a ferious, nay, even fad and melancholy countenance. Were the climate or the foil the radical caufe of this, the effect would be the fame in every individual. But this is not the cafe; under this general character, there are a thoufand peculiar minute varieties in different claffes and individuals, arifing from their fituation, relative to the influence of government, which differs in its effects on thefe claffes, and thefe individuals. Thus we obferve that the peafants fubjects to the Turks are more gloomy than thofe of the tributary countries; that the inhabitants of the country are lefs gay than thofe of the towns; and that thofe on the coaft are more cheerful than fuch as dwell at a greater diftance from it; that in the fame town, the profeffors of the law are more ferious than the military, and thefe again more fo than the people. We may even remark, that in the great cities, the people have much of that diffipated and carelefs air they ufually have with us; becaufe there, as well as here, inured to fuffering from habit, and devoid of reflection from ignorance, they enjoy a kind of fecurity. Having nothing to lofe, they are in no dread of being plundered. The merchant, on the contrary, lives in a ftate of perpetual alarm, under the double apprehenfion of acquiring no more, and lofing what he poffeffes. He trembles left he fhould attract the attention of rapacious authority, which would confider an air of fatisfaction as a proof of opulence, and the fignal for extortion. The fame dread prevails throughout the villages, where each peafant is afraid of exciting the envy of his equals, and the avarice of the Aga and his foldiers. In fuch a country, where the fubject is perpetually watched by a defpoiling government, he muft affume a ferious countenance for the fame reafon that he wears ragged cloaths, and makes a public parade of eating cheefe and olives. The fame caufe, though it has a lefs influence on lawyers, is not, however, without its effect on them;

VOL. II.   N n

but the infolence in which they have been educated, and the pedantry of their manners, render it unneceffary to affign any other.

With refpect to their indolence, it is not furprizing that the inhabitants of the cities and the country, fatigued with labour, fhould have an inclination to repofe. But it is remarkable, that when thefe people are once in action, they exert themfelves with a vivacity and ardour almoft unknown in our climates. This is more particularly obfervable in the fea ports and commercial towns. An European cannot but admire with what activity the failors, with their naked arms and legs, handle the oars, bend the fails, and perform ever manœuvre : with what ardour the porters unload a boat, and carry the heavieft couffes.* Always finging, and anfwering by couplets to one who directs their labour, they perform all their motions in cadence, and redouble their exertions by making them in time. It has been faid, on this fubject, that the inhabitants of hot countries have a natural propenfity to mufic; but in what confifts its anology with the climate? Would it not be more rational to fay, that the hot countries we are acquainted with, having made a confiderable progrefs in improvement and knowledge long before our cold climates, the people have retained fome traces of the fine arts which were formerly cultivated among them. Our merchants frequently reproach this people, and efpecially thofe of the country, with not labouring fo often, nor fo long, as they are able. But why fhould they labour beyond their wants, fince the fuperfluity of their induftry would procure them no additional enjoyment? In many refpects, a man of the lower clafs of people refembles the favages; when he has expended his ftrength in procuring a fubfiftence, he takes his repofe; it is, only by rendering

---

* Sacks made of ftraw, greatly ufed in Afia.

that fubfiftence lefs difficult to acquire, and by exciting him with the temptation of prefent enjoyments, that he can be induced to exert an uniform activity ; and we have feen, that the Turkifh government is of a directly contrary tendency. As to the fedentary life of the natives, what motives has a man to beftir himfelf in a country where the police has never thought either of laying out walks, or encouraging plantations ; where there is no fafety without the towns, nor pleafure within their precincts ; where every thing, in fhort, invites to ftay at home ? Is it aftonifhing that fuch political maxims fhould have produced fedentary habits ? And muft not thefe habits, in their turn become the caufes of inaction ?

The comparifon of our civil and domeftic ftate, with that of the Orientals, will furnifh ftill further reafons for that phlegm which conftitutes their general character. One of the chief fources of gaiety with us, is the focial intercourfe of the table, and the ufe of wine. The Orientals are almoft ftrangers to this double enjoyment. Good cheer would infallibly expofe them to extortion, and wine to corporal punifhment, from the zeal of the police in enforcing the precepts of the Koran. It is with great reluctance, that the Mahometans tolerate the Chriftians in the ufe of a liquor they even envy them ; wine, therefore, is not habitual or familiar, except in the Kefraouan, and the country of the Druzes ; and their repafts there have a cheerfulnefs which brandy does not procure even in the cities of Aleppo and Damafcus.

A fecond fource of gaiety among us, is the free intercourfe between the two fexes, which prevails more particularly in France. The effect of which is, that even without any particular views, the men endeavour to obtain the good opinion of the women, and ftudy to acquire the manners moft likely to enfure it. Now, fuch is the nature, or fuch the education of the fex, that the firft merit in their eyes is to be able to amufe them ; and nothing is fo certain of fucceeding with them, as fprightlinefs and mirth.   Hence we have contracted a habit of trifling, politenefs and frivolity, which is become the diftinguifhing character of the French nation in Europe.   In Afia, on the contrary, the women are rigoroufly fecluded from the fociety of men.   Conftantly fhut up in their houfes, they have no communication but with their hufband, their father, their brother, or at moft with their coufin-german.   Carefully veiled in the ftreets, they dare hardly fpeak to a man, even on bufinefs.   Every body muft be ftrangers to them : it would be indecent to fix your eyes on them, and you muft let them pafs you, as if they were fomething contagious in their nature.   And indeed this is nearly the idea of the Orientals, who entertain a general fentiment of contempt by that fex.   It may be afked, what is the caufe of this ? The fame which operates on every thing ; the laws and government.   In fact, Mahomet, paffionately fond as he was of women, has not, however, done them the honour of treating them in his Koran as appertaining to the human fpecies ; he does not fo much as make mention of them either with refpect to the ceremonies of religion, or the rewards of another life ; and it is even a fort of problem with the Mahometans, whether women have fouls.   The government is ftill more unjuft towards them ; for it denies them the poffeffion of any landed property, and fo completely deprives them of every kind of perfonal liberty, as to leave them dependent all their lives on a hufband, a father, or a relation.   In this ftate of flavery, having nothing at their difpofal, we cannot fuppofe it very neceffary to folicit their favour, or to adopt that gaiety of manners they find fo captivating. The government and laws are, no doubt, the efficient caufe of this fequeftration of the women ; and, perhaps, were it not for the facility of divorces, and the

dread of feeing a wife or daughter carried off by fome
powerful man, the Afiatics would be lefs anxious to
conceal them from ftrangers.

This fituation of the women among the Orientals,
occafions a great contraft between their manners and
ours. Such is their delicacy on this head, that they
never fpeak of them ; and it would be efteemed highly
indecent to make any enquiries of the men refpecting
the women of their family. We muft be confiderably
advanced in familiarity with them, to enter into a converfation on fuch a fubject ; and when we then give
them fome account of our manners, it is impoffible
to exprefs their amazement. They are unable to
conceive how our women go with their faces un-
covered, when, in their country, an uplifted veil is
the mark of a proftitute, or the fignal for a love adventure. They have no idea how it is poffible to fee
them, to talk with them, and touch them, without
emotion, or to be alone with them without proceeding to the laft extremities. This aftonifhment will
fufficiently fhew what opinion they entertain of their
females ; and we need not hefitate to conclude they
are abfolutely ignorant of love, in our fenfe of the
word. That defire on which it is founded, is with
them ftripped of all thofe acceffories which conftitute
its charm ; privation is there without a facrifice, victory without a combat, and enjoyment without delicacy ; they pafs at once from torment to fatiety. Lovers there are prifoners, always watching to deceive
their keepers, and always alert to feize the firft opportunity, becaufe it feldom happens, and is foon loft.
Secret as confpirators, they conceal their good fortune as a crime, becaufe it is attended with no lefs
fatal confequences. Indifcretion can fcarcely avoid
the poniard, the piftol, or poifon. Its deftructive
confequences to the women render them implacable
in punifhing, and, to revenge themfelves, they are
frequently more cruel than their hufbands and their

brothers. This feverity preferves a confiderable degree of chaftity and decorum in the country ; but in
the great towns, where there are more refources for
intrigue, as much debauchery prevails as among us ;
only with this difference, that it is more concealed.
Aleppo, Damafcus, and above all, Cairo, are not
fecond in this refpect to our provincial capitals.
Young girls are referved there as every where elfe, becaufe the difcovery of a love adventure would coft
them their lives ; but married women give themfelves
up to pleafure with the more freedom, to indemnify
themfelves for the long and ftrict reftraint they have
endured, and becaufe they have often juft reafons for
revenging themfelves on their mafters.   In fact, from
the practice of polygamy permitted by the Koran, the
Turks, in general, are enervated very early, and nothing is more common than to hear men of thirty
complaining of impotence.   This is the malady for
which they chiefiy confult the Europeans, defiring
them to give them *Madjoun*, by which they mean
provocatives.   This infirmity is the more mortifying
to them, as fterility is a reproach among the Orientals : they ftill retain for fecundity all the efteem of
ancient times ; and the beft wifh you can make a
young girl, is that fhe may foon get a hufband, and
have a great number of children.   From this prejudice they haften their marriage fo much, that it is not
rare to fee girls of nine or ten years old married to
boys of twelve or thirteen.   It muft however be con-
feffed, that the apprehenfions of libertinifm, and the
feverity with which this is punifhed by the Turkifh
police, greatly contribute to thefe premature unions,
which muft likewife be reckoned among the caufes of
their early impotence.   The ignorance of the Turks
will not fuffer itfelf to be perfuaded on this head, and
they are fo irrational as to force nature, at the very
time their health is impaired by excefs.   This alfo is
to be afcribed to the Koran, in which the amorous

prophet has taken care to infert a precept inculcating the fpecies of duty. Montefquieu, therefore, is in the right, to affign polygamy as one of the caufes of depopulation in Turkey; but it is one of the leaft confiderable, as there are few but the rich who allow themfelves a plurality of women; the common people, and efpecially thofe of the country, content themfelves with one; and perfons are fometimes to be met with, even among the higher ranks, who are wife enough to imitate their example, and confefs that one wife is quite fufficient.

What we are able to learn of the domeftic life of the hufbands who have feveral wives, is neither calculated to make their lot envied, nor to give a high idea of this part of Mahomet's legiflation. Their houfe is a perpetual fcene of tumult and contention. Nothing is to be heard but quarrels between the different wives, and complaints made to the hufband. The four legal married women complain that their flaves are preferred to them, and the flaves that they are abandoned to the jealoufy of their miftreffes. If one wife obtains a trinket, a token of favour, or permiffion to go to the bath, all the others require the fame and league together in the common caufe. To reftore peace, the polygamift is obliged to affume the tone of a defpot, and from that moment he meets with nothing but the fentiments of flaves, the appearance of fondnefs and real hatred. In vain does each of thefe women proteft fhe loves him more than the reft; in vain do they fly, on his entering the apartments, to prefent him his pipe and his flippers, to prepare his dinner, to ferve him his coffee; in vain, whilft he is effeminately ftretched out upon his carpet, do they chafe away the flies which incommode him; all thefe attentions and careffes have no other objeét than to procure an addition to their trinkets and moveables, that if he fhould repudiate them, they may be able to tempt another hufband, or find refource in what becomes their only property. They are merely courtizans, who think of nothing but to ftrip their lover before he quits them ; and this lover, long fince deprived of defires, teezed by feigned fondnefs, and tormented with all the littlefsnefs of fatiety, is far from enjoying, as we may well imagine, an enviable fituation. The contempt the Turks entertain for their women, arifes from this concurrence of circumftances, and it is evidently the effect of their own cuftoms. For how fhould the women retain that exclufive love, which renders them moft eftimable, when fo many fhare in the affections of their hufband ? How fhould they poffefs that modefty which conftitutes their greateft virtue, when the moft fhocking fcenes of debauchery are daily before their eyes ? How, in a word, fhould they be endowed with the manners requifite to make them amiable, when no care whatever is taken of their education ? The Greeks at leaft derive this advantage from religion, that, being permitted to take but one wife at a time, they enjoy more domeftic peace, though perhaps, without approaching nearer to real happinefs.

It is remarkable, that in confequence of the difference in religion, there exifts between the Chriftians and Mahometans of Syria, and indeed of all Turkey, as marked a difference of character as if they were two diftinct nations, living under different climates. Travellers, and our merchants, who on account of the habits of intimacy in which they live with both, are ftill better qualified to decide, agree that the Greek Chriftians are in general wicked and deceitful, abject in adverfity, infolent in profperity, and efpecially remarkable for levity and ficklenefs : the Mahometans, on the contrary, though haughty even to infolence, poffefs however a fort of goodnefs of heart, humanity, and juftice ; and above all, never fail to manifeft great fortitude under misfortune, and much firmnefs of character. This contraft between men, living under the fame fky, may appear furprifing ; but the prejudices of their education, and the influence of the government under which they live, fufficiently account for it. The Greeks, treated by the Turks with all the haughtinefs and contempt which they fhew to their flaves, cannot but at laft affume the charaƈer perpetually afcribed to them : they have been obliged to praƈice deceit, to efcape from violence by cunning, and they have recourfe to the meaneft flatteries, becaufe the weak muft ever court the ftrong ; they are diffemblers and mifchievous, becaufe he who cannot openly revenge himfelf, difguifes his hatred ; cowardly and treacherous, fince he who cannot attack in front, naturally ftrikes behind ; and infolent in profperity, becaufe they who attain wealth or power unworthily, are eager to revenge themfelves by returning all the contempt they have received in the purfuit.   I was one day obferving to a very fenfible monk, that among all the Chriftians, who in more modern times have been advanced to eminent ftations in this country, not one of them has fhewn himfelf worthy of his good fortune.   Ibrahim was meanly avaricious ; Sad-el-Kouri irrefolute and pufillanimous, his fon Randour, ignorant and infolent, and Rezk, cowardly and deceitful : his anfwer was word for word, as follows " The Chriftians have not *hands* " proper to manage the reigns of government, be- " caufe, during their youth they have been continually " employed in *beating cotton.* They refemble thofe " who walk for the firft time on high terraces, they " grow giddy at feeing themfelves fo exalted, and as " they are afraid they fhall be forced to return to " their olives and cheefe, they are in hafte to make " all the profits they can. The Turks on the contra- " ry, are accuftomed to govern ; they are mafters " habituated to their authority, and ufe it as if there " was no fear of their being deprived of it." We muft not forget at the fame time, that the Mahometans have the prejudices of fatalifm inftilled into them from their birth, and have a full perfuafion that every thing

is predeftined.   Hence they experience a fecurity
which moderates both defire and fear, and a refignation by which they are equally prepared for good and
evil ; they are habituated in a kind of apathy, which
equally prevents them from regretting the paft or providing againft the future.   Does the Mahometan fuffer by any misfortune ? Is he plundered ? Is he ruined ? he calmly fays, "It was written," and fubmits
without a murmur, to the moft unexpeated tranfition
from oppulence to poverty : Even on the bed of death,
nothing difturbs the tranquility of his refignation, he
makes his ablution, repeats his prayers, profeffes his
belief in God, and the prophet ; he tranquilly fays to
his fon ; "turn my head towards Mecca," and dies
in peace.   The Greeks, on the contrary, who believe
that God may be prevailed on to change his purpofe,
by vows, fafting, prayer, and pilgrimages, live in the
perpetual defire of obtaining fome new blefling, the
fear of loofing fome good they already poffefs, or tormented with regret for fome duty they omitted.   Their
hearts are a prey to every contending paffion, nor do
they avoid their deftructive effects ; but fo far as the
circumftances in which they live, and the example of
the Mahometans enfeeble the prejudices of their child-
hood.   We may add a remark equally true of both
religions, that the inhabitants of the inland country
have more integrity, fimplicity, and generofity, and
are in every refpect of more amiable manners than
thofe upon the fea-coaft, no doubt becaufe the latter
continually engaged in commerce, have contracted, by
their mode of life, a mercantile fpirit, naturally ini-
mical to all thofe virtues which are founded on a moderation and difintereftednefs.

     After what I have faid of the manners of the Ori-
entals, we fhall be no longer aftonifhed that their
whole character partakes of the monotony of their
private life, and of the ftate of fociety in which they
live.   Even in the cities where we fee moft activity,

as Aleppo, Damaſcus, and Cairo, all their amuſe-
ments conſiſt in going to the bath, or meeting together
in coffee-houſes, which only reſemble ours in name.
There, in a large room, filled with ſmoak, ſeated on
ragged mats, the wealthier claſs of people paſs whole
days in ſmoaking their pipes, talking of buſineſs, in
conciſe phraſes, uttered at long intervals, and frequently in ſaying nothing. Sometimes the dullneſs of this
ſilent aſſembly is relieved by the entrance of a ſinger,
ſome dancing girls, or one of thoſe ſtory tellers they
call *Naſhid*, who to obtain a few Paras, relates a tale,
or recites verſes from ſome ancient poet. Nothing
can equal the attention with which they liſten to this
orator ; people of all ranks have a very extraordinary
paſſion for this ſpecies of amuſement. A European
traveller is not a little ſurpriſed to ſee the Turkiſh
ſailors, when the weather is calm, aſſemble on the
deck, and attentively liſten for two or three hours
together, to a declamation, which the moſt unexpe-
rienced ear muſt at once perceive to be poetry, from
the exaCtneſs of the meaſure and the continually
recurring rhymes. It is not in this alone that the
common people of the eaſt excel ours in delicacy.
The populace even in the great cities, notwithſtanding the turbulence of their diſpoſitions, are never ſo
brutal as we frequently ſee them with us, and they
have the great merit of not being addiCted to drunk-
enneſs, a vice from which our country peaſants are
not free.   Perhaps this is the only real advantage
produced by the legiſlation of Mahomet : unleſs we
may add the prohibition of the games of chance, for
which the Orientals have therefore no taſte ; cheſs
is the only amuſement of this kind they hold in any
eſtimation, and we frequently find among them very
ſkilful players.
   Of all the different ſpecies of public exhibitions,
the only one they know, and which is common at
Cairo alone, is that of ſtrollers, who ſhew feats of

ftrength like our rope-dancers, and tricks of flight
of hand like our jugglers. We there fee fome of them
eating flints, others breathing flames, fome cutting
their arms or perforating their nofes, without receiving any hurt, and others devouring ferpents. The
people, from whom they carefully conceal the fecrets
of their art, entertain a fort of veneration for them,
and call thefe extraordinary performances, which
appear to have been very ancient in thefe countries,
by a name which fignifies *prodigy* or *miracle.* This
propenfity to admiration, and facility of believing the
moft extraordinary facts or tales, is a remarkable
feature in the character of the Orientals. They admit, without hefitation or the leaft fhadow of doubt,
the moft wonderful things that can be told them,
and if we regard the tales current among them, as
many prodigies happen every day as have been afcribed to the age of the *Genii* and Fairies ; the reafon
of which no doubt is, that being totally ignorant of
the ordinary courfe of phyfical and moral caufes,
they know not the limits of probability and impofli-
bility. Befides, having been accuftomed from their
earlieft youth to believe the extravagant fables of the
Koran, they are wholly deftitute of any ftandard of
analogy, by which to diftinguifh truth from falfehood.
Their credulity therefore arifes from their ignorance,
the imperfection of their education, and the nature
of their government. To this credulity the extra-
vagance of imagination which fome have fo much
admired in their romances, is in a great meafure to
be attributed ; but though they were deprived of this
fource, their works would ftill poffefs many brilliant
ornaments. In general, the Orientals are remarkable
for a clear conception, an eafy expreffion, a propriety
of language in the things they are acquainted with,
and a paffionate and nervous ftyle. They have particularly a tafte for moral fentences, and their pro-
verbs fhew they know how to unite the juftnefs of

obfervation, and profundity of the thought to an ingenuity and force of expreffion. Their converfation
appears at firft to have a fort of coldnefs, but when
we are accuftomed to it, we find ourfelves greatly
attached to them. Such is the good opinion with
which thofe who have had moft communication with
them have been impreffed, that the greater part of our
travellers and merchants, who have known them beft,
allow that they find in them a people of a more humane
and generous character, and poffeffing more fimplicity,
and more refined and open manners, than even the
inhabitants of European countries, as if the Afiatics,
having been polifhed long before us, ftill preferved the
traces of their early improvement.

But it is time to terminate thefe reflections; I fhall
only add one more, which is perfonal to myfelf. After having lived near three years in Egypt and Syria;
after having been habituated to fpectacles of barbarifm and devaftation; on my return to France, the
fight of my own country had almoft the fame effect
on me as that of a foreign land; I could not avoid
feeling a kind of furprife, when traverfing our provinces from the Mediterranean to the ocean, inftead
of thofe ruined countries and vaft deferts to which I
had been accuftomed, I faw myfelf tranfported as it
were into an immenfe garden, where cultivated fields,
populous towns, and country feats continually fucceeded each other during a journey of twenty days.
When I compared our elegant and folid buildings, to
the brick and mud-walled cottages I had left behind
me, the opulence and induftry of our cities to the
ruinous and defolate condition of the Turkifh towns,
the plenty, peace, and power of this kingdom, to the
poverty, anarchy, and feeblenefs of the empire of the
Turks; to admiration fucceeded pity, and to pity philofophical meditation. "Whence," faid I to myfelf,
"fo ftriking a contraft between countries fo much
"alike? Why fo much life and activity here, and

" there fo much indolence and neglect? Why fo
" great a difference between men of the fame fpe-
" cies?" Then, remembering that the countries I
had feen fo defolate and barbarous, were once flourifhing and populous, a fecond reflection fucceeded
almoft involuntarily. " If formerly," faid I, " the
" ftates of Afia enjoyed this fplendor, who can af-
" fure us that thofe of Europe will not one day ex-
" perience the fame reverfe?" This thought appeared to me diftreffing, yet perhaps it may be ufeful.
For let us fuppofe that at the time when Egypt and
Syria were at the fummit of their glory, fome one had
delineated to the people and governments of thofe
countries, their prefent deplorable ftate; let us fuppofe he had faid to them, " Such is the humiliating
" decline which muft be the confequence of fuch and
" fuch political errors: thus fhall injudicious laws
" deprive you of all your wealth and all your power."
Is it not probable that thefe governments would have
taken care to avoid thofe fatal miftakes, which muft
conduct them to fuch entire deftruction? What they
have not done, it is in our power to do: their example may be a leffon to us. The great utility of hiftory is, that by reviving the memory of paft events,
it enables the prefent time to anticipate the coftly
fruits of experience. Travels, in this fenfe, are no
lefs ufeful, and have this advantage; that as they
treat of prefent objects, the obferver is better able
than the pofthumous hiftorian, to difcover the relations and caufes of facts, and to explain the whole
working, however complicated of the political machine. By exhibiting together with the prefent ftate
of a country, the nature of the fubfifting government,
the narrative of the traveller may develope the caufes
of its greatnefs and decline, and furnifh us with means
to determine the actual duration of the empire. Seen
under this point of view, Turkey is a country more
efpecially inftructive. The account I have given of

it, fhews how the abufe of authority, by caufing the mifery of individuals, becomes eventually deftructive to the power of a ftate ; and what we may fafely venture to predict, will foon prove, that the ruin of a nation fooner or later recoils on thofe who have been the caufe of it, and that the errors or crimes of thofe who govern cannot fail of their punifhment, even from the very mifery and wretchednefs of thofe whom they have governed.

CONTENTS

OF THE

SECOND VOLUME.

--«-«-«-«-«-«-«-‹‡›-«-‹‡›-»-»-»-»-»-»--

STATE OF SYRIA CONTINUED.

CONTENTS.

SUBSCRIBERS NAMES.

A.

ANDERSON, Anthony L.
Anderfon, Alexander
Anderfon, Doct. P.
Allen, Stephen
Anthony, John
Aftor, John Jacob
Afh, Thomas

B.

Burk, Jofeph B.
Baker, Mr.
Baker, Sarah
Bogert, J. L.
Bogert, Rudolph
Bogert, R.
Benfon, Robert
Buckley, William
Buckley, P.
Brown, John
Brown, Peter
Brown, Mr,
Betts, John
Ball, John
Balmore, Jacob
Bacon, Thomas
Bafely, John
Baldwin, Hannah
Bramer, George
Ballard, John
Berg, Chriftopher
Battlers, I.
Brower, David A.
Baufier, Henry
Bowne, Samuel
Bell, Robert C.
Bancker, Gerard
Beach, Lazarus, Newfield, 20 copies

C.

Campbell, John
Campbell, James
Conhoven, Francis
Crolius, John
Coddington. William
Corrington, Jofiah
Cox, John
Caldwell, John R.
Codwife, George
Codwife, Mr.
Crook, Jofeph
Clark, T.
Carbray, Daniel
Cozine, Auguftus B.

Carter Jonathan]
Cafterline, Mr.

D.

Dominick, George F.
Defeat, Henry
Dipur, Aaron
Dilks, Thomas
Day, Abraham
Doty, James
Davis, Richard
Degrad, efq. John Peter
Dayton, Abraham
Darracg, B.
Degrove, Robert C.
Drake, Samuel

E.

Elmendorf, Coenrad
Eaton, Thomas
Earle, Sylvefter

F.

Fifher, Leonard
Fardon, Thomas
Furman, Richard, Efq.

G.

Grant, Peter
Greaton, James
Gueft, Louis
Goodheart, George
Gaffner, Thomas
Gibbons, James
Greer, William
Gelfton, David

H.

Hawkins, Matthew
Hedden, Jafper
Heard, Charles
Hicks, John
Hilton, B.
Hallentake, Ifaac
Heeler, Abraham
Hickle, Robert
Hubbard, Mifs
Hendrickfon, Jacob
Hutchins, Ino.
Houfeman, Jacob
Hagerman, Jacob
Hogflefh, Mr.
Hays, Henry
Hager, Benjamin
Hurtin, Sarah
Hoyt, Monfon
Haydock, Henry

SUBSCRIBERS NAMES.

J.

Jones, Owen
Jones, E. R.
Jeffup, Oliver
Jarvis, James
Jacobs, William

K.

Knapp, Ebenezer
Kipp, Thomas F.
Kuntzie, I. C.
Kemble, Andrew B.
Knox, I.

L.

Leveridge, John
Lock, Henry
Luff, Mr.
Lorillard, Jacob
Loudon, Samuel C.
Lampier, George
London, Z.
Lafher, Ino.

M.

Morrifon, Martin
M'Donald, Mr.
M'Donald, John
Myers, Jacob
Myers, Henry
Minufe, Andrew
Minufe, George
Morgan, Margaret
Minthorn, Philip
Mount, Robert
Meeks, Jofeph
Mott, Jacob S.
M'Carty, Peter
Minger, Louis
M'Gregor, Ino.
Marriner, Edward
M'Dougall, Hugh
Minard, Ifaac
M'Key, George
Mertlet, Mons.
M'Kerfon, Ino.
Millin, Quintin

N.

North, Benjamin
Neilfon, William
Neftle, Chriftopher
Nicoll, Edward

P.

Paddock, Peter
Prince, Abraham
Prince, Robert
Parfals, Thomas
Pauling, Eleanor
Pullis, George
Pricket, Albert
Price, Jofeph
Price, Mr.
Pitt, Ino.

Parker, Sidney
Philips, Rev. I.

R.

Reed, William
Roberts, Enos
Roberts, George
Riddell, John
Randolph, Jeremiah
Ruffell, Abraham
Rogers, Leonard
Randall, John
Renard, John B.
Rutger, Col. Henry

S.

Shatzel, William
Shields, Edward
Sutton, Noah H.
Swain, James
Sickles Henry
Shady, John
Smith, George
Smith, James A.
Spinage, John
Scott, David
Stevens, John
Sykes, Ifaac
Schuyler, P.
Seamon, Thomas
Shippey, Jofiah

T. U. V. W.

Tuttle, Seth
Thompfon, William
Tallman, John
Tallman, P.
Thurfton, Peter
Timpfon, Thomas
Underhill, Peter
Utt, John
Vanderbilt, Oliver
Valentine, Charles
Way, John
Winthrop, Peter
Wells, Jofhua
Whitehand, John
Wilcocks, Samuel
Welch, George
Weeks, Levi
Wayland, Seth
Ward, Thomas
Williams, John
Watfon, John
Wilkinfon, Richard
Wallis, John
Warner, George G.
Wilfon, Capt. Philip
Wood, Ebenezer
Wilder, T.
Walton, Gerrard
Webb, Thomas—Albany, 20 copies.

Printed in Great Britain
by Amazon

44849382R00175